Teenage Pregnancy and Parenthood

D0162033

Teenage parenting, particularly mothering, is commonly seen as both personally and socially undesirable. Governments across the world demonstrate concern about teenage pregnancy figures, setting targets and sponsoring campaigns to lower rates of teenage pregnancy, and this view is reflected across society and throughout the media.

Teenage Pregnancy and Parenthood explores a broad range of perspectives on pregnancy and parenting at a young age from a number of international and cultural contexts, and looks at interventions and examples of good practice. Bringing together contributions from leading international academics in the field, this book discusses amongst other topics:

- sexual health and unwanted pregnancy among adolescents;
- young mothers as peer educators in school-based sex education;
- teenage pregnancy and social exclusion;
- the needs of young girls with emotional and behavioural problems;
- teen fathers – deconstructing patriarchy and masculinity.

Teenage Pregnancy and Parenthood explores the contexts in which the critique of young parenthood is often conducted. It draws attention to the assumptions underlying policy positions and argues that these limit an effective consideration of adolescent sexuality and gender roles in society. It is invaluable reading for academics and postgraduate students, as well as policy-makers and practitioners in health, sex education, youth care and related areas.

Helen S. Holgate is a sexual health counsellor, trainer and registered nurse with considerable experience of working with people of all ages in relation to sexual health, including young people, who are in need of information and counselling about pregnancy and related issues. Her PhD thesis provided a discourse analysis of the contexts and experiences of young mothers.

Roy Evans is Professor of Education at Brunel University. He has been actively involved in research and publications in the general area of children and young people 'at risk', including young deaf children's education, drug education, inclusive education, early childhood education, specific learning difficulties and autism, for more than 35 years.

Francis K. O. Yuen is Professor of Social Work at California State University, Sacramento. He has published in the areas of family health social work practice, programme evaluation and grant writing, diversity, and disability.

Teenage Pregnancy and Parenthood

Global perspectives, issues and interventions

Edited by Helen S. Holgate,
Roy Evans and Francis K. O. Yuen

Routledge
Taylor & Francis Group

LONDON AND NEW YORK

First published 2006
by Routledge
2 Park Square, Milton Park, Abingdon, Oxon OX14 4RN

Simultaneously published in the USA and Canada
by Routledge
270 Madison Ave, New York, NY 10016

Routledge is an imprint of the Taylor and Francis Group, an informa business

Typeset in Gill Sans and Times New Roman by Prepress Projects Ltd,
Perth, UK
Printed and bound in Great Britain by TJ International Ltd, Padstow,
Cornwall

British Library Cataloguing in Publication Data
A catalogue record for this book is available from the British Library

Library of Congress Cataloging in Publication Data
Teenage pregnancy and parenthood: global perspectives, issues and
    interventions / edited by Helen S. Holgate, Roy Evans and Francis
    K. O. Yuen.
    p. cm.
    Includes bibliographical references and index.
    1. Teenage parents. 2. Teenage parents – government policy. 3. Teenage
    pregnancy. I. Holgate, Helen S., 1966– II. Evans, Roy. III. Yuen, Francis K.
    O.
    HQ759.64.T44 2006
    306.87–dc22
    2006006578

ISBN10: 0-415-34625-8 (hbk)
ISBN10: 0-415-34626-6 (pbk)
ISBN13: 978-0-415-34625-2 (hbk)
ISBN13: 978-0-415-34626-9 (pbk)

Contents

     implications for sex education in Hong Kong   95
     BILLY C. O. HO AND DENNIS S. W. WONG

     Introduction 95
     Adolescent sexuality in Hong Kong: a trend analysis in figures,
         1981–2001 95
     Unwanted pregnancy 97
     Sexually transmitted infections (STIs) 99
     HIV infection 101
     Sex education for adolescents in Hong Kong 102
     What's wrong with sex education for young people in
         Hong Kong? 103
     Dilemmas encountered in delivering sex education for
         young people 106
     Setting an agenda on sex education for young people in
         Hong Kong 107
     Conclusion 109

7   **Sisters doing it for themselves: young mothers as peer**
     educators in school-based sex education   112
     JUDI KIDGER

     Researching young mothers as sex educators 114
     'It could happen to anyone' – new responses to old messages 116
     Tackling social exclusion – tales from young mothers 120
     Conclusion 125

8   **Controversial issues surrounding teen pregnancy: a**
     feminist perspective   129
     NANCY SHIELDS AND LOIS PIERCE

     The social construction of teen pregnancy as a social problem 129
     The ideology of adolescence 131
     Who has the right to control fertility? 132
     Sex education 133
     Knowledge about birth control and sexually transmitted infections
         (STIs) 135
     Who pays for teen pregnancy? 136
     Abortion 138
     Quality of teen parenting 139
     A negative bias 141
     "Invisible" teen fathers 142
     Conclusions 144

Contributors

Chrystal C. Ramirez Barranti, PhD, MSW, is associate professor in the Division of Social Work at California State University, Sacramento, where she has taught social work practice courses at the undergraduate and graduate levels. Dr Barranti has over 20 years of experience in direct practice with children, youth, elders and families. Her research and scholarly efforts have included interprofessional education and practice, programme evaluation, domestic violence and Mexican immigrant families.

Nona Dawson is a teacher and research fellow at the University of Bristol. She has worked researching teenage parents and their children for many years. This has included work on the education for teenage parents within the UK and Europe and the psychosocial characteristics of teenage parents and their children. She may be contacted on Nona.Dawson@bristol.ac.uk

Roy Evans is Professor of Education and Head of the Education Department at Brunel University, West London. He has researched and published widely in early childhood education and inclusive education. His concern for maginalised groups has found expression through numerous research enquiries focussing on educational provision for young children who are profoundly deaf, those with autistic spectrum disorders and specific learning difficulties, and children whose life circumstances impact their educational achievement and life chances. He has been Chief Editor of the international journal *Early Child Development and Care* since 1978 and was the founding editor of the *International Journal of Adolescence and Youth*. He has given international key note lectures on protective strategies for children and young people at risk for over 30 years.

Rosio Gonzalez is Executive Director of Catholic Charities of Idaho and former executive director of Casi Foundation for Children. She holds an MSW from the School of Social Work at Washington University (1997) and a BSW from San Jose State University (1995). She formerly was Quality Assurance Director for Grace Hill Settlement House in St Louis, Missouri.

Chi On (Billy) Ho, PhD, is currently a lecturer in social work in the Division of Social Studies, City University of Hong Kong. His research interests are youth sexuality, HIV prevention and sex education. He has been conducting sex education for young people in Hong Kong for over 10 years.

Helen Holgate RGN, MEd (Guidance and Counselling), PhD, has worked extensively in the field of sexual health as a practitioner offering counselling and health education to people of all ages relating to all aspects of sexual well-being. Amongst her experiences as a facilitator she has worked on a Teenage Pregnancy Prevention project which provided the inspiration for her PhD thesis. This focused on young mothers, providing a discourse analysis of context and experience.

Alison Hosie is an independent research consultant who is currently focusing on sexual health relating to young people with learning disabilities and pregnancies to women living with Type 1 diabetes and epilepsy. Prior to this Alison was a research associate at Newcastle University where she was involved in a number of research projects which focused on the educational experiences of pregnant young women and young mothers of school age in England. Alison's qualifications include a BA in Social Policy and an MSc in Medical Sociology. Her PhD focused on a comparative policy analysis relating to teenage pregnancy.

Judi Kidger is a research associate in the Department of Social Medicine at the University of Bristol. Her research interests centre on health education, particularly in the school context, the causes and consequences of teenage pregnancy and parenthood, school-related risk and protective factors for adolescent mental health, and peer-led health initiatives. Her current research is an investigation of emotional health interventions in secondary schools. Her recent publications include papers in the *British Educational Research Journal* and in *Sex Education*.

Serge C. Lee is a social work professor at California State University, Sacramento. He is the first Hmong American to have a doctoral degree in social welfare and the first Hmong American to have attained the rank of full professor. His areas of specialization include child welfare, mental health of Southeast Asians, international social work and cross-cultural diversity issues. He is nationally and internationally known in refugees health and human services. He is serving as a special consultant to the National Institute of Mental Health Services, Substance Abuse and Mental Health Services Administration–Refugee section and holds a three-year offsite guest professor appointment with Guizhou University for Nationalities, People's Republic of China. He is also coordinating an MSW Southeast Asian focus program at the Division of Social Work at California State University, Sacramento. In August 2004, he was commissioned by the US Department of State and the Center for Disease Control to investigate suicide incidences at a refugee camp in Thailand.

David Nylund, PhD, MSW, is an assistant professor of social work at California State University, Sacramento, and a clinical supervisor at La Familia Counseling Services and Alicante School. David earned his doctorate in Cultural Studies at the University of California, Davis, where he studied masculinities and queer theory. His dissertation project was an examination into the popularity of sports talk radio programs and their link to masculinity and homophobia and will be published by SUNY Press as a book in their Sport and Culture series. David is the co-editor (with Craig Smith) of *Narrative Therapies with Children and Adolescent* and the author of *Treating Huckleberry Finn: A New Narrative Approach with Kids Diagnosed ADD/ADHD*. In addition to publishing various articles and book chapters on narrative therapy and cultural studies, David presents his work throughout North America, Europe and Japan.

Lois Pierce is the Director of the School of Social Work at the University of Missouri–St. Louis. Her research focuses primarily on child welfare including child abuse and neglect and adoptions. She has published numerous articles and several book chapters on these and other topics.

William Rainford is assistant professor, School of Social Work, Boise State University. He holds a PhD in social welfare from the University of California at Berkeley (2002), an MSW from the School of Social Work at Washington University (1996) and a BSW from San Jose State University (1995). He has completed research on women who have been sanctioned for failure to comply in the Temporary Assistance to Needy Families programme. Currently, he is examining employment outcomes for women welfare clients in an arch-conservative TANF programme. Rainford has authored and co-authored articles on punitive welfare programmes, social development as a theory of social welfare and asset accumulation for families with children with disabilities. In addition to his academic work, Rainford is a legislative advocate for Catholic Charities of Idaho and governmental liaison for Interfaith Sanctuary Homeless Shelter in Boise, Idaho.

Peter Selman is Reader in Social Policy and Visiting Fellow in the School of Geography, Politics & Sociology at Newcastle University, where he teaches courses in comparative social policy and adoption. His main areas of research interest are child adoption, teenage pregnancy, and demographic change and public policy. He is currently Chair of the Network for Intercountry Adoption, member of the Board of Trustees of the British Agencies for Adoption & Fostering and a member of the Newcastle PCT Teenage Pregnancy Support Sub Group. During the past six years he has directed two major research projects for DfES (*Monitoring of the DfES Standards Fund Teenage Pregnancy* with Alison Hosie and Suzanne Speak) and the Teenage Pregnancy Unit (*The Education of Pregnant Young Women and Young Mothers in England* with Nona Dawson and Alison Hosie), as well as several local evaluations of teenage pregnancy initiatives. His other most recent publication is 'Scapegoating and Moral Panics: Teenage Pregnancy in Britain and the United States' in S. Cunningham-Burley and L. Jamieson (eds) *Families and the State: Changing Relationships* (Palgrave, 2003).

Margaret Sherrard Sherraden is professor, School of Social Work, University of Missouri in St. Louis, and Research Professor, Center for Social Development, Washington University. She holds a PhD in sociology from Washington University (1989), an MA from the School of Social Service Administration at the University of Chicago (1974) and a BA from Beloit College (1972).

Past research includes a Fulbright-funded study of health and poverty policy in Mexico (1987) and research on birth outcomes among Mexican immigrants in Chicago. She has recently completed an in-depth interview study of participants in a matched savings programme of Individual Development Accounts (IDAs), and a study of the tri-national North American Community Service initiative. Currently she is leading research on school-based children's savings accounts. She is past President of the 100-year-old Missouri Association for Social Welfare, a voluntary education and policy organization. Sherraden is author, with Cynthia K. Sanders and Michael Sherraden, of *Kitchen Capitalism: Microenterprise in Low-Income Households* (State University of New York Press, 2004) and co-editor, with William Ninacs, of *Community Economic Development and Social Work* (Haworth Press, 1998).

Nancy Shields is associate professor and Chair of the Department of Sociology at the University of Missouri–St. Louis. She has published numerous articles and book chapters related to applied sociology, including papers on domestic violence, community violence and the social psychology of education. She is currently conducting comparative research (with Kathy Nadasen, Lois Pierce and Sharyn Spicer) on children and community violence in Cape Town, South Africa, and St. Louis, Missouri.

Dennis S.W. Wong, PhD, is currently an associate professor at the Department of Applied Social Studies at City University of Hong Kong. Before joining tertiary education, he was a social worker. His current research interests focus on youth problems, juvenile delinquency and youth policy. Apart from publishing papers in local and international journals, he has been active in public policy consultancy such as harm reduction strategies, HIV/AIDS and drugs treatment approaches, and use of a whole school approach to prevent school bullying.

Zha Blong Xiong, PhD, is associate professor, Department of Postsecondary Teaching and Learning, College of Education and Human Development, University of Minnesota. He has done extensive research on parent–adolescent relationships and parent education in Southeast Asian families in the United States. His publications include papers on Southeast Asian fathering, parent–adolescent conflicts, and family secrets, and can be found in journals such as the Journal of Psychology, Families in Society, and Hmong Studies Journal. He also co-authored a research-based parent education curriculum *Helping Youth Succeed: Bicultural Parenting for Southeast Asian Families*. Besides research and publications, he also serves on the Board of Directors for the Hmong Archives, Minnesota Council on Family Relations, University of Minnesota Children, Youth and Family Consortium and the Saint Paul's Children Collaborative.

Francis K.O. Yuen, DSW, ACSW, is professor in the Division of Social Work at California State University, Sacramento. His practice and research interests are in the areas of family health social work practice, children and families, disability, grant writing, programme evaluation and international social work. He is editor of the *Journal of Social Work in Disability & Rehabilitation*. He has authored and edited many journal articles and books, including *Social Work for the Twenty-First Century: Challenges and Opportunities* (2006) and *Practice with Children and Families: A Family Health Approach* (2005). He is also a co-editor for *Handbook on Emotional and Behavioural Difficulties* (2004) and a co-author for *Practical Grant Writing and Program Evaluation* (2003).

Acknowledgements

I am grateful to my co-editors, Roy Evans and Francis Yuen, for all they have taught me during the lengthy process that has culminated in the production of this book. Sincere thanks to all the contributors for their chapters and patience. To my dear family and friends, thanks are due for their tolerance and support. Thanks also to the team at Taylor & Francis for their commitment to the project. Most of all, my thanks and admiration go to all the young parents who have directly and indirectly contributed to this book.

Helen Holgate

We would like to thank all the outstanding authors and practitioners who have contributed to this book. Their professionalism and dedication to academic excellence are vividly reflected in their high-quality writing. They share their expert knowledge and genuine concerns towards the well-being of our young people. I would also like to recognise my students, who have consistently reminded me of the value of learning and the joy of teaching.

Francis Yuen
Roy Evans

Introduction

Helen Holgate, Roy Evans and Francis Yuen

Teenage pregnancy and parenthood is a complex contemporary issue. Although current statistical evidence collected within the European Union (EU) and the USA suggests that absolute numbers of teenage mothers are falling, the number of infants born to young mothers is still large and the number of recorded concep- tions even larger. Moreover, the available statistics, while reflecting a decline in teenage pregnancies, clearly indicate that the rate at which the reduction in num- bers is occurring is variable across Europe, with the United Kingdom still show- ing the highest number of births relative to its population. Generally construed as a 'problem' not only for the young mother and the child but also for society at large, numerous writers have attempted to explore and identify the possible reasons why an adolescent becomes pregnant. Research and writing reflect both the complexity of the issues surrounding young motherhood and the pertinence of differing theoretical frameworks to the development of an understanding of the issues. Inevitably, the varying analyses reflect the disciplinary bases from which researchers launch their accounts, incorporating their particular worldview and moral position and, powerfully, the principles and values that guide their own psy- chological engagement with the phenomenon. Landy and Walsh (1988) suggested that three major types of explanation have emerged to account for young (as low as at 11 years of age) motherhood, as follows:

- lack of information about contraception and knowledge of its availability to young teenagers;
- socio-cultural factors such as poverty and cultural acceptance;
- psychological and psychodynamic perspectives.

There is no suggestion in Landy and Walsh's (ibid.) analysis that these are mutually exclusive. However, O'Connor (1990) would add a fourth category re- lating to the availability and quality of 'education for parenthood' courses within the curriculum of schools. She argues that despite a professed belief in the family as a stabilising influence on society such a topic has been a neglected, low-status area of the curriculum (ibid.: 85). The opportunity for exploring parenting as the outcome of a serious, long-term, stable emotional relationship through discussion within peer groups of adolescent girls and boys may thus be missed. Within the requirements of the National Curriculum in England and Wales, there is little doubt that the biology of human reproduction is explored, but the relationship of this to sex education in the fullest sense remains tenuous.

The perception of young motherhood as a problematic issue cannot be divorced from the political, moral and economic fabric of individual societies at particular points in time. In post-scientific societies young mothers become positioned as 'deviant' (i.e. their behaviour is socially undesirable) as a consequence of factors that appear to have emerged as 'givens' on the basis of social research. Some of this research is quite dated but has continued to shape perceptions. Some current perceptions emerge as outcomes of detailed studies of young mothers and their children. These have focused on parenting behaviours and personal–social outcomes as well as the psychological, motivational and academic futures for the children themselves. Whether young mothers show age-specific kinds of mothering behaviours is perhaps less significant than the degree to which clinically determined inappropriate mothering and a social welfare-dependent future is disproportionately evident in this age group. Research suggests that, although the group defined as young mothers is not homogeneous, these young women are the products of their own natural family configuration. Within this research a recurring theme emerges of absent or emotionally distant biological fathers, and dysfunctional or broken homes (e.g. Ulvedal and Feeg 1983). However, little research has been undertaken to explore the *processes* at work or the way in which these interact. Major theoretical perspectives are relatively silent about the connection between family dynamics and teenage sexual behaviour.

Attributions of low self-esteem and a tendency to external locus of control were reported on 20 years ago by, for example, Thompson (1984) and the Group for the Advancement of Psychiatry (1986), the latter commenting that 'unmarried teenage mothers seldom become pregnant for sound or emotionally healthy reasons' (p. 21). Moreover, the natural development of a young woman to adulthood through accomplishing the growth tasks of adolescence is prematurely halted as she becomes someone's mother whilst still relatively a child herself.

The issue for professionals is whether teenage mothers are likely to be able to provide the warm and nurturing environment that they themselves may have been denied. Numerous past studies (e.g. Epstein 1980; Roosa 1983) have reported that, compared with older women, teenagers know less about effective child rearing during their first successful pregnancy and show a preference for a more physical style of infant stimulation and a less verbal style of interaction. In addition, discipline declines and child rearing generally becomes harder as infancy leads into toddlerhood (McAnarney 1985). As a group, teen parents are regarded as disproportionately 'at risk' for multiple social problems, even if they get married, and their offspring are 'at risk' for immature development, emotional and behavioural difficulties, and neglect. Whilst there is an acceptance that the birth of a child to a young mother is not inevitably a high-risk situation, the outcomes depend substantially on the level of support available to the child and his or her parents.

A further significant consideration for professionals and policy-makers alike is that the birth of a child provides a disruption to, if not termination of, the mother's own education. Whilst a more enlightened policy on schooling means that some teenage mothers can return to school to complete education towards qualifications, this is by no means always feasible, with the result that the young mother frequently finds herself at a disadvantage in the employment market. Poverty, and with it the lack of choice in life futures, is a common experience of young mothers, especially those who are unsupported by the child's natural father or other care-taking adult in the home. Numerous studies within a wide international literature have amply demonstrated the impact of social disadvantage on the life chances of the young child and the implications for educational success. Using data from a national cohort study (the 1958 National Child Development Study), Davie *et al.* (1972) compared children of adolescent mothers with children of older mothers and found that the children of young mothers evidenced more emotional and behavioural difficulties. This was, and remains, the most comprehensive cohort study to have been undertaken in the UK, although the later 1970 birth cohort study directed by Neville Butler (e.g. Butler *et al.* 1986) at Bristol University (the Child Health and Education Study) has provided additional insights to the factors that affect the resilience of socially disadvantaged young children. Osborn (1990) used the 5-year and 10-year follow-up data to explore factors associated with resilience, risk and protection within a group of socially disadvantaged children defined within the national cohort. Osborn (ibid.: 44) observes that:

> Children of young mothers are at increased risk of educational and behavioural problems, which is partly attributable to the mother's and father's immaturity in the parental role, but may also be related to the economic insecurity of parents at an early stage in the adult life cycle. In the present analysis, the vulnerability of children in low SES families was increased still further if the mother was under 25 when the child was 5.

Concepts of risk, vulnerability and protection have come to dominate the literature concerned with interventions designed to improve the life chances of children born into potentially disadvantaging circumstances. Research over more than 30 years has revealed the potentially disadvantaging outcomes for a child born to a teenage or young mother. These transcend the practical impacts of poverty that arguably are shared by all unsupported mothers who cope alone. A multidisciplinary research literature points up the possible risks to the young child, which include academic underachievement, general immaturity, emotional and behavioural difficulties and disrupted social relations. However, vulnerability can be counterbalanced through effective interventions designed to minimise the impact of risk by supporting and enhancing protective factors in the child's environment. Here the professional challenge is to recognise the individuality and uniqueness of each family unit and to identify supportive strategies that give the mother and child a fair chance of success. Critical to the success of such interventions is the willingness of public social agencies to recognise the multifaceted nature of the difficulties faced by young mothers and their need for coordinated multiprofessional support. One difficulty is constructed by the views and attitudes of the wider society to the issue of teenage pregnancy. Nowhere is the negative characterisation of young mothers more evident than in the positions adopted by government and media. Whilst the media celebrated social inclusiveness as a cornerstone of public policy, young mothers continue to be cast as undesirables . . . in so far as teen pregnancy is deemed unacceptable. Holgate (2005) has analysed the multiple negative perspectives arising from national social agencies and the media and illustrated how public perception is shaped by negative stereotyping.

Notwithstanding the research evidence to which we have referred above, absent from virtually all current policy pronouncements is any notion of personal agency that may be both rational and determining in the context of young mothers' lived experience or any recognition that teenage pregnancy and young motherhood could be an acceptable life choice. Such omissions contribute to the construction of the young mother as deviant: frequently marginalised by the social agencies that they could look to for support, they are equally frequently demonised by the media. Their partner in the construction of motherhood is usually ignored: there is relatively little research literature on young fatherhood or fathers of children born to or conceived by young mothers. The social consequences of young motherhood arise often because 'young' may be synonymous with 'lone'. When unsupported either economically or emotionally, the issues faced by teen mothers are seldom different in kind from the issues that face women of more mature years when forced to cope alone with limited resources. Individuals in society may nevertheless respond quite differently to the two situations, reflecting perhaps a public perspective that regards the latter as unfortunate but the former as irresponsible.

This book has been compiled as a contribution to the ongoing international debate surrounding young pregnancy and parenthood. In different countries, the positions taken by governments and other social institutions on issues of teenage parenting share common features of concern.

Contributions to this edited volume have been selected to embrace a range of perspectives on young pregnancy and parenting from a number of international and cultural contexts. The book also seeks to present a contemporary perspective based on current research. Chapters have been selected both to define the intellectual contexts in which the critique of young parenthood is often conducted and to draw attention to the discourses that frame the policy positions and the extent to which these discourses limit an effective consideration of adolescent sexuality and gender roles in society. Education in formal institutions, peer education and interventionist strategies aimed at reducing the rate of teenage pregnancy and parenthood are dealt with in separate chapters. An important contribution is achieved through a chapter on the needs of young girls with emotional and behavioural problems with regard to young pregnancy. Young fatherhood is taken as the focus of two chapters that provide an important contribution and extension to the current debates.

The book consists of 11 chapters. In the first chapter Helen Holgate and Roy Evans present an introduction to teenage pregnancy and parenthood. This chapter acts as a scene setter, providing the reader with a statistical and policy framework for the UK that provides a useful backdrop to the following chapters. Moreover, it begins to describe some of the multiple theoretical positions and issues that are pertinent to the topic, some of which are elaborated upon in the subsequent chapters.

In recognising that cultural values can provide a specific dimension to issues of teenage pregnancy and parenthood it has been of particular value to be able to include two chapters addressing the issues as they relate to two specific cultures. Serge Lee, Zha Blong Xiong and Francis Yuen (Chapter 2) present a chapter that describes and discusses the Hmong in the USA as a community experiencing dramatic change whilst attempting to maintain its values, among them the tradition whereby young people are expected to get married in their early teens. Margaret Sherraden, Rosio Gonzalez and William Rainford provide additional perspectives on these issues in their chapter, which focuses upon pregnancy and childbearing among Latino adolescents, and consider social policy implications specific to the community (Chapter 3).

Five chapters are related directly to the arena of social exclusion and education. Nona Dawson (Chapter 4) introduces the contextual framework for the education of young mothers in the UK by detailing current education policy and the issues and tensions that this, in turn, generates for young mothers and their children. Peter Selman and Ali Hosie (Chapter 5) discuss the UK government's response to teenage pregnancy and parenthood as laid out in the Teenage Pregnancy Strategy (Social Exclusion Unit 1999), which is then related to the government's aim of reducing social exclusion, which pays particular attention to policy aimed at reintegrating school-aged mothers into education. The next chapter explores the tensions and dilemmas inherent in delivering sex education in Hong Kong, a country described by Billy Ho and Dennis Wong (Chapter 6) as modern yet conservative but which is experiencing rapidly changing sexual attitudes and behaviour among its youth. The theme of approaches to education is further developed in Chapter 7, in which Judi Kidger examines the role of young mothers as agents in the development of peer-delivered school-based sex education. Kidger considers the value of this approach both to young mothers acting as agents and to those receiving the education provided by them and highlights the tensions in this process. The last of the education-based chapters, Chapter 11, considers the needs of girl students with emotional and behavioural difficulties as they relate to their educational needs around teenage pregnancy. Chrystal Ramirez Barranti discusses the challenges facing human service providers and teachers in regular and special education including the need for educational strategies to prevent girls with emotional and behavioural difficulties from dropping out of school.

Nancy Shields and Lois Pierce in Chapter 8 deliver a feminist perspective upon some of the controversial issues surrounding teenage pregnancy, including cross-racial adoption and abortion. They explore some of the common discourses and separate from fact some of the myths that teenage pregnancy and parenthood has generated. In their conclusion they call for greater research attention to be given to teenage fathers in a bid to create a more balanced picture of the issue.

The chapters by Suzanne Speak (Chapter 9) and David Nyland (Chapter 10) take up the perspective on young fathers and add a much needed dimension to the literature on young parenthood. Suzanne Speak's chapter explores the roles and aspirations of young, single non-residential fathers, and in doing so aims to dispel some of the myths surrounding young single fathers. Utilising a narrative therapeutic approach David Nyland focuses upon the experiences of teen fathers and examines the barriers to effective teen father parenting. Both chapters contribute to redressing the imbalance of the teenage pregnancy and parenthood literature. Importantly, both chapters offer suggestions that seek to improve the potential of young fathers.

In our opening remarks we referred to research literature of some long standing that has shaped ideas around the topic of young mothers. This book will bring this literature up to date and provide a more rounded contemporary perspective which we hope will be of value to practitioners and to all young mothers and fathers, who often struggle for recognition and a voice.

References

Butler, N., Golding, J., with Howlett, B.C. (1986) *From Birth to Five: A Study of the Health and Behaviours of Britain's 5-Year-Olds*, Oxford: Pergamon Press.

Davie, R., Butler, N. and Goldstein, H. (1972) *From Birth to Seven*, London, Longman.

Epstein, A.S. (1980) 'New Insights into Problems of Adolescent Parenthood,' *Bulletin of High/Scope* 5, Spring.

Group for the Advancement of Psychiatry (1986) *Crises of Adolescence: Teenage Pregnancy: Impact on Adolescent Development*, New York: Brunner/Mazel.

Holgate, H. (2005) 'Young Motherhood: A Discourse Analysis of Context and Experience', unpublished PhD thesis, Brunel University, London.

Landy, S. and Walsh, S. (1988) 'Early Intervention with High-risk Teenage Mothers and their Infants', *Early Child Development and Care* 37, 27.

McArnarney, E. (1985) 'Adolescent Pregnancy and Childbearing: New Data, New Challenges', *Pediatrics* 75, 973–5.

O'Connor, L. (1990) 'Education for Parenthood and the National Curriculum: Progression or Regression?', *Early Child Development and Care* 57, 85.

Osborn, A.F. (1990) 'Resilient Children: A Study of High Achieving Socially Disadvantaged Children', *Early Child Development and Care* 62, 23–48.

Roosa, M.A. (1983) 'A Comparative Study of Pregnant Teenagers' Parenting Attitudes and Knowledge of Sexuality and Child Development', *Journal of Youth and Adolescence* 12, 213–24.

Social Exclusion Unit (1999) *Teenage Pregnancy*, London: The Stationery Office.

Thompson, R.A. (1984) 'The Critical Needs of the Adolescent Unwed Mother', *The School Counsellor* 31, 460–6.

Ulvedal, K. and Feeg, V.D. (1983) 'Profile: Pregnant Teens who Choose Childbirth', *Journal of School Health* 53, 229–33.

Chapter 1

Sexuality and young motherhood

Discourses and definitions

Helen Holgate and Roy Evans

The purpose of this chapter is to provide an overview of the 'meaningful' contexts within which teenage parents operate, and the power of social discourse in defining them as problematic. The following chapters take a more specific focus upon the varied and complex issues emanating from the issue of teenage pregnancy and motherhood. Initially, however, we need to note that teen pregnancy, and subsequently teenage motherhood, is often placed in the public consciousness alongside other facets of adolescent life experience such as drug and alcohol abuse, gang violence and delinquency. These are all aspects of deviant behaviour within the confusion of adolescent development that are best prevented, since they constitute a threat to the very fabric of society if allowed to flourish unchecked, as well as to the health and well-being of the young people themselves. They represent a cost to society – an actual financial cost through restitution and rehabilitation, an opportunity cost through the loss to society of economic activity and a moral cost. Our young people appear to have rejected many of the moral precepts that shaped destinies and formed the principled basis of interpersonal relationships in past generations.

Research into each of these different aspects of adolescent deviance often implicates disadvantageous socio-economic, class-based and familial structural factors in the early experience of many young people at risk, suggesting that deviance is a reaction to exclusion, actual or felt, an attempt to deny social invisibility and to leave a footprint that others can see. Programmes of preventative education are often less effective than hoped, particularly when delivered in schools, as their ability to change some aspect of the psychosocial environment of the young person on an enduring basis is essentially limited. By early adolescence most young people will have acquired, or have begun to acquire, a set of attitudes and dispositions to their environment based on their actual life experiences. For many growing up in urban environments, their behaviours are normalised within the harshness of life as they experience it. Poverty has to be seen within the overall dynamic of lack of opportunity, inappropriate role models and lack of a sense of future. Exclusion is less a positive act than an endemic socialised experience. Exclusion relates to lack of personal power and lack of choice, real or felt, an inability to shape one's future within the status quo. Many pregnant teenagers who go on to become teen mothers emerge from such disadvantaged backgrounds. Their reasons for becoming pregnant are sometimes complex, but despite this they are frequently demonised by the media as deliberate queue jumpers seeking social housing. For government the issues are not so easily accounted for or dismissed. How should a modern social democracy respond to the causes and effects of teenage pregnancy? To treat it is as a subject to be solved by education is clearly indefensible; the fact that the level of teenage pregnancy in the UK is the highest in Europe is clearly a matter for policy development and professional action. Political objectives are ultimately serviced through professional agencies whose particular ideologies and practices influence the outcomes in human terms for better or worse. The current government has set out its policy objectives for life politics, amongst which a reduction in the number of young mothers is a key element. This is unsurprising since successive political parties in the UK have defined it as a social problem (Griffin 1993) since the 1980s.

The Third Way is constituted as the value base for the New Labour, and as such the discourse features in its policies, documents and speeches (Fairclough 2000). It is defined as a new politic that:

> stands for a modernised social democracy, passionate in its commitment to social justice and the goals of the centre-left, but flexible, innovative and forward looking in the means to achieve them. It is founded on the values which have guided progressive politics for more than a century – democracy, liberty, justice, mutual obligation and internationalism.
>
> (Blair 1998)

The Third Way pays particular attention to family life, crime and the breakdown of the family and is concerned to engage with 'life politics', which are about:

> how we should respond to a world in which tradition and custom are losing their hold over our lives, and where science and technology have altered so much of what used to be 'nature'.
>
> (Giddens 2000: 40)

Within the ideological rationale of the Third Way is a new discourse, specific to New Labour, that of social exclusion, which has been described as becoming increasingly detached from the concepts of poverty and inequality (Gillies 2005). The reduction of social exclusion is one of the key priorities in New Labour policy, constituting a target for the Social Exclusion Unit (SEU) and embodied within policies, including the New Deal welfare-to-work policy (Department for Work and Pensions 2005) and Bridging the Gap (Social Exclusion Unit 1999a), which aims to get young people not in education, employment or training into work. The SEU was established in 1997 as a unit within the Cabinet Office. Its role is summarised thus:

The work of the SEU includes specific projects to tackle specific issues and wide ranging projects to assess past politic and ideas for future trends.

(Social Exclusion Unit 2004)

The remit of the SEU includes unemployment, discrimination, poor skills, low income, ill health, family breakdown and teenage pregnancy. In including young pregnancy the government has for the first time developed a specific strategy for 'tackling' the issue. This inclusion is centralised in the 'cross-government' (Teenage Pregnancy Unit 2005) Teenage Pregnancy Unit (located within the Department of Education and Skills), whose role is the implementation of the Teenage Pregnancy Strategy. The strategy centres on two aims (Social Exclusion Unit 1999b: 6):

- reducing the rate of teenage conceptions, with the specific aim of halving the rate of conceptions among under-18s by 2010;
- getting more teenage parents into education, training or employment, to reduce their risk of long-term social exclusion.

Underpinning these goals lies a set of contested assumptions: first, that young pregnancy represents a problem; second, that the problem has reached such an extent that rates should be reduced (Phoenix 1991a; Birch 1996; Luker 1996; Davies *et al.* 2001); and, third, that the solution to the problem of young parents being at risk of social exclusion lies in education, training and, ultimately, employment (Kidger 2004). At this stage it is useful to briefly consider the statistical evidence informing the above policy aims.

The Social Exclusion Unit (1999b: 12) cites the following statistical data as the basis for evidence of a problem:

In England, there are nearly 90,000 conceptions a year to teenagers; around 7,700 to girls under 16 and 2,200 to girls aged 14 or under. Roughly three-fifths of conceptions – 56,000 – result in live births . . . within Western Europe, the UK now stands out as having the highest rate of teenage births.

Despite the picture presented in this statement it is valuable to recognise that 'teenagers today are far less likely to have a baby than was the case 20 years ago' (Corlyon and McGuire 1997: 1). In the 1970s the figure fluctuated around 50 births per 1,000 teenagers in England and Wales. During the 1980s there was a rise in the proportion of teenage women becoming pregnant, but by the late 1990s the figure had decreased to less than 30 births per 1,000 (Singh and Darroch 2000). These statistics demonstrate a chronological mismatch between the highest rates of teenage pregnancy and parenthood and the creation of the Teenage Pregnancy Unit (Arai 2003a). Equally, the aim of reducing rates of young pregnancy and parenthood coincides with a time of concern that the ratio of young to elderly people is in decline (the number of children aged under 16 in the UK fell by 18 per cent between 1971 and 2002 whilst in the same period there was a 27 per cent increase in the number of people age over 65; Summerfield and Babb 2004).

The latest progress reports from the Teenage Pregnancy Unit (2004) state that all 30 points of the Teenage Pregnancy Strategy Action Plan are being implemented. According to the report's key points, data for 2002 show that in England conception rates among the under-18s have fallen by 8.6 per cent since 1998, with an additional decrease of 11.2 per cent in conception rates for the under-16s in the period 1998–2001. Data for 1997–99 show that 29.7 per cent of young parents were in education, training or work in 2002–04, compared with 23.1 per cent in 1997–99.

Is young teenage pregnancy and motherhood a problem?

The issue of young pregnancy and parenthood is constructed as problematic to the extent that 15 of the 28 countries that form the membership of the Organization for Economic Co-operation and Development (OECD) are trying to reduce their rates (United Nations Children's Fund 2001). Policy-makers in the UK have cited evidence which suggests that the UK has the highest rate of teenage births in Western Europe, with 'rates twice as high as in Germany, three times as high as in France and six times as high as in the Netherlands' (Social Exclusion Unit 1999b). According to current data compiled by Eurostat, the Statistical Office of the European Union, during the period 2002–03, live births in women under the age of 19 years in Germany totalled 26,522, compared with 3,324 in the Netherlands and a provisional figure in the UK of 49,633 (Eurostat 2005). No data were available for France. The countries with the lowest rates of young pregnancy and parenthood are Korea, Japan, Switzerland, the Netherlands and Sweden, each of which experiences teen birth rates of less than 7 per 1,000 women (United Nations Children's Fund 2001).

The UK in the twentieth century witnessed an overall downward trend in fertility rates, from 115 live births per 1,000 women aged 15–44 years at the beginning of the century to 57 per 1,000 women in the same age group by the end of the century. In the interim period there were peaks in the birth rate following the world wars and in the 1960s. In 2004 there was an upturn in birth rates; young women in the under-20 age group accounted for 45,094 out of a total 639,721 births in England and Wales, or 7.04 per cent.

Despite the focus given to rates of young pregnancy and parenthood, a close reading of the statistics reveals a decline in the teenage birth rates in most areas of the industrialised world, including the UK, in the last 25 years. Even against a background of reducing birth rates generally, the decline is often much greater among the younger age groups. However, this picture has not deterred New Labour from comparing UK rates unfavourably with those of other European countries as justification for its goal of reducing rates of young pregnancy and parenthood.

Arai (2003b) has criticised this approach as inappropriate because inter-country comparisons ignore variations in conception and abortion rates. The point that the rate of teenage abortion in the UK also needs to be taken into account is made by Lee *et al.* (2004), whose methodological approach uses high-level statistical analyses of complex datasets, in conjunction with qualitative analyses of individual accounts of experiences, to examine the rationale employed by some young women to continue with a pregnancy, and by others to abort, and the factors that influence their decisions. They concluded that decision-making appears to be affected by a number of factors, including the views of family and community and the availability of services, with the key factor being social deprivation, which is reflected by data demonstrating that among under-18-year-olds the highest rates of conceptions and lowest rates of terminations are in the more deprived areas in the UK. A further point demonstrated by Arai (2003b) is that in comparing rates of young pregnancy and parenting between countries it is assumed that the experience of other countries can be compared with that of Britain, which is unrealistic on the grounds that the UK is demographically and socio-economically distinct, rendering comparison impossible. Similarly, religious and cultural attitudes within countries are varied; thus Korea's low rate of young pregnancy and parenthood has been partly attributed to its strong social disapproval of premarital sex, which places young pregnant women in considerable financial and social difficulty (United Nations Children's Fund 2001).

This section has provided some statistical context to the issue of young pregnancy and parenthood and a discussion of some of the tensions arising from the use of statistics to justify the problematisation of the issue. It is now worth considering related tensions in the defining of 'young' as well as in the discourses surrounding 'mothering' specifically.

What is a young mother?

There are a number of inconsistencies in the terminology used to describe a young mother (Dennison and Coleman 1998). Among the terms used are 'young mother' (Phoenix 1991a; Levine *et al.* 2001), 'adolescent mother' (Jorgensen 1993; Samuels *et al.* 1994; Birch 1997), 'children who have children' (Family Planning Association 1994), 'schoolgirl mother' (Horwitz *et al.* 1991; Dawson 1997) as well as 'teenage mother' (Sharpe 1987; Hudson and Ineichen 1991; SmithBattle 1995; Allen and Bourke-Dowling 1998). The abundance of terms contributes to the lack of clarity and general confusion surrounding the issue. Language is important – it reflects social processes and structures (Wodak 1996) – thus the choice of labelling terminology is significant to the way in which the described issue, person or people comes to be interpreted. 'Adolescent', 'teenage' and 'schoolgirl' mother more clearly suggest an age-related and developmentally related interpretation, whilst 'young' mother is more open to interpretation, allowing for an appreciation of the differentiation in all aspects of maturity.

Studies employing the listed definitions have incorporated research with young mothers between the ages of 13 and 24. The upper parameter is clearly outside the definition of teenager or schoolgirl. It is open to debate whether it also equates with the concept of a young or adolescent mother, or even post-adolescent mother, as some theorists would have it.

Societal definitions of age

The differences discussed above reflect a generalised lack of consistency regarding age-related terminology and definitions. There is no consistent or universal definition of a young person in the UK infrastructural institutions such as the education, legal, health and welfare systems, so it remains unclear by which criteria an age construct is measured in a given situation. Fundamental to the issue of teenage pregnancy is the assumption that there is such a phenomenon as 'teenage' (Macleod 2003).

In 1970, the age of majority (the age at which a person is eligible to vote in an election) was reduced from 21 to 18. At this age a person can also legally buy alcohol, gamble in a licensed betting shop, be tried in an adult court, and marry and leave home without parental consent.

At 16 a person can (amongst others) legally leave full-time education, enter full-time employment, have sexual intercourse, smoke tobacco, pay tax and National Insurance and with parental consent marry and leave home (Electoral Commission 2003).

An area of particular relevance to this theme is the age of consent. The Criminal Law Amendment Act 1855 increased the age of consent (defined as the age at which a person can give consent to sexual intercourse) for heterosexuals from 13 to 16, where it remains. In 2001 the age of consent for homosexuals was brought into line with this, being reduced from 21 (Stonewall 2004). It is a contradiction that, although people under 16 are not legally able to have sex, the age of consent does not preclude them obtaining contraception. This can be accessed confidentially as, within medical guidelines, a young person can consent to medical treatment if he or she is deemed sufficiently mature to fully understand the implications of a proposed treatment (Brook Advisory Service 2005).

This brief synopsis of the UK age parameters demonstrates the inconsistencies within which young people, and professionals working with them, must operate. These inconsistencies are reflected within the literature on young pregnancy and motherhood that is described in the preceding section as being unclear and unclearly defined.

Discourses of adolescence

Adolescent sexuality lies within the overarching framework of theories of adolescence. This section considers the construction of adolescence as a distinct age-related period.

The definitive terms described, i.e. teenage mother, adolescent mother and schoolgirl mother, locate a young mother as a woman who becomes a mother during the period between childhood and adulthood. This time has come to be known as 'adolescence'. The construction of a period of time called adolescence is of recent development (Furstenberg 2000). The way in which it is defined is culturally and historically specific. For example, adolescence in Western nations relates to a progression through the education system and the transition to the labour market. This coincides with various other transitions equally symbolic of the passage to adulthood, for example the transition from virginity to sexual activity (ibid.).

Multiple interrelated components constitute levels of development, including physical and psychological maturity. Physical changes occur in the body that represent a progression to physical maturity, a process that has been identified as speeding up during the twentieth century. This acceleration is partly attributed to higher standards of nutrition and improved environmental circumstances (Tanner 1961). An example of the progression to physical maturity is menarche in women. A commonly cited cause of the protraction of adolescence is the belief that menarche is, on average, occurring earlier although, according to Whincup et al. (2001), any reduction in the average age at menarche over the last 20 or 30 years is less than 6 months. Furthermore, evidence from Dann and Roberts (1993) gathered by survey over a period of 16 years suggests that the mean age at menarche is increasing, reversing any previous downward trend. In any event, it remains the case that in the UK one in eight girls is likely to experience menarche while at primary school (Whincup et al. 2001). The arguable earlier onset of menarche has been discussed as a contributory factor in the supposed rise in the number of young pregnancies.

Increasing numbers of young people are staying in the education system for longer (Department for Education and Skills 2005). This defers their progression to economic independence, previously recognised as a demarcation between the world of adolescence and adulthood.

The arguable decrease in the average age at menarche and the deferral of entry to economic independence, combined with other factors, including changing relationship patterns whereby adolescent marriage is less normative (Furstenberg 2000), leads to the understanding that the duration of adolescence in Western nations is extending and becoming increasingly complex (Morrow and Richards 1996). In recognition of this, the concept of stages of adolescence has developed, whereby the process is divided into three subdivisions (Kohen-Raz 1983: 10):

- pre-adolescence – the age span between the onset of pubertal changes until menarche;
- adolescence proper – from menarche until the end of the pubertal process, defined as the manifestation of drastic deceleration in physical growth and equilibration of the menstrual cycle and fertility;
- post-adolescence – from that point until the attainment of adult status, defined as the attainment of sexual, legal and work responsibilities, despite the vagueness of these definitions within their fields.

This formulaic conceptualisation of adolescence may be of help in focusing definitions of adolescence. However, the protraction of adolescence and the accompanying conflict in roles has resulted in adolescence becoming constructed as a 'category of exclusion', neither childhood nor adulthood, but simultaneously both (Macleod 2003). The result of this is that young people are experiencing an increasing mismatch between their expectations and ambitions and the reality of their everyday transitional experiences (Morrow and Richards 1996).

Discourses of sexuality

As concepts of adolescence have altered, so have concepts of sexuality. It is now salient to focus on discourses of sexuality as they influence and relate to the formation of subjectivities (Foucault 1990). The subject is more than a product of the discourses of institutional regimes; subjects are dynamic and multiple, positioned in relation to the particular discourses and practices that produce them (Henriques 1998). These practices are continuously changing and so our subjectivities change as we relate and intersect with other practices. Sexuality is a component of our subjectivities, and the way in which it is experienced is also affected by multiple interrelated discourses.

Knowledge of sexuality and sexual moralities has been constitutive and constituting in relation to the changing structure of the family, the role of religion, an increasingly multicultural society, changes in the way 'society' is constructed and perceived, improvement in accessibility of contraception and increasing advances in technology. The impact of this can be seen in the changing structures of the family, for example, affecting patterns in marriage and divorce rates, changes to family structure in terms of number and gender of parents and changing patterns in rates of childbirth and their relationship with marriage (Gittins 1993). It is, therefore, within a complex and dynamic landscape that we must explore the construction of young pregnancy and motherhood, 'a dimension' of which is understood through the lens of sexuality. Jackson (1982: 163) describes the centrality of sexuality to our lives:

> Sexuality is an important area of social life. It is closely related to the most fundamental of social divisions, that of gender, and to one of the most basic social institutions, the family.

Jackson understands relationships with sexuality as reflecting gender and familial divisions. The significance of the role of sexuality and its relationship with social policy as an institution that influences, and is influenced by, the social divisions defined by Jackson remains largely ignored and under-researched (Carabine 1996). Arguably, as a result of this, and despite the significance of sexuality, omnipresent in the West are conflicting and confused ideologies about childhood and adolescent sexuality. This manifests as anxiety, imbibing sexuality with a special status whereby instead of being a simple everyday activity it is entwined in polarised understandings as being associated with extreme pleasure or extreme danger (Jackson and Scott 2004).

The framework of sexuality as 'special' informs the way in which children and young people are enabled (or disabled) in developing their sexuality. A binary of the sexually innocent and the dangerously aware is constructed within which young people are expected to self-locate. The sexually 'innocent' construct is increasingly enforced by the heightened anxiety witnessed in response to perceptions of sexual abuse and the increased awareness of child sex offenders, especially in relation to information technology and the worldwide web (ibid.). The conceptualisation of children as holding a sexual innocence that can be stolen or removed is historically specific, as demonstrated by the change in the age of consent, from 13 to 16 years, 150 years ago.

The boundaries of sexuality are conflicted. The conceptualisation of children as sexually innocent opposes the increasing sexualisation of, in particular, young women. Jackson (1982) discusses the historical processes leading to the state in which young children and women were social inferiors, living under the patriarchal authority of men. Prior to the nineteenth century women and children were expected to participate fairly equally in life. By the nineteenth century the bourgeois man wanted a wife to serve as a visible symbol of his economic and masculine success; thus began the establishment of the roles of the cosseted wife and her children. Boys were encouraged to leave behind their child-like qualities in order to supersede their fathers and become a 'man', whereas girls were trained to stay at home to satisfy the needs of other men. Part of the process of becoming a man included developing a masculine sexuality that is associated with activity and performance. Girls, however, were encouraged to remain child-like, innocent and vulnerable, an image that still constitutes part of the current conflicted representations of female sexuality. In order to maintain the innocence of children, sexual information was/is withheld and concealed from them. The complex management of young women's sexuality is seen as a central factor in determining the role and position of women (Ward 1995) and, therefore, as contributing to the oppression of children and, sequentially, women (Jackson 1982).

Changing discourses of sexuality highlight the continuing contested nature of sexuality whilst influencing personal and institutional attitudes to sexuality. In the education system this is demonstrated by an education curriculum that embodies the conflict between repressing child sexuality and regulating sexual behaviour whilst all along representing political desires to regulate sexual liberty (Monk 1998). As such, the classroom is constructed as a location for programmes of moral education with the aim being that it will enable children to regulate their own sexual behaviour in accordance with traditional norms (ibid: 254).

Thus, the institutional framework of education plays a significant role (Althusser 2001) in the formation of subjectivities that are individually and collectively accomplished through participating in social, material and discursive practices (Potter and Wetherell 1987).

Continuing from a historical perspective, second-wave feminism is seen to have contributed a new dimension to sexuality discourses that have arguably improved the formation of young women's lives and subjectivities. Equal opportunity discourses and legislation suggest a wealth of opportunity to young women never before in existence. The advent of the contraceptive pill afforded some women greater sexual freedom in protection against pregnancy by their own control. Whilst these concepts remain highly contested, the arrival of the Girl Power concept in the 1990s added a further dimension to the construction of femininity. Girl Power stemmed from a movement within youth culture to reclaim the word 'girl' and reinvest it with a sense of power and energy previously associated with the masculine-orientated punk music movement of the 1970s (Aapola *et al.* 2005). It has resulted in further development in the discourse of femininity. Another facet to this discourse is the way in which young (and increasingly younger) women are targeted with relentless amounts of sexualised marketing. Young women today are faced with the complex task of locating themselves within these ever-expanding and changing discourses.

Murcott (1980) has argued that young pregnancy and parenthood is located as a problem at the intersection of ideologies of reproduction and childhood.

Discourses of reproduction and motherhood

Historically women's identities have been inextricably linked to, and defined by, their relationship with motherhood (Silva 1996). At a physical level reasons for this are evident – women can be impregnated, carry and bear children. Post birth other people can accomplish the role of child carer. It is the biological association between women and the outcome of (hetero)sexual activity that connects women with the institution of motherhood that is treated as a given fact instead of as the possible outcome of specific social processes (Smart 1996). This consideration has arguably done little to diminish the strong connection between women and motherhood.

Motherhood is constructed in such a way as to serve political and psychological purposes (Phoenix and Woollett 1991). The implicit interpretations and the personification of the purposes of motherhood are based upon patriarchal ideology about reproduction and the role of women (Gittins 1993). Whilst 'the state' is not unitary ideologically or practically, a number of state institutions (such as health, education and welfare agencies) are designed to enforce and enact government policy. Mothers are, to varying degrees, subject to the control of these institutions guided by a dominant discourse and ideology. Manifestations of dominant discourses are seen in policy, legislation and in the discursive interpretations of mothering. Collectively they may be described as the process through which mothering becomes 'moralised, medicalised, psychologised, psychiatrised, and more recently legalised' (Ambert 1994). Paramount in recent and contemporary policy discourse is the need for parents to provide economic support and care for their children (Phoenix and Woollett 1991). Current policy places an emphasis upon economic independence, with its agenda of getting people off welfare and into work (Fairclough 2000). Parents unable to provide economically for their children represent a burden to the state in terms of benefits and welfare. The majority of parents reliant on state assistance are mothers. This leads to a focus on mothers, and particularly lone mothers and young mothers, as costly and heavily reliant on the state. Whilst welfare receipt may be the experience of some lone and/or young mothers, it is not that of all. The effect, however, through the many interrelated aspects of policy production and promulgation, is the demonisation of all young mothers.

In a critique of New Labour's welfare project, Lister (2001: 245) argues that two characteristics, 'a populist tendency to woo rather than to lead the electorate and a pragmatic "what works" approach', undermine its more progressive policies and result in a reactionary stance whilst partially ignoring structural inequalities. This is demonstrated by the instrumentation of policy that ensures that the nuclear family framework remains the idealised, dominant and privileged paradigm despite the increased numbers of men and women parenting outside the traditional nuclear family framework (Summerfield and Babb 2004). The issue of varied and changing cultural and societal attitudes towards young parenthood is rarely mentioned in the young pregnancy and parenthood literature yet would seem to be critical to the debate. Little recognition is made that in some religious and cultural groups early motherhood is positively sanctioned (Birch 1997). Moreover, in recognising the vast differentiation in cultural and religious attitudes towards young pregnancy and parenthood, consideration must also be paid to the complexity of these attitudes that are influenced by changes and advances in society (Chapters 2 and 3).

Psychological constructions of motherhood provide a framework for motherhood that demonstrates the articulation between knowledge and power to suggest 'ideas about the circumstances in which motherhood should occur and how mothers should interact with their young children' (Phoenix and Woollett 1991: 21). Examples of current psychological theory would include the theoretical construction of a 'right age' at which to mother.

Dominant psychology-based theory about how motherhood should occur, like political ideology, is expressed through state institutions, the media and public discourse. Although psychological discourses of motherhood are not enforceable, they are in a strong position to inform, and lend credence to, political discourse and practice. Research into mothering has been critiqued as focusing upon, and reinforcing, androcentric, patriarchal middle-class perceptions (Walkerdine and Lucey 1989; Phoenix and Woollett 1991). Studies have focused on a limited or single-dimensional understanding of mothering, as opposed to considering the multiple influences on the way in which women mother. The result of this is acceptance and normalisation of particular prescribed standards in mothering.

Standards for mothering are not routinely articulated, but are covertly expressed through institutional and personal discourses (Phoenix and Woollett 1991). What counts is not only what is said about that which constitutes a good or bad mother, but what remains unsaid, therefore research focusing upon mothers who are in some way deviant, or pathological, by default creates an understanding of mothers that are not. Lone mothers are frequently considered deviant, and thus constitute a 'wrong' sort of mother (Roseneil and Mann 1996); another 'wrong' sort of mother are lesbian and single mothers, as demonstrated by an Australian parliamentary debate over the drafting of legislation aimed at preventing lesbian and single women accessing *in vitro* fertilisation techniques (Smith 2003). And young mothers are another example of the 'wrong' sort of mother.

Accepted ideas about standards for mothering are historically and culturally specific. As noted earlier, young women now are less likely to have a baby than they were 20 years ago (Corlyon and McGuire 1997). Moreover, the options that were available to young single women who did get pregnant 30 years ago were more limited than they are today; many married to keep within the acceptable moral standards of the time in order to avoid discrimination, thus maintaining a degree of invisibility. The advent of oral contraception and the gradual emergence of equal opportunities in the workplace have both contributed to women's deferment of their reproductive careers. This is reflected in trends in childbearing. The number of first pregnancies occurring among women in their 30s and 40s has increased, while first pregnancies among women in their 20s or younger have decreased. The average (mean) age at first birth in the UK is currently 27.4 years, representing an increase over previous years (Office for National Statistics 2004). Extension of reproductive opportunity is assisted by an increase in availability of reproductive technology enabling a greater number of women who experience difficulties in conceiving the opportunity to have children. This has resulted in higher numbers of women becoming mothers at a later age. This framework explains why the dominant age at which women have their first child is in the late 20s. Women who mother outside of this framework, i.e. 'young' or 'old' mothers, are less prevalent and constructed as deviant (Berryman 1991; Phoenix 1991a,b).

The 'right time' numbers one of the circumstances in which motherhood idealistically should occur. Another is that it should take place within a 'steady' relationship, ideally marriage, in order to form a 'family'. Moral and policy discourses around lone mothers demonstrate this conceptualisation (Harding 1996). The early 1990s bore witness to a moral panic about lone motherhood, fed by a discourse linking lone motherhood with the generation of a moral underclass. This interrelates with a moral discourse centred on the 'breakdown of the family' (Roseneil and Mann 1996). In this context the 'family' refers to the Westernised institution of the nuclear family as a household of a couple and dependent children. The existence, role and nature of family have been extensively debated and are a focus for feminist thought. New Labour's Third Way discourse features the family as an extension of its conceptualisation of community (Fairclough 2000) whereby both are central to the organisation and functioning of society. Smart (1996: 56) argues that the 'traditional family' is 'a nineteenth century construction that was dependent upon clear strategies of disempowering women and binding them to motherhood and the private sphere'. History therefore creates a perception of normalcy through a socio-political description of women's role and place in life. Women operating outside of the dominant discourse come to be construed as deviant.

The 'traditional family' – which conforms to the roles, responsibilities and expectations of men and women as gender specific – is changing in terms of its dominant presence in most Western societies. Bearing witness to this change is the increasing proportion of households comprising a couple without children, the massive increase in reconstituted families with complex familial relations and the increase in lone-parent households (Summerfield and Babb 2004). This situation developed despite the moral panics of the 1990s and discrimination against lone mothers. Roseneil and Mann (1996) argue that lone mothers are active agents, as opposed to victims, in their decisions leading to motherhood. Recognition of this suggests that some women operate in a culture in which they feel able to make the choice to parent independently, outside the confines of the 'traditional family'. The debate about lone mothers therefore needs to shift its emphasis from denying their rights or existence to one that seeks to recognise their particular perspectives and needs. Within this debate the particular needs of young mothers is an essential component.

Lone mothers and young mothers share attributes – motherhood, exclusion and often single parenthood. They share the problems associated with career development, economic independence and stigmatisation by society. Exploring and understanding the way in which lone mothers have been constructed contributes to the understanding of the construction and experiences of young mothers. Edwards and Duncan (1996) describe two key discourses of lone motherhood. The first of these features lone mothers as a moral and financial threat to society. The second sees them as a social problem. These standpoints bear close resemblance to those of young motherhood.

The dominant political and psychological ideologies of motherhood result in the construction of a good–bad mother binary whereby women who mother within the dictates of the dominant ideological position are considered 'good mothers' while those who operate outside them are 'bad mothers' (Ladd-Taylor and Umansky 1998). Ideologies of motherhood are historically, socially and culturally specific (Ambert 1994) so the binary is dynamic yet inherent in the construction of mothers and motherhood.

The conceptualisation of the good–bad mother places a narrow emphasis on the relationship between mother and child(ren), the underlying assumption being the existence of mothers and mothering. Biologically, mothers exist, although 'mothering' is arguably a social construct. As Silva states this is important because:

> What mothers do whilst mothering matters strongly because, whether mothers make autonomous choices or fall under the domination of men, they continually recreate mothering and the conditions under which mothering happens.

> (Silva 1996: 33)

Concluding comments

This chapter has raised and begun to explore a number of issues that demonstrate the depth and breadth of all that constitutes teenage pregnancy and motherhood. Included within these issues we began with a discussion of the construction of teenage pregnancy as a problem, basing our argument upon the statistical evidence supporting the problematisation. We have considered the difficulties inherent in defining a young mother and continued by framing this within the broader picture that shapes personal and institutional discourses of young mothers, including discourses of sexuality, adolescence and reproduction and motherhood.

The conceptualisation that there is a 'right' time and a 'right' framework in which to mother reflects an oversimplification of the complexities of motherhood. Perceptions of what constitutes the 'right' time and framework are historically and culturally specific. It is clear that there is a need for people to be in a position to make informed choices and evaluate their desires and circumstances as they relate to potential parenthood within a framework of insightfulness and knowledge.

Education has a role to play in the process of enabling young people to make informed life choices by providing them with a space in which to explore the realities of parenting. This process should be undertaken in a way that recognises the contexts of the lives of the young people being worked with because these will shape the subjectivities of all. Such educational programmes need to recognise and reflect the power inherent in media discourses that represent motherhood as a luxury lifestyle option whereby babies and children are seen as a type of fashion accessory whose purpose is to enhance the social and glamour capital of the bearer. The reality of parenting, specifically motherhood, is personal whilst also being simultaneously shaped by the dominant political and psychological discourses of mothering. It is therefore impossible to facilitate a fully informed decision to become a mother as the concept can arguably be understood only from a position of experience. In response to the multiplicity of discourses of mothering there is a call for women to share their multiple realities of the experience of motherhood and to claim the power inherent in this gained knowledge (Maushart 1999).

A major consideration in the educational facilitation of informed choice-making regarding parenthood is the discourses of sex and relationships. Jackson and Scott (2004) have described discourses of sex as being imbibed with a 'special status' whereby sex is constructed as something extraordinary to be treated differently whilst Monk (1998) has drawn attention to the nature of contemporary sex education policy, which, when combined with the legal framework for sexual activity, results in a conflict between the desire to repress and to regulate young people's sexual behaviour. These conflicted and controversial discourses must be examined and reconsidered if sex and relationship education is to be effective in achieving the goal of helping young people to make informed choices regarding their sexual health, including decisions about potential parenthood.

Policy needs to recognise the significance of the contexts in which all women mother, in which circumstances of class and socio-economic background are meaningful and powerful (Walkerdine and Lucey 1989). This recognition can be demonstrated in a number of ways. First, policy-makers need to examine the body of research evidence that demonstrates that young pregnancy and parenthood is a class issue and consider the implications of this, particularly as it relates to educational expectations and aspirations which have been described as central in the decision-making process when a young woman is pregnant and considering a termination (Lee *et al.* 2004). Second, in recognising that for some young women motherhood is a desirable choice, policy needs to examine its locale when constructing the position of all mothers. Finally, at a practical but crucial level, the lives of many young mothers and their children could be made considerably more manageable if they were to receive adequate financial support when required. When considering the provision of welfare to young mothers, policy-makers should take account of the research evidence that demonstrates the longitudinal picture of young mothers as being similar to older mothers in economic productivity terms, albeit in a different pattern (Noble *et al.* 1998). Furthermore, the provision of practical housing is essential in promoting physical and psychological health in young mothers and their children.

The role of young fathers must be considered in policy, a point made by our colleagues Speak (Chapter 9) and Nyland (Chapter 10) later in this book. The needs of young fathers, like those of young mothers, require analysis and understanding from their perspectives in order to facilitate an egalitarian approach to young parenthood. There remains much work to be done if we are to achieve New Labour's goal of inclusion.

References

Aapola, S., Gonick, M. and Harris, A. (2005) *Young Femininity: Girlhood, Power And Social Change*, Basingstoke: Palgrave Macmillan.

Allen, I. and Bourke-Dowling, S. (1998) *Teenage Mothers Decisions and Outcomes*, London: Policy Studies Institute.

Althusser, L. (2001) *Lenin and Philosophy and Other Essays*. New York, Monthly Review Press.

Ambert, A. (1994) 'An International Perspective on Parenting: Social Change and Social Constructs', *Journal of Marriage and the Family* 56, 529–43.

Arai, L. (2003a) 'Low Expectations, Sexual Attitudes and Knowledge: Explaining Teenage Pregnancy and Fertility in English Communities. Insights from Qualitative Research', *The Sociological Review* 51, 199–217.

Arai, L. (2003b) 'British Policy on Teenage Pregnancy and Childbearing: the Limitations of Comparisons with other European Countries', *Critical Social Policy* 23(1), 89–102.

Berryman, J.C. (1991) 'Perspectives on Later Motherhood', in *Motherhood, Meanings, Practices and Ideologies* (eds A. Phoenix, A. Woollett and E. Lloyd), London: Sage, pp. 103–22.

Birch, D. (1996) *The Child That Rocks the Cradle*, London: Youth Support.

Birch, D. (1997) 'The Adolescent Parent – a Fifteen Year Longitudinal Study of School Age Mothers and their Children', *Journal of Adolescent Health and Welfare* 10(1), 17–25.

Blair, T. (1998) *The Third Way: New Politics for the New Century*, London: Fabian Society.

Brook Advisory Service (2005) *Your Rights: Your Rights to Receive Contraceptive Treatment*, Brook Advisory Service (available from http://www.brook.org.uk/content/M1_4_treatment.asp).

Carabine, J. (1996) 'Heterosexuality and Social Policy', in *Theorizing Heterosexuality* (ed. D. Richardson), Milton Keynes: Open University Press, pp. 55–74.

Corlyon, J. and McGuire, C. (1997) *Young Parents in Public Care: Pregnancy and Parenthood Among Young People Looked After by Local Authorities*, London: National Children's Bureau.

Dann, T.C. and Roberts, D.F. (1993) 'Menarcheal Age in University of Warwick Young Women', *Journal of Biosocial Science* 25, 531–8.

Davies, L., McKinnon, M. and Rains, P. (2001) 'Creating a Family: Perspectives from Teen Mothers.', *Journal of Progressive Human Services* 12(1), 83–100.

Dawson, N. (1997) 'The Provision of Education and Opportunities for Future Employment for Pregnant Schoolgirls and Schoolgirl Mothers in the UK', *Children and Society* 11, 252–63.

Dennison, C. and Coleman, J. (1998) 'Teenage Parenthood', *Children and Society* 12, 306–14.

Department for Education and Skills (2005) *Participation in Higher Education*, London: Department for Education and Skills.

Department for Work and Pensions (2005) *New Deal*, London: Department for Work and Pensions.

Edwards, R. and Duncan, S. (1996) 'Rational Economic Man or Lone Mothers in Context? The Uptake of Paid Work', in *Good Enough Mothering? Feminist Perspectives on Lone Motherhood* (ed. E.B. Silva), London: Routledge, pp. 114–29.

Electoral Commission (2003) *How Old is Old Enough? The Minimum Age of Voting and Candidacy in UK Elections*, London: The Electoral Commission.

Eurostat (2005) *Live Births by Marital Status and Mother's Age at Last Birthday*, Luxembourg: Eurostat.

Fairclough, N. (2000) *New Labour, New Language?*, London: Routledge.

Family Planning Association (1994) *Children Who Have Children*, London, Family Planning Association.

Foucault, M. (1990) *The History of Sexuality,* Volume 1: *An Introduction* (trans. Alan Sherridan), Harmondsworth: Penguin.

Furstenberg, F. (2000) 'Sociology of Adolescence and Youth in the 1990s: A Critical Commentary', *Journal of Marriage and the Family* 62, 896–910.

Giddens, A. (2000) *The Third Way and its Critics*, Cambridge: Polity Press.

Gillies, V. (2005) 'Meeting Parents' Needs? Discourses of "Support" and "Inclusion" in Family Policy', *Critical Social Policy* 25(1), 70–90.

Gittins, D. (1993) *The Family in Question: Changing Households and Familiar Ideologies*, Basingstoke: Macmillan.

Griffin, C. (1993) *Representations of Youth*, Cambridge: Polity Press.

Harding, L.M.F. (1996) ' "Parental Responsibility": the Reassertion of Private Patriarchy?', in *Good Enough Mothering: Feminist Perspectives on Lone Motherhood* (ed. E.B. Silva), London: Routledge, pp. 130–47.

Horwitz, S., Klerman, L. *et al.* (1991) 'Intergenerational transmission of school-age parenthood', *Family Planning Perspectives* 23(4), 168–72.

Henriques, J. (1998) 'Social psychology and the politics of racism', in *Changing the Subject: Psychology, Social Regulation and Subjectivity* (eds J. Henriques, W. Hollway, C. Urwin, C. Venn and V. Walkerdine), London: Routledge, pp. 60–90.

Hudson, F. and Ineichen, B. (1991) *Taking It Lying Down: Sexuality and Teenage Motherhood*, Basingstoke: Macmillan.

Jackson, S. (1982) *Childhood and Sexuality*, Oxford: Basil Blackwell.

Jackson, S. and Scott, S. (2004) 'Sexual Antinomies in Late Modernity', *Sexualities* 7, 233–48.

Jorgensen, S.R. (1993) 'Adolescent Pregnancy and Parenting', in *Adolescent Sexuality* (eds T. Gullotta, G. Adams and R. Montemayor), Thousand Oaks: Sage, pp. 103–40.

Kidger, J. (2004) 'Including Young Mothers: Limitations to New Labour's Strategy for Supporting Teenage Parents', *Critical Social Policy* 24, 291–311.

Kohen-Raz, R. (1983) *Disadvantaged Post-Adolescents: Approaches to Education and Rehabilitation*, London: Gordon and Breach.

Ladd-Taylor, M. and Umansky, L. (1998) *'Bad' Mothers. The Politics of Blame in Twentieth Century America*, New York: New York University Press.

Lee, E., Clements, S., Ingham, R. and Stone, N. (2004) *A Matter of Choice? Explaining National Variation in Teenage Abortion and Motherhood*, York: Joseph Rowntree Foundation.

Levine, J., Pollack, H. and Comfort, M. (2001) 'Academic and Behavioural Outcomes Among the Children of Young Mothers', *Journal of Marriage and Family* 63, 355–69.

Lister, R. (2001) 'New Labour: a Study in Ambiguity From a Position of Ambivalence', *Critical Social Policy* 21, 425–47.

Luker, K. (1996) *Dubious Conceptions: The Politics of Teenage Pregnancy*, Cambridge, MA: Harvard University Press.

Macleod, C. (2003) 'Teenage Pregnancy and the Construction of Adolescence', *Childhood* 10, 419–37.

Maushart, S. (1999) *The Mask of Motherhood*, London: Pandora.

Monk, D. (1998) 'Sex Education and the Problematization of Teenage Pregnancy: A Genealogy of Law and Governance', *Social and Legal Studies* 7, 239–59.

Morrow, V. and Richards, M. (1996) *Transitions to Adulthood: a Family Matter?*, York: Joseph Rowntree Foundation.

Murcott, A. (1980) 'The Social Construction of Teenage Pregnancy: a Problem in the Ideologies of Childhood and Reproduction', *Sociology of Health and Illness* 2(1), 1–23.

National Statistics (2006) *Live births: 1938–2004, Age of mother in 5 year age-groups: within/outside marriage and sex, all live births and female births only*, Newport: Office for National Statistics.

Noble, M., Smith, G. and Yi Cheung, S. (1998) *Lone Mothers Moving In and Out of Benefit*, York: Joseph Rowntree Foundation.

Office for National Statistics (2004) *Population Trends*, London: Office for National Statistics.

Phoenix, A. (1991a) *Young Mothers?*, Cambridge: Polity Press.

Phoenix, A. (1991b) 'Mothers under Twenty: Outsider and Insider Views', in *Motherhood: Meanings, Practices and Ideologies* (eds A. Phoenix, A. Woollett and E. Lloyd), London: Sage, pp. 86–102.

Phoenix, A. and Woollett, A. (1991) 'Motherhood: Social Construction, Politics and Psychology', in *Motherhood: Meanings, Practices and Ideologies* (eds A. Phoenix, A. Woollett and E. Lloyd), London, Sage, pp. 13–27.

Potter, J. and Wetherell, M. (1987) *Discourse and Social Psychology: Beyond Attitudes and Behaviour*, London: Sage.

Roseneil, S. and Mann, K. (1996) 'Unpalatable Choices and Inadequate Families: Lone Mothers and the Underclass Debate', in *Good Enough Mothering? Feminist Perspectives on Lone Motherhood* (ed. E.B. Silva), London: Routledge, pp. 191–210.

Samuels, V., Stockdale, D. and Crase, S. (1994) 'Adolescent mothers adjustment to parenting', *Journal of Adolescence* 17, 427–43.

Sharpe, S. (1987) *Falling For Love: Teenage Mothers Talk*, London: Virago Press.

Silva, E.B. (1996) 'The transformation of mothering', in *Good Enough Mothering? Feminist Perspectives on Lone Motherhood* (ed. E.B. Silva), London: Routledge, pp. 10–36.

Singh, S. and Darroch, J.E. (2000) 'Adolescent Pregnancy and Childbearing: Levels and Trends in Developed Countries', *Family Planning Perspectives* 32(1), 14–23.

Smart, C. (1996) 'Deconstructing Motherhood', in *Good Enough Mothering? Feminist Principles on Lone Motherhood* (ed. E.B. Silva), London: Routledge, pp. 37–57.

Smith, J.L. (2003) ' "Suitable Mothers": Lesbian and Single Women and the "unborn" in Australian Parliamentary Discourse', *Critical Social Policy* 23(1), 63–88.

SmithBattle, L. (1995) 'Teenage Mothers' Narratives of Self: an Examination of Risking the Future', *Advanced Nursing Science* 17(4), 2 –36.

Social Exclusion Unit (1999a) *Bridging the Gap: New Opportunities for 16–18 Year Olds Not in Education, Employment or Training*, London: Social Exclusion Unit.

Social Exclusion Unit (1999b) *Teenage Pregnancy*, London: Stationery Office.

Social Exclusion Unit (2004) *About Us – Social Exclusion Unit*, London: Office of the Deputy Prime Minister.

Stonewall (2004) *Age of Consent: Changing the Law*, London: Stonewall.

Summerfield, C. and Babb, P. (2004) *Social Trends 34*, London: Office for National Statistics.

Tanner, J.M. (1961) *Education and Physical Growth*, London: University of London Press.

Teenage Pregnancy Unit (2004) *Implementation of the Teenage Pregnancy Strategy Progress Report*, London: Teenage Pregnancy Unit.

Teenage Pregnancy Unit (2005) *Teenage Pregnancy Unit*, London: Teenage Pregnancy Unit.

United Nations Children's Fund (2001) *A League Table of Teenage Births in Rich Nations*, Florence: UNICEF Innocenti Research Centre.

Walkerdine, V. and Lucey, H. (1989) *Democracy in the Kitchen: Regulating Mothers and Socialising Daughters*, London: Virago Press.

Ward, M.C. (1995) 'Early Childbearing: What is the Problem and Who Owns It?', in *Conceiving the New World Order: The Global Politics of Reproduction* (eds F. Ginsburg and R. Rapp), Berkeley, CA: University of California Press, pp. 140–58.

Whincup, P.H., Gilg, J.A., Odoki, K., Taylor S.J.C. and Cook, D.G. (2001) 'Age of Menarche in Contemporary British Teenagers: a Survey of Girls Born between 1982 and 1986', *British Medical Journal* 322, 1095–6.

Wodak, R. (1996) *Disorders of Discourse*, London: Longman.

Chapter 2

Explaining early marriage in the Hmong American community

Serge C. Lee, Zha Blong Xiong, and Francis K. O. Yuen

Introduction

Explanations offered to understand the practice of early marriage by the Hmong in the USA must take into account the complexity of the culture and its previous ecological environment. Early marriage is defined as a recognizable, socially sanctioned marriage that involves at least one partner who is under the age of 18. Hmong who live in the USA and in other Western countries (i.e., Australia, France, and Canada) originally migrated from Laos after the end of the Vietnam War in 1975.

Laos is a land-locked country in South-East Asia located south of China, west of Vietnam, east of Thailand, and north of Cambodia, with an estimated population of 3.6 million prior to 1975 (Lee 1996). Although the origins of the Hmong (Miao) people across the globe have yet to be determined, the Chinese recorded history was the first to mention the Hmong who lived along the Yellow River Valley during the Shang dynasty between the sixth and eleventh centuries BC (Dekun 1991). During the early nineteenth century, after several decades of conflict with the Chinese and others, thousands of Hmong emigrated to northern Vietnam, then to the northern part of Laos and other South-East Asian countries, including Burma and Thailand. Most Hmong who resettled in Laos dwelled in villages in mountainous regions at altitudes between 3,000 and 7,000 feet above sea level (Mottin 1980; Quincy 1995), and integration with the Lao people was limited.

During the Vietnam War (i.e., from 1961 to 1975), the Hmong were recruited by the US Central Intelligence Agency (CIA) to serve as secret armies in the "special forces." Under the leadership of General Vang Pao, their mission was to block the Ho Chi Minh Trail along the Plain of Jars (Quincy 1995). In 1975, after the communist regime took over Laos, Vang Pao and a small contingent of his close associates managed to leave the country. *In absentia*, Vang Pao and his followers were publicly denounced as "contaminated crops" and sentenced to death by the new government. This "search and destroy the contaminated crops" order was applied to all Hmongs who were on the opposing side. In order to avoid the harsh persecutions, thousands of Hmong left Laos to seek freedom and democracy. Even now, more than 30 years later, this type of sentiment continues to prevail in

Laos. The communist government of the Lao People's Democratic Republic still describes the former combatant Hmong enemies as "bad elements."

Today, there are an estimated 186,310 Hmong living in the USA. They are among the fastest growing immigrant populations and are one of the youngest Asian populations in the USA, with 48 percent of Hmong aged between 5 and 19 (US Census 2000 as cited by the Hmong National Development and Hmong Culture and Resource Center 2004). The median age of the Hmong population is 16.1 years, compared with 35.3 for the US population. Owing to high fertility rates and early marriage, the Hmong population in the USA has quadrupled since 1980 (i.e., from 47,430 in 1980 to 186,310 in 2000), with a majority (over 70 percent) of the population concentrated in three states, California (65,000), Minnesota (41,800), and Wisconsin (33,791). Because of this rapid population growth, it is projected that by 2020 the number of Hmong people in the USA will reach 1 million (Xiong *et al.* 2004).

Prevalence of early marriage and teen pregnancy

Based on two of the authors' personal knowledge as members of the Hmong community, the age at marriage among the Hmong is often less than 18. Early marriage is a prevalent issue for Hmong Americans. Dunnigan *et al.* (1996) and Donnelly (1994), who have studied the US Hmong, found that the majority of people in their samples, especially females, married between the ages of 13 and 23, with an average age at marriage of 16. McNall *et al.* (1994) conducted a longitudinal study of Hmong students in Minnesota, beginning in 1987 when participants were in the ninth grade, and found that by the end of high school 70 percent (34 out of 49) of Hmong women were married. Similarly, Mottin (1980) observed that the Hmong in Thailand also typically marry at a young age, 12 years for girls and 14 for boys.

Hmong teenagers who live in Laos and other South-East Asian societies continue to marry soon after the onset of adolescence; in contrast, their counterparts in Western countries typical delay marriage until the late teens.

Giving birth immediately after marriage is not uncommon among the Hmong, since having children is one of the primary goals of marriage (McNall *et al.* 1994). Symonds (1984) studied 40 married Hmong mothers and found that most first gave birth when they were between the ages of 15 and 17. McNall *et al.* (1994) also found that, by the end of high school, more than half of the married women already had at least one child. Similarly, Rumbaut and Weeks (1986) found that the fertility rate of the US Hmong was the highest among the Vietnamese, Cambodian, and Laotian groups. In 1986, there were 1,769 children under 4 years of age per 1,000 Hmong women, compared with only 309 children of similar age group per 1,000 non-Hmong Asian women. Recently, Lee (unpublished, 2004) and Xiong *et al.* (2004) found that, on average, the time between first marriage and the birth of the first child was 1.62 years, suggesting that the Hmong do not long postpone childbearing after marriage. The Hmong people value large families, and young couples usually have several children.

The effects of early marriage and early childbearing on young couples in this community are not fully known and available findings are contradictory. Goldstein's (1985) ethnographic study of a group of young Hmong women found that "up to 80 per cent [of the girls] leave high school before graduation" (p. 3) due to child care issues. On the other hand, almost 10 years later, McNall *et al.* (1994) found that despite marrying early and having children before completing high school, most Hmong married women performed well in school and graduated. Some even chose to pursue postsecondary education. The extent to which the effects of early marriage and childbearing affect young Hmong people's life choices deserves further study by the professional and academic communities.

Why do many young Hmong marry before finishing school?

Several socio-cultural factors play a significant role in motivating young Hmong persons to decide to get married early. The next section further discusses these socio-cultural factors within the contexts of the Hmong tradition, custom, and current situations.

The Hmong culture and its kinship system

The primacy of the Hmong culture in the past, as well as the present, is based on its kinship system. Marriage is the key to the fulfillment and sustainability of the kinship system. The Hmong kinship system includes two kin categories, *kue tee* and *neng cha*.

Kue tee refers to members who share the same ascribed name and/or the same ancestor-worshipping rituals. *Kue tee* includes two levels of relationships: the lineage and the clan.

The more intimate relationship of the *kue tee* occurs at the lineage level. Barney, an anthropologist who studied the Hmong in South-East Asia, reports that, "members of the same lineage, who can trace their common descent from a known ancestor, refer to lineage mates by a common term meaning 'my olders and youngers'" (Barney 1967: 276). Each lineage chooses a few lineage leaders based on their service, age, and some other qualities. Together the leaders are responsible for facilitating and mediating internal lineage affairs (i.e., family problems, spousal disputes, and weddings). These leaders also represent the lineage to other lineages. In the Hmong community, members of the lineage usually consult a lineage leader on matters regarding marriage, funerals, and social disputes before seeking outside help (Xiong *et al.* 2004).

The less intimate level of the *kue tee* involves the clan. Clan is a term used to refer to members who share a common ascribed or last name, or *xeng (xeem)*. As Barney (1967) reports, "The clan name refers to descent from a mythical ancestor, and common membership in a clan serves as a bond of kinship and friendship between people who would otherwise be strangers" (p. 275). In the USA, there are approximately 18 Hmong clans. Because of the often unfounded fear of persecution and rejection by the American society, or to facilitate rapid acculturation into the American ways of life, some individuals and families have changed their Hmong clan names by adopting some other non-clan-related Hmong last names. Usually, rather than adopting a completely Americanized last name, these individuals and families use their father's or grandfather's given name, or part of it, as the family name. As a result they permanently change their last name to this family's middle name. However, even if they change their name, the majority of the Hmong still consider themselves members of their native clan and continue to be involved in clan activities to some extent.

Within this well-defined social structure, clan-endogamous marriage, i.e., marriage between members of the same clan, is prohibited regardless of the remoteness of the relationship or geographical distance (Westermeyer *et al.* 1997). For example, Kou Vang was born into the Vang clan in the USA; he is prohibited by Hmong custom from marrying Zoua Vang, who is also part of the same Vang clan even though she lives in Australia, regardless of the absence of any blood relationship between them. Because of this cultural taboo, people are expected to mate and marry outside the clan. Ironically, they also practice clan exogamy, which allows marriage between first and second cousins so long as they have different last names and belong to different clans.

Marriage between clans forms the second kin category, called *neng cha*. *Neng cha* consists of individuals of different clans who often reside in the same village and have social ties to other clans through relationships formed by marriage. Specifically, *neng cha* are the in-laws from the wives' side of the family. However, this conjugal relationship is important not only to the groom and his family of origin, but also to his lineage and clan.

In Laos, *kue tee* and *neng cha* link people and villages together into a big family and kinship network in which everyone is related and differentiated either by the clan and lineage affiliations or through marriage. Thus, marriage is a key mechanism that strengthens the "village family." It formalizes people's relationships for cultural preservation or political or economic gains, and promotes cultural and ethnic identities.

This "village family" structure is further strengthened through the cultural norm of gaining or losing face. Within this collectivist culture, the need to preserve face and maintain a social harmony with others in the community is vital (Yuen and Nakano-Matsumoto 1998). Social disharmony or *tou shia* (sad mind) and face saving are closely related. Individuals' behavior reflects on the family and individuals are expected to behave accordingly. This is done to maintain social harmony and gain face, or at least to avoid losing face. Individual actions that disturb social harmony result in everyone who shares the same lineage identity losing face. Face saving is often achieved at a great cost both individually and collectively (Yuen and Nakano-Matsumoto 1998). The consequences of losing face are severe and affect the individual, the families, the linkage, and the clan. Consider the following scenario.

Xao is a 15-year-old Hmong man who is considered obedient to his parents and a good student in school. He is willing to help out his parents around the house, since he does not have a sister. In Hmong culture, it is customary to have a big family usually including both male and female children. One day, without warning, Xao brought home a 14-year-old Hmong girl, Nou, whom he wanted to be his bride. Nou had had some problems in school and at home. She had run away from home several times to live with her uncle in order to avoid conflict at home. Although Xao's parents, Mr. and Mrs. Cher Pao, disapproved of the marriage, according to Hmong custom, they must accept the bride into their house as their potential daughter-in-law. Most importantly, Mr. Cher Pao is obligated by Hmong custom to accept Nou into his house until such time as the two families have the opportunity to meet and discuss the proposed union between the young couple. As soon as Nou is accepted by the Cher Pao family, she not only becomes their daughter-in-law to-be, but also automatically becomes an additional member of the family. If Nou is not properly accepted and the rituals of welcoming a new daughter-in law are not followed through, the finalization of the marriage could become difficult. In fact, it could be perceived as offending not only Nou but her clan as well.

Because of these cultural obligations, Mr. Cher Pao quickly grabbed a few incense sticks, as a substitute for a live chicken, and performed a "chicken ceremony" for the couple, a spiritual rite that "officially" accepts the bride into the groom's family. Mr. Cher Pao also quickly called a lineage meeting (*sha lah*) to discuss the situation before proceeding with any other plans. This is a typical protocol for all marriages. Within an hour, several men from the lineage had gathered in the Paos' house for the meeting. During the meeting, Mr. Cher Pao indicated that he wanted his son to go to college first before marriage. Additionally, he believed that his son deserved a better wife. However, because the bride had been "officially" married to his son, turning the bride away would violate the wedding rituals, which in turn would show disrespect to the bride, her parents, and her lineage group. Any wrong steps could potentially result in a feud between two lineage groups and would quickly extend to the clan level, which involves several related lineages. This situation could discredit the integrity of the lineage and clan leaders of the groom's family, resulting in shame and loss of face (Yuen and Nakano-Matsumoto 1998). Because of these complications, the lineage decided that Mr. Cher Pao should accept the marriage and arrange the wedding ceremony.

These socio-cultural complications, coupled with old and young Hmong people's acceptance of and attitudes toward early marriage, have sustained and perpetuated early marriage among the Hmong even in a modern postindustrial society. Nevertheless, some parents and young people have tried to discourage early marriage. They are, however, vulnerable to being assigned the label of causing social disharmony (*tou shia*) and to the fear of being singled out for not conforming to the cultural norms including customary laws (*kev cai cha yee*).

Pursuit of an easier life: tao zong

The concept of pursuing an easier life or *tao zong* is closely related to early marriage. In Laos most Hmong people are farmers. Farming demands long hours of manual work and is labor intensive, requiring everyone in the family to participate. It is normal for children to help out with both family and farming chores during their adolescent years. In addition, children are expected to care for their parents even after they have their own families. For most parents the pathway to an easier life in their later years, and to financial and social security (Yuen and Nakano-Matsumoto 1998), is through their children. Consequently, Hmong parents tend to encourage their children to get married as soon as they are biologically capable of becoming parents. An old Hmong saying states, "The sooner you get married, the sooner you get to rest." In other words, the sooner one gets married and bears children, the sooner one can enjoy the benefits of having children. Children are educated early to be responsible, obedient, and loyal to the family. Traditionally, girls were taught to get up early in the morning to gather water and feed the animals. Then they were to care for younger siblings, sew, and embroider clothes. Boys were socialized to lead the practice of ancestor worship and other spiritual rites, fish, hunt, farm, and scout for suitable lands to be cleared for various types of crops (Westermeyer *et al.* 1997).

A traditional Hmong female's role demands are tied to domestic responsibilities and her place is in the house. It is important to socialize a girl to become a "good" girl. A good girl is to grow up to be a good wife, and a good wife would make a good daughter-in-law. A good daughter-in-law is someone who possesses attributes such as good temper, patience, self-control, diligence, and responsibility, and is a hard worker. She is not independent or self-assertive and does not exhibit critical thinking or intelligence. This attitude is similar to that expressed by the old Chinese belief that "A woman without education is a good disposition." Parents and male children are taught to look for these qualities in a prospective wife and daughter-in-law, not ambition, independence, assertiveness, and education (Goldstein 1985; Donnelly 1994).

A family without a teenage girl is a family in which the parents, especially the mother, are burdened with endless household responsibilities. Thus, the sooner a son brings home a diligent and hard-working bride, the sooner the parents are able to reduce their responsibilities. A mother who has a daughter-in-law will no longer have to worry about getting up early in the morning to pound the rice, carry the water, cook meals, and prepare food for the family and animals. This new family member also represents extra help on the farm. Because of this idea of pursuing an easier life, younger sons are encouraged to marry older girls, and sometimes such marriages are arranged (Geddes 1976; Savitridina 1997). Families that have daughters accept the cultural norm that daughters are "temporary" and will marry out into their new homes. It is better to prepare them well and early to marry into good families than for them to become old maids living in their parents' homes. Traditionally, parents have not invested in daughters' education. It is more desirable to pool family resources to support the sons who will carry the family name than to invest in the daughters. Why invest precious family resources in daughters, who will leave the house and benefit the in-laws instead?

During the second half of the twentieth century, education became an alternative pathway to achieving an easier life in Laos. Yet few Hmong had the same opportunity as most people in Laos to pursue an education. Girls in particular were not allowed by their parents to receive formal schooling as this conflicted with the demands of family and farm work (Donnelly 1994; Kunstader 2004). Although most boys were encouraged to enroll in village schools, many stopped going after completing their primary education, i.e., sixth grade. Secondary education required children to board at city schools. Boarding at city schools required parents to fund room and board, clothing, and school supplies, costs that were simply too high for many poor parents to meet. As there is no formal higher education, i.e., college, in Laos, the term higher education is used to describe education grades 7 through 12. Even today, there is no baccalaureate (comparable to 4 years at college in the USA) level or higher level education in Laos. Unable to continue high school and obtain a better job in the city, most adolescent boys end up staying in their home village to follow the traditional path of farming and getting married early. A similar path continues to predominate among the Hmong community in the USA. Many Hmong Americans have voiced their concerns and beliefs that there is a strong link between early marriage and school failure and many parents tell their high-school children that if they cannot pursue higher education then they should get married and begin raising a family. The common message "an early start gets an early rest," passed on from one generation to the next, continues to have an impact on young Hmong people's decision to get married early.

An interesting trend that has, however, emerged in recent years is that more Hmong American females are continuing their education at college while fewer Hmong American males are doing so. It is thought that many Hmong males are following a traditional role as the provider for the family, which necessitates entering the workforce immediately after high school. Hmong females, in contrast, view education as a unique opportunity to escape their traditional role and to become successful and achieve independence through a means, i.e., education, that is valued and sanctioned by the Hmong community. Consequently, many of these females have delayed marriage.

Marriage as an escape route and rescuing someone in trouble

The reasons for the perpetuation of the practice of early marriage among the Hmong community in the USA are twofold. Young Hmong are both the products of their parents' past cultural practices and at the same time casualties of their own attempts to escape from or resolve family problems. Growing up in America, and being faced with competing cultural values and practices, is not easy for the children of Asian immigrant parents (Yuen and Nakano-Matsumoto 1998; Portes and Rumbaut, 2001; Xiong *et al.* 2001).

In Hmong families, children are expected to be bright, obedient, and responsible, and to help out the family. Hmong American girls are more burdened than their male counterparts. They face pressure to do well in school and also to work tirelessly around the house. Some parents even perceive their daughters as the last resource to rescue the family and to rise above many negative socio-cultural conditions. These young girls often act as surrogate parents to their younger siblings. They take on multiple tasks that their parents lack the necessary English skills to perform, such as filling out forms, translations, and attending parent–teacher conferences (DuongTran *et al.* 1996; Pardeck and Yuen 1997; Yuen and Nakano-Matsumoto 1998). They are, however, supervised closely at home to protect their own reputation as well as that of their family in order to enhance their marital chances (Donnelly 1994). Ngo (2002) found that South-East Asian teenage girls experience more dissatisfaction with their parents than do teenage boys. Portes and Rumbaut (2001) assert that parent–adolescent conflict around family responsibilities is higher among South-East Asians than in other immigrant groups. Ironically, however, parents perceive their daughters as more responsible and dependable than their sons, and theyare therefore viewed as a reliable, and perhaps the only, resource to allow the families to rise above many negative socio-cultural conditions.

The unique Hmong family environment also serves as a major contributing factor for some young marriages. Girls in particular use marriage as a tool to get away from their parents and their sometimes difficult and complex family life. Ngo (2002) conducted an ethnographic study of nine Hmong college students in the USA and reported that the Hmong women she interviewed claimed that they used marriage to escape parental authority. Her study findings are similar to those of Donnelly (1994), who reported that girls frequently felt overprotected and were rarely allowed to date or party with their peers. Boys, on the other hand, have few household responsibilities and use their advantage to rescue girls who have a troubled family life, as exemplified by the story of 15-year-old Xao described earlier in this chapter.

Findings on early marriage: two studies in California and Minnesota

In order to further understand the prevalence of, and the reasons contributing to, early marriage in the Hmong community, we conducted two surveys among 230 married and single Hmong Americans in California and Minnesota during the summer of 2004. Participants were recruited using convenience samples from the Hmong community and Hmong college students.

The California sample comprised 107 participants, ranging in age from 13 to 67 (mean = 30.5, SD = 13.8) years, with a median age of 27 years. Fifty-four (50.5 percent) respondents described themselves as youth, while 53 (49.5 percent) said they were parents. The term "youth"' is commonly used in Hmong culture to refer to males and females who either have never been married or who are married only by custom (i.e., have participated only in a traditional Hmong marriage, which is not legally binding in the American justice system) and have no children. The term "parents" refers to males and females who are not only married (legally or by custom) but have at least one child. Thus, married teenagers were classified as parents and not youths.

The Minnesota sample comprised 126 participants, with an age range of 12–67 (mean = 27.9, SD = 13.9) years and a median age of 21 years (compared with a median age of 16 years for the overall Hmong Americal population; US Census Bureau 2000 as cited in Hmong National Development 2004). Seventy (55.6 percent) respondents said that they were in the youth group and 53 (42.1 percent) described themselves as being in the parent group. Three participants (2.4%) declined to state whether they were in the youth or the parent group.

In both studies, participants were asked several questions pertaining to their age at marriage and their reasons for getting married early if they married before the age of 18. Overall, the reported mean marital age in the two samples was 20.7 years (SD = 4.4), with a median marital age of 19.5 years. In contrast to the literature reviewed, only 39.6 percent (42 of the 106 parents) of respondents said that they married at age 18 or younger. This finding is consistent with the findings of Lee and Yuen (unpublished, 2005), who, in a study of 50 young adult Hmong aged 18–30, found that 82 percent were single. We used analysis of variance (ANOVA) to compare age at first marriage for men and women. The difference between the sexes was not statistically significant, especially in the group who first married at 13–19 years and those who first married at 20 and over. These statistics seem to suggest that Hmong in America have started to delay marriage.

Young respondents, aged 13–27, were asked for their response to the following statement: "If my girlfriend or boyfriend was being treated badly at home, I would marry my loved one to help him or her out." Sixty percent (74 out of 124) of the young unmarried respondents reported that they either agreed or strongly agreed with this statement. These escape and rescue attempts are closely intertwined with cultural values and practices that have continued to contribute to the perpetuation of early marriage.

We also examined the Hmong cultural belief that it is universally acceptable and developmentally appropriate for boys and girls to get married as soon as they are sufficiently mature. The evidence revealed that young people's decision to get married while of high-school age is typically supported by their siblings. For example, 53 percent (n = 27) of youth participants in the survey agreed that if they had a brother or sister who wanted to get married before completing high school, they would support his or her decision. In addition, 71 percent ($n = 37$) of adults said that they would support their children's early marriage decision.

To determine the economic consequences of early marriage for Hmong Americans, two specific variables pertaining to the Californian participants were extrapolated for analysis: age at first marriage and estimated income for the immediate past year. Age at first marriage was divided into two categories: marriage between the ages of 13 and 18, described as "early marriage," and marriage at age 19 or later, described as "delayed marriage." Among participants who got married early the average annual family income was US$27,500 (SD = US$23,500), with a median income of US$25,000 and a range of US$0–80,000. The results in the delayed marriage group were very different. This group reported an average annual family income of US$46,000 (SD = US$30,000), with a median income of US$44,000 and a range of US$1,000–100,000. In other words, average annual income was $19,000 lower in the early marriage group than in the delayed marriage group. An independent *t*-test revealed that the difference in income between the two groups was highly significant ($t = -12.673$, d.f. = 87, $P < 0.001$). However, it should be borne in mind that the analysis failed to control for many confounding variables such as level of education, geographic location, and other factors.

Conclusion

The current study findings reflect the prevalence as well as the changing face of early marriage among Hmong in the USA. Although early marriage is still acceptable to many young Hmong, more are delaying marriage. Many have witnessed both positive and negative social, economic, and educational consequences of getting married early. Early marriage in the Hmong community over the last two decades has changed in both form and nature. In the early twenty-first century, the Hmong American community will face new challenges and be presented with new opportunities.

First, an open dating system similar to that which takes place in mainstream American society will become more prevalent. Young Hmong will prefer to date in an open fashion without fear of stigma. Hmong girls who date should not be viewed as lacking dignity and pride or be suspected of being sexually promiscuous. Dating and courtship should be mainstreamed into the Hmong community. They should be properly perceived as socially sanctioned ways of gaining a better mutual understanding and developing the romantic love that may eventually lead to the decision to marry.

Second, the relationship between early marriage and educational attainment and family economic security may need to be further examined. Early marriage might be a viable and sensible practice in a preliterate, agricultural, and traditional society in Laos. However, the negative consequences of early marriage without sufficient academic or vocational preparation have forced some to question its appropriateness and utility in postmodern technology-age American society. The abundance of educational and vocational development opportunities in the USA offers many alternatives to youngsters of different abilities and aptitudes. Early marriage is less of a guarantee of an easier life in one's later years than having an appropriate academic or vocational preparation.

Third, it is difficult to change a custom that has been practiced for centuries in a static system of a close-knit community. In the "village family" everyone is connected to, and affected by, everyone else. Few would risk oneself and one's family being isolated and abandoned by explicitly standing up against the lineage and clan in an effort to refuse early marriage. The lack of strong convictions and motivations to despise the group decision and cultural norm has perpetuated the practice of early marriage. In order to make a change to this traditional practice, lineages and clans need to assess whether early marriage will generate desirable outcomes for the future generations of Hmong in America. Thus, Hmong Americans should reconsider the meaning and impact of early marriage in the Hmong community. At the same time, community leaders and elders should address the need to allow individuals to make decisions for themselves or their children without the fear of being isolated and ostracized. Minimizing the connection between personal marital choice and the linkage or the clan is another big challenge for Hmong elders. This is a drastic paradigm shift that may take generations to accomplish.

Fourth, Hmong educators, professionals, and community leaders could take a more active role in serving as mediators between Hmong teenagers and parents. Interestingly, Hmong parents are becoming more supportive of their children delaying marriage for education; it is the teenagers who do not object to the practice of early marriage.

Finally, there is a need for the Hmong American communities to properly discuss and address the issue of marriage including early marriage and its correlation with divorce. By custom in Hmong society, a stable marriage between a young couple served as a functional transition from childhood to adulthood, thus preserving the clan's lineage systems. Just a generation ago, divorce was very rare, an almost unheard of event. Now, although no data have been collected on the prevalence of divorce among young Hmong American couples, observations and reports from Hmong communities suggest that an increasing number of early marriages are resulting in divorce. If a clear correlation between early marriage and divorce can be proved, then concern about the increased divorce rate among young Hmong couples may lead to discussion within the community on early marriage.

Only 30 years ago Hmong Americans were mostly illiterate; now the community includes doctors, professors, lawyers, politicians, civic leaders, professionals, and microeconomic entrepreneurs. As McNall *et al.* (1994) have pointed out, even Hmong who married early did not stop pursuing their higher education. In addition, data from the US Census (2000) indicate that the proportion of people under the age of 25 who have never married is significantly higher among the Hmong (31.5 percent) than in the US population as a whole (14.9 percent) (Hmong National Development 2004). Grover and Todd (2004) reported that in the 1990s home ownership among Hmong Americans was below 10 percent, but in 2000 the rate jumped to about 39 percent nationally and to about 54 percent in the three large states where most Hmong currently reside. Hmong families have emerged from an agricultural society and have begun to adapt to the postindustrial, technological, and professional American society. While some young Hmong may still be embracing the practice of early marriage, more are choosing to delay marriage in exchange for education opportunities and socio-economic growth.

References

Barney, L.G. (1967) "The Miao of Xiengkhouang Province, Laos," in *Southeast Asian Tribes, Minorities, and Nation* (ed. P. Kunstadter), Princeton, NJ: Princeton University Press, pp. 271–94.

Dekun, W. (1991) "A Brief Introduction to the Hmong of China," *Hmong Forum* 2, 1–15.

Donnelly, N. (1994) *Changing Lives of Refugee Hmong Women*, Seattle: University of Washington Press.

Dunningan, T., Olney, D., McNall, M.A. and Spring, M.A. (1996) "Hmong," in *Refugee in America in the 1990s: A Refugee Handbook* (ed. D.W. Haines), Wesport, CT: Greenwood Press, pp. 191–212.

DuongTran, Q., Lee, S., and Khoi, S. (1996) "Ethnic and Gender Differences in Parental Expectations and Life Stress," *Child and Adolescence Social Work Journal* 13, 515–26.

Geddes, W.R. (1976) *Migrants of the Mountain: The Cultural Ecology of the Blue Miao of Thailand*, Oxford: Clarendon Press.

Goldstein, B.L. (1985) "Schooling for Cultural Transitions: Hmong Girls and Boys in American High Schools", PhD dissertation, Department of Educational Policy Studies, University of Wisconsin–Madison.

Grover, M., and Todd, R.M. (2004) "Hmong Home Ownership: Up Sharply in the 1990s but Still Lagging in the Central Valley," in *Hmong 2000 Census Publication: Data and Analysis*, Washington, DC: Hmong National Development.

Hmong National Development (2004) *Hmong 2000 Census Publication: Data and Analysis*, Washington, DC: Hmong National Development, Inc. and the Hmong Cultural and Resource Center.

Kundstadter, P. (2004) "Hmong Marriage Patterns in Thailand in Relation to Social Change," in *Hmong/Miao in Asia. Chiang Mai* (eds N. Tapp, J. Michaud, C. Culas, and G.Y. Lee), Thailand: Silkworm Books, pp. 375–420.

Lee, G.Y. (1996) "Cultural Identity in Post-modern Society: Reflections on What is a Hmong?," *Hmong Studies Journal* 1(1), 1–15.

Lee, S.C. (2004) "Views and perspectives of early marriage in Hmong American communities." Unpublished manuscript.

McNall, M., Dunnigan, T., and Mortimer, J.T. (1994) "The Educational Achievement of the St. Paul Hmong," *Anthropology and Education Quarterly* 25(1), 44–65.

Mottin, J. (1980) *The History of the Hmong*, Bangkok: Odeon.

Ngo, B. (2002) "Contesting 'Culture': The Perspective of Hmong American Female Students on Early Marriage," *Anthropology and Education Quarterly* 33, 163–99.

Pardeck, J., and Yuen, F. (1997) "A Family Health Approach to Social Work Practice," *Family Therapy* 2(24), 115–28.

Portes, A. and Rumbaut, R. G. (2001) *Legacies: The Story of the Immigrant Second Generation*, New York: Russell Sage Foundation.

Quincy, K. (1995) *Hmong, History of a People*, Cheney, WA: Eastern Washington University Press.

Rumbaut, R., and Weeks, J.R. (1986) "Fertility and Adaptation: Indochinese Refugees in the United States," *International Migration Review 20*, 428–466.

Savitridina, R. (1997) "Determinants and Consequences of Early Marriage in Java, Indonesia," *Asia-Pacific Population Journal* 12(2), 3–25.

Symonds, P.V. (1984) "A Flower for the Bee: Hmong Perceptions of Adolescent Pregnancy," Masters Thesis: Brown University, Providence, RI.

Westermeyer, J., Bouafuely-Kersey, M., and Her, C. (1997) "Hmong children," in *Transcultural Child Development: Psychological Assessment and Treatment* (eds G. Johnson-Powell and J. Yamamoto), New York: John Wiley and Sons, pp. 161–82.

Yuen, F.K.O. and Nakano-Matsumoto, N. (1998) "Effective Substance Abuse Treatment Approaches for Asian American Adolescents," *Early Child Development and Care* 147, 43–54.

Xiong, Z.B., Detzner, D.F., and Rettig, D.K. (2001) "Southeast Asian Immigrant Parenting Practices and Perceptions of Parent–Adolescent Conflicts," *Journal of Teaching Marriage and Family: Innovations in Family Science Education* 1(1), 27–45.

Xiong, Z.B., Eliason, P.A., Detzner, D.F., and Cleveland, M.J. (2004) "Southeast Asian Immigrants' Perceptions of Good Adolescents and Good Parents," *Journal of Psychology* 139, 159–75.

Chapter 3

Hacia un futuro más seguro[1]

Pregnancy and childbearing among Latina adolescents

Margaret S. Sherraden, Rosio Gonzalez, and William Rainford

Latino adolescents constitute 15 percent (2.4 million) of the under-18 population and are now the largest minority teen group in the USA (US Census Bureau 2001a). Furthermore, the proportion of adolescent Latinos is expected to rise in the coming decades. It is expected that by 2020 one in five teenagers in the USA will be Latino (Day 1996; Dickson 2001). As their numbers grow, the well-being of this group has become a focus of public policy debate. This chapter examines pregnancy and childbearing among Latina teenagers in the USA.

Since 1991, adolescent pregnancy and childbearing rates in the USA have steadily declined. Latina teenage birth rates also declined, but at a slower rate than among African American and white adolescents. Birth rates for all 15- to-19-year-olds declined by 33 percent, between 1991 and 2002, from 61.8 per 1,000 women to 41.6 per 1,000 (Martin *et al.* 2005: 5) (Figure 3.1). Among adolescent Latinas, the birth rate fell by 21 percent (from 104.6 to 83.4 per 1,000) (Martin *et al.* 2005: 42).[2]

Research results on sexual activity among Latino adolescents are mixed and suggest that rates vary by immigrant generation and level of acculturation. Compared with white adolescents, rates of sexual activity are higher in the more acculturated groups (second- and third-generation Latinos) but lower in first-generation Latinos. According to nationally representative data collected from Youth Risk Behaviour Surveys (YRBS) carried out between 1990 and 1995, 62 percent of adolescent Latino males are sexually active, compared with 49 percent of adoles-

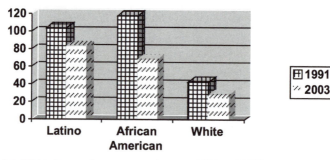

Figure 3.1 US birth rates for teenagers by race, 1991 and 2002.

cent white males. For females, the corresponding figures are 53 percent for Latina adolescents and 49 percent for white adolescents (Warren *et al.* 1998). Between 1990 and 1997 the proportion of white adolescents who were sexually active fell from 52 percent to 44 percent, whereas their Latino counterparts showed little change, the figure falling only from 53 to 52 percent (Annie E. Casey Foundation 1998). In addition, an analysis by Brener *et al.* (2002) found that between 1991 and 2001 the proportion of all high-school students who reported sexual experience decreased by 16 percent, compared with a decline of only 9 percent among Latino students. The proportion of high-school students who reported having four or more sexual partners fell by 24 percent overall and by 11 percent among Latinos (Brener *et al.* 2002). However, as these data were collected in high schools, the samples may have been biased toward more acculturated groups. In contrast, Remez (1991) found that Latino adolescents born in Mexico and residing in the USA were less likely than US-born Mexican adolescents or non-Hispanic white adolescents to engage in sexual activity at a young age. Likewise, Harris (1998) found that first-generation Latino immigrant adolescents were older at age of first sexual intercourse and were less likely to have had intercourse than second and later generations of Latino adolescents. Torres and Singh (1986) found that Latino adolescents had the lowest rate of premarital intercourse (30 percent) of all racial groups; for comparison, the rate among white adolescents was 36 percent. Confounding findings on sexual activity, Torres and Singh (1986) also reported that Latino adolescents are five times more likely to be married than white adolescents.

Latina teenagers are more likely than teenagers from other groups to give birth. The birth rate among adolescent Latinas in 1999 was 94 per 1,000, nearly double the national average for all adolescents (Dickson 2001). During the 1990s, births to all US adolescents decreased by over 30 percent, compared with a decrease of only 20 percent among Latinas (Hamilton *et al.* 2003). Should we be concerned? Early pregnancy and childbearing have long-term risks (Pabon 1998; Gillock and Reyes 1999). For example, adolescent mothers encounter challenges obtaining adequate health care (Nguyen *et al.* 2003). As a result, pregnant teenagers often face significant health threats, including high rates of sexually transmitted infections and HIV infection (Centers for Disease Control and Prevention 1999). Their children often have major health problems (Baldwin and Cain 1980). Teenage mothers also have to contend with psychological challenges brought on by caring for their infants when they themselves have not reached adult maturity (de Anda *et al.* 1990). Further, adolescent mothers struggle to financially support themselves and their babies (Maynard 1996). The outlook for adolescent mothers is likewise often challenging. Many adolescent mothers fail to continue their education, having dropped out of high school to give birth to and raise their children (Ahn 1994; Klepinger *et al.* 1995). Adolescent mothers are thus less likely to successfully build stable economic opportunities for themselves and their children (Maynard 1996). Adolescents' birth families, often already financially stretched, frequently must assume additional financial and emotional responsibilities for supporting pregnant adolescents and their babies, thereby exacerbating the family's poverty (Haveman *et al.* 1997). Birth fathers offer insufficient material and emotional support because of their own economic struggles (Zayas *et al.* 1987).

Unfortunately, the discourse on teen pregnancy and childbearing has led to an exclusive focus on decreasing rates of pregnancy and childbearing without calling for improvements in overall well-being and future opportunities for adolescents, including teen mothers and fathers (Geronimus 2003). Public policy resources have tended to focus on abstention, sex education, and contraception (Aneshensel *et al.* 1990). While these are important and necessary aspects of teen pregnancy prevention, they do not address the way that adolescents (and their parents) view their future, including their motivation to delay early pregnancy and childbearing. Failure to address future economic opportunity may leave Latina adolescents with little hope of improving their socio-economic status, which in turn may lead them to fail to delay childbirth.

In this chapter we examine the evidence and causes of teen pregnancy and early childbearing among Latino youth. We begin by addressing diversity within the Latino community and implications for teen pregnancy and childbearing rates. Following this, we analyze factors that contribute to adolescent pregnancy and childbearing in Latino communities. We then explore investment strategies that empower Latino youth to make decisions in their own and their families' best interests. We conclude with a discussion about the politics of teen pregnancy and childbearing among Latinos.

Diversity of the Latino population

Despite widespread perception that US Latinos are a homogeneous group, there are important differences in national origin, geographic destination, and immigration status that mask important issues and distinctions. Thus, despite the many cultural and linguistic similarities, Latinos originate from 23 countries, including what is now the USA. Within the adolescent Latino population, approximately 66 percent are of Mexican descent, 15 percent are of Central American or South American descent, 9 percent are of Puerto Rican descent, 4 percent are of Cuban descent, and 6 percent are of other Latino origin (US Census Bureau 2000; Thierren and Ramirez 2001) (Figure 3.2). There is also variation by settlement, with the largest numbers of Latinos in the south-west, Illinois, and New York. Over half of all Latinos live in California and Texas (17.7 million), and most others live in New York, Florida, Illinois, Arizona, and New Jersey (9.2 million). Overall, Latinos are more likely than other populations to live in metropolitan areas (Bonilla 2001). These geographic settlement patterns are changing, however, with large increases in Mexican-origin immigrants in the Deep South, south-east, and Midwest.

Approximately 40 percent of Latinos are foreign born, and many more have family members who are foreign born. (Puerto Ricans are US citizens, and therefore are not counted as foreign born.) Citizenship and language barriers are key

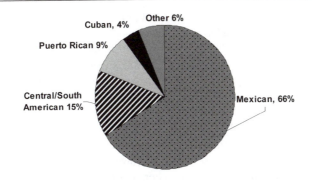

Figure 3.2 US Latino adolescent population by national origin of family.

issues for the foreign-born. Almost one-quarter (24 percent) of adolescent Latinos currently residing in the USA were born outside the country, mostly in Mexico (US Census Bureau 2001a). Some of these adolescents and members of their families lack legal immigration documents. Although exact numbers are impossible to know, it is believed that between 300,000 and 500,000 undocumented immigrants enter the USA each year. Mexicans account for approximately 57 percent of immigrants without legal immigration documents, while other Latin Americans account for another 25 percent (US Immigration and Naturalization Service 2002).

These ethnic differences have important implication for different subgroups (Pedraza-Bailey 1985; Portes and Rumbaut 2001). To illustrate, the circumstances of Mexican American immigrants, whose ancestors occupied the US south-west for centuries, differ from those for Puerto Rican citizens who grew up migrating between the US mainland and Puerto Rico. Similarly, the circumstances of El Salvadoran refugees who fled war in Central America differ from those of Cubans who joined the Mariel boatlift in 1980. These varying contexts affect the experiences of each of these groups, including the demographic characteristics of the group itself, political rights, settlement patterns, social networks, access to services, and acculturation patterns. These, in turn, influence patterns and outcomes of teen pregnancy and childbearing. We will turn to some of these implications shortly.

Reflecting this diversity, pregnancy and birth rates vary widely among Latino groups. In 2004, adolescent Latinas of Mexican descent had a birth rate of 93 births per 1,000, adolescents of Puerto Rican descent had a birth rate of 61 per 1,000 births, and adolescents of all other Latina descents had a birth rate of 60 per 1,000 births (National Campaign to Prevent Teen Pregnancy 2005). In addition, birth rates among adolescent Latinas vary by place of settlement, being 38 per 1,000 in California, 67 per 1,000 in Texas, and 219 per 1,000 in North Carolina (Sutton and Matthews 2004).

Birth rates also vary by generation of immigration. This is not surprising, given the wide range of immigration and acculturation experiences of the Latino population across generations. For instance, Ford (1990) found that the longer Latino immigrants have lived in the USA, the lower their fertility rate. Immigrants who have recently arrived in the USA are likely to have fertility rates closely resembling those of the country of origin (Kahn 1988). Currently, over one-third of US Latina residents are foreign born (i.e., first-generation immigrants) (US Census Bureau 2000). Furthermore, approximately 39 percent of all Latino youth born in the USA have parents who immigrated to the USA (i.e., second-generation immigrants) while almost 48 percent were born to parents who were born in the USA (i.e., third-generation immigrants) (Hernandez and Chaney 1998). Second-generation Latinos of Mexican descent have lower fertility rates than their counterparts who were born in Mexico (Stephen and Bean 1992; Bean *et al.* 1998). Interestingly, studies have found that the third generation of Mexican immigrants actually has higher fertility rates than the second generation (Bean *et al.* 1998).

Factors contributing to adolescent pregnancy and childbearing among Latinas

Access to health care and support services

Access to health care and services is important in preventing pregnancy and caring for mothers and newborns. Latinas are less likely to have health care coverage or a regular source for health care, and are more likely to delay care or use hospital emergency rooms for primary care than other ethnic groups (Kullgren 2003). Between 1998 and 2001, 18 percent of 12- to 17-year-olds had unmet medical needs (Scott and Ni 2004). Research suggests that lack of health care results from a combination of factors, including lack of health insurance, the high cost of medical care, lack of education, language barriers, undocumented immigrant status, long waiting lines in clinics, lack of transportation, unsuitable access hours, and lack of child care (Giachello 1994; Zambrana *et al.* 1995).

One-quarter of Latino children under the age of 18 lack insurance, compared with 14 percent of black children and 8 percent of white children (US Census Bureau 2003; Scott and Ni 2004). The foreign-born are particularly likely to lack health insurance. Changes in welfare policy mean that even legal immigrant children are ineligible for public health insurance for 5 years, and undocumented immigrants are disallowed altogether (Urrutia 2004). Brown *et al.* (1998) found that 55 percent of Mexican-born children had no health insurance compared with 29 percent of US-born children of immigrant parents and 18 percent of children with parents of Mexican descent who were born in the USA. The reason most often cited for not being insured is high cost. Low health insurance rates and no usual place for health care contribute to lower use of health services and poorer health status (Brown *et al.* 1998). The result is clear, as the Urban Institute (2004) found: two-thirds of uninsured children in the USA whose health is described only as fair or poor are Latino.

Directly related to poor health care access is the finding that Latinas are less likely than other population groups to use contraceptives. While only 29 percent of all US adolescents use no form of contraception, this figure rises to 47 percent among Latinas (Brener *et al.* 2002). Nationally, 44 percent of all adolescents reported always using a condom in the previous year, compared with less than one-third of adolescent Latinos (Dickson 2001). Further, Latinas wait longer than white females after first sexual intercourse before beginning to use contraceptives (Becerra and Fielder 1985; Scott *et al.* 1988; Aneshensel *et al.* 1990; DuRant *et al.* 1990; Padilla and Baird 1991).

Adolescent Latinas are also less likely than other adolescents to have received sex education or discussed sex and reproductive health with others (Becerra and Fielder 1985; de Anda 1985; DuRant *et al.* 1990; Padilla and O'Grady 1987). In an exploratory study, De Anda *et al.* (1990) found that few Mexican American adolescents understood their physical development or sexual relations. For those who talked to others about sex and reproductive health, friends were the main source of information (Becerra and Fielder 1985; de Anda *et al.* 1988).

Lower rates of therapeutic abortions among Latinas than among whites contribute to higher rates of childbearing. In 1995, 20 percent of abortions performed in the USA were carried out in Latinas, a higher rate than in African Americans but lower than in whites (Henshaw and Kost 1996). There are important differences by ethnic group and immigrant generation, with the highest rates among Puerto Rican women and other US-born Latinas (Aneshensel *et al.* 1990; Erickson and Kaplan 1998). However, researchers also note that adolescents are relatively unlikely to have abortions compared with older women (Aneshensel *et al.* 1990; Kaplan *et al.* 2001). While lower abortion rates contribute to increased birth rates for Latinas, they are not the only explanation. Other factors, including cultural, environmental, and social variables, also contribute to the phenomenon, as discussed below.

Poverty

Researchers have consistently noted higher rates of pregnancy and childbirth among poorer adolescents. According to one study, 83 percent of adolescents who have babies are from poor families even though they are only slightly more likely to have sexual intercourse than wealthier adolescents (Cass 1994). In 1999, poverty was higher among Latinos than in many other groups. Approximately 21 percent of Latinos overall were poor (US Census Bureau 2000), with especially high rates among Puerto Ricans (31 percent) and Mexicans (24 percent) (US Census Bureau 1999).

Income poverty is high among Latinos, but asset poverty is even higher. In fact, the average net worth of Latino households fell by 30 percent between 1992 and 1998 (from US$4,300 to US$3,000 in inflation-adjusted dollars) and, overall, Latinos held only 4 percent of the household wealth of whites (Friedrich and Rodriguez 2001). Financial wealth among Latino families in 1998 was zero. Home ownership, a principal source of stability and wealth, is below 50 percent and

declining, remaining lower than the national average for all Americans of 68 percent (Friedrich and Rodriguez 2001; Bowdler 2004). Such low household wealth
suggests that families have little financial security, and almost no money to help
young people pay for advanced education and training.

At the same time adolescent Latinas are often ineligible for or face barriers
in receiving financial, food, and housing assistance. More than one-fourth (28
percent) of Latinos eligible for monetary support under the Temporary Assistance
to Needy Families (TANF) scheme did not receive it, a higher rate of non-receipt
than in any other ethnic group (Zedlewski 2002). Furthermore, most legal immigrants now entering the country and all undocumented immigrants are ineligible
for welfare services. Fix and Passel (2002) argue that a confluence of factors,
including confusing forms and language barriers, and fears about reprisal, both
real and imagined, also prevent many Latinos from applying for benefits.

Education

School experiences, school achievement, and educational aspiration influence patterns of adolescent pregnancy and childbearing. Young women engaged in school
are less likely to get pregnant (O'Connor 1999). Unfortunately, the educational
situation for Latino youth is discouraging. More than two in five Latinos do not
hold a high-school diploma or General Educational Development (GED) creden-
tial (US Census Bureau 2000). Although high-school completion rates increased
overall in the 1990s, there was only a small improvement among Latinos (from
21 to 22 percent) (National Research Council 2006). Rates of high-school graduation are particularly low among Latinos of Mexican descent (US Census Bureau
2000; Bonilla 2001).

Moreover, only one in ten Latinos over 24 years of age has a bachelor's degree
or higher qualification (US Census Bureau 2000). Only 47 percent of foreign-born
Latinos enroll in college compared with 79 percent of foreign-born Asians, and
Latinos are proportionately less likely to complete a four-year degree (Fuligni
and Hardway, 2004). Finally, data for Latinos of Mexican descent suggest that
educational attainment increases in the second generation, but stalls between the
second and third generations, with significant consequences for economic well-
being (Groggier and Trejo, 2002: 11–13). Second- and third-generation women
are less likely than men to obtain a first or postgraduate degree (Vélez-Ibáñez
2004: 7).

In the USA, many Latinas attend large, overcrowded schools staffed by relatively inexperienced teachers, and, in addition, have to face safety concerns, problems
with gangs, and language difficulties (Zambrana *et al.* 1995; Fuligni and Hardway
2004). Many schools attended by a large number of Latinos are underfunded,
overcrowded, ethnically segregated, and isolated (Trueba 1998). In two studies
carried out in Chicago, Latino youth described academic problems, intermittent
attendance, racist experiences, safety problems, and an overall dislike of school
(Darabi and Ortiz 1987; Sherraden and Barrera 1997a). Poor-quality schools and

social exclusion prepare young people for low-wage and unstable employment, offering little incentive to stay in school. Unfortunately, for many Latino adolescents, the rewards to education may not be clear. Young people observe that some adults with high-school or college degrees earn little more than those without. Even with high educational aspirations, postsecondary education and training, including college, may not be achievable for academic or financial reasons. Many young Latinos, while not formally "dropping out" of school, never really "drop in" (Darabi and Ortiz 1987). Some young Latinas view pregnancy and motherhood as a reasonable alternative to poor schools (Sherraden and Barrera 1997a). Further, if pregnancy and childbearing interrupts schooling, re-entering school or balancing school with motherhood is challenging and often discouraged.

Culture

Culture is a tempting explanation for high pregnancy and childbearing rates among Latinas. Tello (2000) argues that culture is the primary driving force behind sexual decision-making for young Latinos, including its various components: the extended family system, a strong work ethic, independence, and internalized oppression derived from daily exposure to prejudice and discrimination. Flores *et al.* (1998) argue that pregnancy and motherhood are highly valued in the Latino community and that "sexual behaviour is influenced by strong cultural values and social norms that obligate the young woman to behave in culturally expected ways" (see also Brindis 1997). Others find that young Latinas talk about motherhood as a positive choice (Sherraden and Barrera 1997b). They report that they gain respect from family members (often despite initial disapproval) and status in the eyes of friends. During pregnancy and for a time after the baby is born, they find themselves the center of attention and the recipient of gifts.

Research emphasizes the protective aspects of culture in pregnancy and childbearing. Research on Mexican-origin women, for example, suggests that traditional cultural values appear to have protective effects on babies and that acculturation to US mainstream culture threatens some of the positive effects. For example, despite higher levels of poverty, less health insurance, and lower use of health services (Treviño *et al.* 1996; Brown *et al.* 1998), Latinas have better birth outcomes than many other groups (Scribner and Dwyer 1989; Guendelman *et al.* 1990). The infant mortality rate, for example, is 6.8 among all Latinas, compared with 7.1 among all women, 5.7 among whites, and 13.5 among African Americans.[2] Traditional "everyday" pregnancy practices (Sherraden and Barrera 1997b), family support (Sherraden and Barrera 1996), good nutrition (Guendelman and Abrams 1995), abstention from harmful substances (Guendelman and Abrams 1995; Zambrana *et al.* 1995), and other factors may advantage the immigrant generation in terms of birth outcomes.

Acculturation seems to attenuate some of these protective forces. For younger Latinas in particular, acculturation, especially in the face of limited economic mobility, may lead some to abandon their parents' cultural norms and values in favour of mainstream US culture. US-born women of Mexican descent, for example, initiate sexual intercourse at earlier ages, have higher levels of sexual activity, and have more sexual partners than the Mexico-born (Darabi and Ortiz 1987; Aneshensel *et al.* 1990; Marín *et al.* 1993; Reynoso *et al.* 1993).

Acculturation in the second and succeeding generations has also been linked to increased incidence of smoking and drinking (Gilbert 1987; Marín *et al.* 1989; Campbell and Kaplan 1997). As Rumbaut (1997: 934) observes, "the longer time in and exposure to the United States, the poorer are the physical health outcomes and the greater the propensity to engage in each of the risk behaviors mentioned."

Acculturation, however, is not a simple process (Weigers and Sherraden 2001). Sometimes women born in Mexico display characteristics associated with the second generation. As Rumbaut (1997) reports, some immigrants arrive in the USA already more or less "Americanized." Anecdotal evidence suggests that the profile of pregnant Mexican immigrant adolescents is increasingly similar to US-born youth. In other words, they are more likely to be living independently, and to smoke, drink, and be sexually active. The prevailing view that young Latinas are naive and protected is clearly changing as the forces of globalization and urbanization impact youth in other countries. Data on women born in Puerto Rico also suggest that reproductive patterns and birth outcomes conform more to the experiences of acculturated adolescent Mexicans, although, as we noted earlier, the historical and structural circumstances of migration between Puerto Rico and the US mainland are a unique case and deserve more attention from researchers (Rumbaut 1997).

Similarly, the US-born do not always conform to the "acculturated" model. Portes and Zhou (1993) refer to this as "segmented assimilation." They describe three paths of assimilation: one path into the mainstream middle class, one path into poverty, and a third path toward ethnic advancement and solidarity. Which path is taken depends on the structural constraints and opportunities that confront youth at the time and place of their arrival, including US receptivity and immigration policy, current economic conditions, ethnic prejudice, discrimination, and resources provided by their immigrant ethnic community. For example, Suro (1998) points out that many of the "stepping-stone jobs" that helped earlier immigrants get a leg up in US society have disappeared for young immigrants, replaced by low-paying service jobs with little opportunity for mobility. Sherraden and Barrera (1997a) found that families played an important role in mediating opportunities for their US-born daughters, but their ability to protect, support, and provide opportunity was largely shaped by their economic circumstances.

Coercion and sexual violence

Although coercion is not a factor in most adolescent pregnancies, it is an important factor in some (Erickson 1998). Fathers of babies born to adolescent mothers are often older. In an ethnographic study of 32 adolescent Latina mothers, de Anda *et al.* (1990) found that fathers were an average of 5 years older than the mother. This is not surprising, given studies that have found similar results for sexually active adolescent females in general. For example, Darroch and Landry (1999) found that 29 percent of sexually active adolescent females had a partner who was 5 years older. In age-differential relationships in which the female is the younger partner, male power and control may undermine the woman's ability to negotiate sexual intercourse and the use of contraception. An older male partner may pressure the adolescent into participating in unprotected sexual activities, basing the encounter on ideas of trust and fidelity (Lesser *et al.* 2001). In another study, many adolescent Latinas who were planning to have sex reported that they felt pressured into doing so by their boyfriend, suggesting that coercion is a factor influencing engaging in sexual activity (Flores *et al.* 1998).

According to Sylvester (1996), adolescents who engage in sexual relationships with older men are more likely to have a history of sexual abuse. In a study conducted by Boyer and Fineman (1992), 535 young women who had become pregnant in adolescence were surveyed regarding previous child abuse. Almost two-thirds of the respondents disclosed histories of abuse. Over half (55 percent) had been sexually molested, 42 percent were victims of attempted sexual assault, and 44 percent had been raped. After the assault, these adolescents experienced increased sexual risk-taking compared with non-abused adolescent females, including starting consensual sexual intercourse at least a year earlier, being more likely to use alcohol or other addictive drugs, and practicing unsafe sex more often (Boyer and Fineman 1992).

Of further concern, an unknown proportion of adolescent pregnancies and births are the result of incest and rape. Although there is a lack of data on Latina adolescents, the US Department of Justice (2003) reports that between 1991 and 1996 two-thirds of all rape victims were under the age of 18. In addition, adolescents were more than twice as likely to be victims of sexual assault as older victims. Among immigrants, language barriers, dangers associated with border crossing, undocumented status, and living with non-relatives are a few of the factors that may make Latinas vulnerable to rape. In a study conducted by the Centers for Disease Control (Abma *et al.* 1997), 18 percent of Latinas under the age of 16 years disclosed involuntary sexual intercourse. National studies indicate that the younger the victim, the more probable that the perpetrator is either a relative or a person known to the victim. However, how many of these sexual assaults result in the birth of a child is unknown and remains a research priority.

Life chances

Although the reasons for adolescent pregnancy and childbearing are complex, the most important reason may be whether or not an adolescent female tries *not* to get pregnant (Conrad 1996). This decision is influenced in large measure by her perception about her options for the future (Thomas 1996).

Researchers looking at adolescent pregnancy and childbirth among African American youth suggest that having a baby represents a compelling dream for a better future among youth with low expectations for their future. In contrast, Anderson (1991: 397) describes young people with higher expectations:

> Young people who are raised with a sense of opportunity and are able realistically to picture a better life are often successful in avoiding the draw of the street culture. For girls, the belief that they can be somebody in the wider community prevails over the lure of becoming somebody by having a prize baby at age fifteen.

Geronimus (2003) found that early fertility may be adaptive for young African American mothers growing up in high-poverty urban areas. Denunciation of adolescent childbearing is based on the assumption that poor minority youth have the same prospects as middle-class white youth. Choices about teen fertility are made in a social and economic context. Socio-economically advantaged youth are more likely to heed appeals to delay early childbearing because they are encouraged and reinforced by a constellation of resources and opportunities.

> At their best, these resources – the material, the institutional, the health-related, and the ideological – support and reinforce the parents, while also facilitating their children's engagement in academic, extracurricular, and social pursuits that promote their development and eventual socio-economic success.
>
> (Geronimus 2003: 890).

As we have seen, young Latinas often grow up in a family and community environment where life chances are limited by poverty and discrimination, in communities with poor-quality schools, and in families in which adults have jobs which pay less than a living wage. Brindis (1997: 8) writes:

> Early childbearing among Latinas appears to be strongly related to limited perceived life options. Black, White, or Latina young women with below-average academic skills coming from families with below-poverty incomes are about five times more likely to be adolescent mothers than those with solid skills and above-average family incomes.

At the same time, Latinas grow up in a cultural context that views pregnancy and childbearing favourably. In this context, pregnancy and childbirth may be a rational option from both an economic as well as a cultural perspective.

To encourage delayed pregnancy and childbearing, education and career opportunities have to be perceived as better choices than pregnancy and motherhood. If the rewards for graduating from high school are unhappy job options (e.g., hotel housekeeper, piecework, low-skilled manufacturing, restaurant work), there is little incentive to remain in school. Incentives and avenues to greater opportunity, however, are more likely to lead more young people to choose school.

Program and policy implications: toward investment in youth

Pregnancy prevention programs range from broad-based education programs to programs that target "at-risk" youth. Some focus on sexual behavior and some focus more broadly on youth development (Kirby 2001). Some have been demonstrated to be effective, but most have not been studied. Research on "abstinence only" approaches, widely supported in the current policy environment (Wertheimer and Papillo 2004), is largely inconclusive (Kirby 1997, 2001). In a review of major studies on teen pregnancy prevention, Kirby (2001) found that successful programs focus on sexual behaviors as well as other aspects of the young person's life. Some adopt a case management and social support approach, or a youth development approach. In combination with other support services, many have positive effects on sexual behavior and pregnancy rates (Erickson 1998).

There is even less research on the outcomes of policy initiatives for Latinos. There is some evidence, for example, that cognitive behavioral group interventions that emphasize skill building and mastery work well with adolescents, including Latinos (Blythe et al. 1981; Barth 1989; Franklin and Corcoran, 1999). Harris and Franklin (2003) found that a culturally consonant school-based approach based on social learning theory and problem solving resulted in higher school performance and better attendance among adolescent Latina mothers.

To be widely effective, however, pregnancy prevention programs should be part of a broader strategy to invest in youth. As Luker (1991: 83) points out, "Teenage pregnancy is less about young women and their sex lives than it is about restricted horizons and the boundaries of hope. It is about race and class and how those realities limit opportunities for young people." Empty promises about the rewards of delayed childbearing and more education will not be convincing to young people or their parents. If real opportunities for education, training, and better jobs are available to young Latinos, the message about delaying pregnancy and childbearing will hold greater sway. Services must reach individuals, but in the context of family and the broader community (e.g., church, school). Below we outline some of the key components of an investment strategy.

Improve education and career opportunities

A key to prevention of adolescent pregnancy is high-quality education. Schools should improve safety, teaching quality, and access to technology that will engage young people and better prepare them for higher levels of education, training, and careers. In response to pressures on young people to get jobs and contribute to family income, more vocational training and apprenticeship opportunities are likely to be effective. Certainly, poorly funded schools need additional funding and rollback of affirmative action programs should be reversed.

Schools must work hard to help young people understand they can succeed (Romo and Falbo 1996). It is important for teachers and other adults who work with youths to be role models for young Latinas, especially for those whose parents received little education, do not speak English, do not understand the US educational system, and in general, are not in a strong position to encourage further schooling. Parents also need to learn about the range of opportunities that are available to their children that may not have been available to them. Particular attention should be paid to what Vélez-Ibáñez (2004: 16) refers to as the "second-to third-generation gap" in educational attainment, especially for women.

In most cases, education and training beyond high school will be required to obtain jobs that pay well and have decent benefits. In addition to scholarships and other incentives for low-income youth to undergo postsecondary training and education, savings programs for higher education may be effective in encouraging young people to stay in school and to pursue higher education (Clancy *et al.* 2004).

Increase access to health education and health care

Latinos experience serious health risks while being the most medically underserved population in the USA (Meza 2000). Improving access to health and sex education, health services, and contraception is clearly an important aspect to preventing adolescent pregnancy and assuring the health of adolescent mothers and their babies. Despite strong cultural proscriptions on premarital sex, those adolescents who are engaged in sexual relations must have access to health education and contraception.

Moreover, more health education, including sex education, is needed in schools and in the community (see below). This, according to de Anda and colleagues (1990), is needed especially at young ages, when adolescents are at particularly high risk. Others suggest that adolescents need incentives to participate, a supportive peer group, positive relationships with adults and peer mentors, skills to cope with peer influences, and explicit and accurate information about sexual activity and risky behaviors (Romo and Falbo 1996).

Reform immigration policy

Approaches to adolescent pregnancy and childbearing must take into account immigration policy. Although most young Latinas are citizens, one or more family members frequently are not. As a result, many Latinas, regardless of their own citizenship status, are placed in a vulnerable position. While this chapter cannot explore the many options for immigration reform, opportunities should not be curtailed for youth because they are not US citizens, or because they live with someone who is not a US citizen. Access to basic human needs, including health care and education, is a critical factor in an investment strategy for youth development, and without it efforts to prevent early pregnancy and childbearing will not succeed.

Adopt a multigenerational perspective

A multigenerational perspective in policy and programs recognizes the importance of family and can build on the cultural importance and strengths of the Latino family. In pregnancy prevention, it is important to recognize the influence of family. Specifically, attitudes toward contraception, sex education, early pregnancy, and marriage among young Latinas and their family members must be taken into account when designing pregnancy prevention programs for Latina teenagers. Moreover, it is likely that education about pregnancy prevention will be ineffective for many youth unless parents and other family members are included.

Dickson (2001) estimates that 80 percent of adolescent Latinas and their babies live within an extended family. There is evidence that co-residence with parents may elevate the well-being of both the adolescent and her baby. Unger and Cooley (1992) found that co-residence increases the likelihood that an adolescent mother will complete her education. Further, such an arrangement may reduce the probability of poverty, early marriage, and additional births for the adolescent mother (Furstenberg and Crawford 1978; Trent and Harlan 1994).

Close interaction between a pregnant teenager and her mother, in particular, may have important positive effects. Sherraden and Barrera (1996) suggest that spending time with her mother during pregnancy provides a teenager with a positive attitude toward pregnancy and motherhood and results in better nutrition and "everyday" care during pregnancy. Apfel and Seitz (1991) suggest that co-residing with the baby's grandparents has a positive effect on teenagers' parenting skills.

However, some researchers have identified potentially negative effects of co-residence. Some adolescent mothers who live with their parents may experience impediments to their psychosocial development. Further, dissonance between teenagers' responsibilities within the household and their developmental needs may lead to negative parenting styles (East and Felice 1996; Wakschlag et al. 1996; Kalil et al. 1998). Certainly, if abuse and neglect are present in the family of origin, co-residence with the offending parent(s) should not take place.

Include fathers

Although this chapter cannot adequately address the role of young fathers, research suggests that young Latino fathers share similar goals as Latina adolescent mothers regarding their children. This includes a desire to be fully involved in the child's life (Becerra and de Anda 1984; Zayas et al. 1987; de Anda et al. 1990; Marsiglio 1993; Allen and Doherty 1996). In an ethnographic study of adolescent Latino fathers, Lesser et al. (2001) found that young Latino fathers are willing and able to make profound changes in their lifestyles in order to support and parent their infant children. But Latino adolescent fathers face many of the same financial, educational, and interpersonal challenges as young mothers that interfere with their ability to remain involved in positive ways with the mother and their baby. These findings suggest that many Latino youth are in long-term committed relationships, and further suggests that fathers should be integrally involved in planning for education, career, reproduction, and child rearing. Nonetheless, additional research is needed to explore how to further involve Latino adolescent fathers in pregnancy prevention and parenthood programs.

Adolescent Latina mothers are more likely to be married (26 percent) than adolescent African American mothers (5 percent), but they are less likely to be married than adolescent white mothers (41 percent) (Dickson 2001). However, there is wide variation within the Latina population. For example, 35 percent of adolescent mothers of Mexican descent and 20 percent of adolescent mothers of Puerto Rican descent are married (Dickson 2001).

Reflect cultural values and attitudes

A challenge for practitioners is how to deliver health services, contraception, and sex education in a way that is culturally appropriate. Using a strengths-based approach that values cultural heritage and attitudes but addresses the contextual reality of adolescents' lives in the USA may help adolescents and their families balance mainstream US and Latino cultural views on sexuality and sexual behavior. Strategies should emerge from the Latino community and include the voices of religious, educational, health, and grassroots leaders.

Certainly, the first step is to create policy that ensures quality educational opportunities for adolescent Latinas (Driscoll *et al.* 2001). But education as intervention is merely the first step. The importance of family and the greater likelihood of marriage argues for a "family education and support model" rather than the more typical "adolescent case management model." For Latinas separated geographically from their family of origin (especially those in the first generation of immigrants), a family education and support model should include substitute supports.

While birth control, abortion, and sexual education remain taboo subjects for many traditional Latino families that adhere to conservative religious teachings, other approaches that are more culturally appropriate can be the focus of intervention with these families. Primarily, these interventions can and should focus on providing avenues to economic opportunities for the family, as well as pathways to educational attainment for the young Latina in particular, in the hope of providing her with a strong incentive for delaying childbirth. Using the strength of the traditional family as its core unit of intervention, programs can build upon the family's sense of protective investment around the young Latina in this way. Intervention focused on economic opportunity must include tangible and social support for the family. Often, it is the case that the young Latina's independent economic future is co-opted by the current pressing household needs of the family, especially that of child care and domestic obligations.

Although there is much more to be learned, there is some evidence that it is important for young Latinas to understand their heritage and culture as they adapt to US culture, and to retain or gain fluency in Spanish as they acquire English skills (Buriel 1984; Rumbaut 1997). Trueba (1998) argues that an ability to successfully negotiate a binational and bicultural world is based on solid Mexican values, which he believes are "the result of a carefully executed plan of education engineered primarily by the mothers, who monitor schooling and defend their language and culture by creating vast networks on both sides of the border" (p. 260). Some have even suggested that young Latinas who have the opportunity to spend some time in their country and community of origin may be more resilient. Whether this provides a safe place during a vulnerable period in life, grounding in cultural heritage, or simply a different perspective on the world and their lives (any combination of the three), it appears to have a positive impact in some cases (Sherraden and Barrera 1997b).[3] It may be that young people are better able to make informed choices when they feel secure and sure about their cultural heritage.

Conclusion

As Latinos have emerged as the largest ethnic minority group in the USA and the proportion of Latino adolescents increases, more attention has focused on their fertility. Evidence that pregnancy and childbirth rates among Latinos are declining at a slower pace than for other ethnic groups raises the level of concern. Further, as the population of Latinos continues to increase, Latina adolescent pregnancy will remain problematic as a policy concern in the USA. By the year 2050, one-quarter of the nation will be of Latino heritage (Driscoll *et al.* 2001). The children of adolescent mothers will have grown up under the pressing weight of poverty and limited opportunity. If policy does not quickly and effectively address the lack of economic opportunity for young Latinas, the problem of adolescent pregnancy among Latinas could easily grow.

More research is needed to fully understand Latina teen pregnancy and how to respond with appropriate policies and programs. Variations in rates by ethnic origin and immigrant generation are still not understood. Culture and religion also play key roles; nonetheless, our knowledge about how these different patterns and factors affect pregnancy and childbearing remains limited. Lack of data and analysis on the role of Latino family, including the role of fathers and families of origin, hampers our understanding, as does the influence of sexual coercion and sexual violence on teen pregnancy and childbearing.

While more research will lead to greater understanding, it is important that we address the issues that we currently understand. How can we provide opportunities for Latina and Latino youth to shape their lives in positive ways? What policies and programs will enable them to make positive choices for themselves? What resources will assist them to become productive members of families, communities, and society? This review suggests that greater social and economic opportunity and culturally competent health care services will facilitate positive choices about pregnancy and childbearing. Public policy efforts should focus on improving the life chances of these young people instead of focusing blindly on reducing adolescent pregnancy.

From a political perspective, Chavez (2004) observes that "the popular discourse of Latina reproduction is decidedly alarmist." The specter of large numbers of Latina immigrants arriving in the USA to have babies and use scarce social services is being used politically to support anti-immigrant and anti-immigration policies. These reactions could become even more pointed in discussions about *adolescent* pregnancy and childbearing. Perhaps, as Chavez argues, we ought to be asking instead about the implications of fertility *declines*.

> Shifting assumptions that valorise white women's fertility levels no matter how low they drop would alter the way Latina fertility is represented ... Would it be just as possible to make the following observation: the abnormally *low* fertility rates of Anglo women are leading to demographic changes and increased pressure for immigration? [emphasis in original]
>
> (Chavez 2004: 185)

As Ozawa (1999) writes, in an aging society we rely on smaller proportions of young people to support a growing aging population. Moreover, the demographic evidence suggests that younger generations will be overwhelmingly non-Anglo, including a large proportion of Latinos. In this context, as a society we should appreciate and reward motherhood. A more productive approach to Latina teen pregnancy and childbearing would be to emphasize investment in young Latinas to ensure their ability to make the best choices for themselves and their children. This would be an investment in the welfare of all Americans.

Notes

1 In English "Towards a more secure future."
2 Among girls aged 10–14 years, the declines were greater. The birth rate for all groups declined by 57 percent (from 1.4 to 0.6 per 1,000); among Latinas the rate fell by 46 percent (from 2.4 to 1.3 per 1,000), among African Americans it declined by 67 percent (from 4.9 to 1.6 per 1,000), and among non-Hispanic whites it fell by 60 percent (from 0.5 to 0.2 per 1,000) (Martin *et al.* 2005).
3 African American families have historically used a similar strategy, sending their children to live for periods of time (summers or longer) "down south" with grandparents and other relatives.

References

Abma, J., Chandra, A., Mosher, W., Peterson, L., and Piccinino, L. (1997) "Fertility, Family Planning, and Women's Health: New Data from the 1995 National Survey of Family Growth," *Vital Health Statistics* 23(19), 1–114.

Ahn, N. (1994) "Teenage Childbearing and High School Completion: Accounting for Individual Heterogeneity," *Family Planning Perspectives* 26(1), 17–21.

Allen, W. and Doherty, W. (1996) "The Responsibilities of Fatherhood as Perceived by African-American Teenage Fathers," *Families in Society* 77(2), 142–55.

Anderson, E. (1991) "Neighbourhood Effects on Teenage Pregnancy," in *The Urban Underclass* (eds C. Jencks and P.E Peterson), Washington, DC: Brookings Institution, pp. 375–98.

Aneshensel, C., Becerra, R., Fielder, E., and Schuler, R. (1990) "Onset of Fertility-related Events During Adolescence: a Prospective Comparison of Mexican American and Non-Hispanic White Females," *American Journal of Public Health* 80, 959–63.

Annie E. Casey Foundation (1998) *Kids Count Special Report: When Teens Have Sex, Issues and Trends*, Baltimore: Annie E. Casey Foundation.

Apfel, N. and Seitz, V. (1991) "Four Models of Adolescent Mother–Grandmother Relationships in Inner-city Families," *Family Relations* 40, 421–9.

Baldwin, W. and Cain, V. (1980) "The Children of Teenage Parents," *Family Planning Perspective* 12(1), 34–43.

Barth, R.P. (1989) *Reducing the Risk: Building Skills to Prevent Pregnancy*, Santa Cruz, CA: ETR Associates/Network Publications.

Bean, F.D., Swicegood, C.G., and Berg, R.C. (1998) "Mexican-origin Fertility: New Patterns and Interpretations," *Social Science Quarterly* 81, 404–20.

Becerra, R.M. and de Anda, D. (1984) "Pregnancy and Motherhood among Mexican American Adolescents," *Health and Social Work* 9, 106–23.

Becerra, R. and Fielder, E.P. (1985) "Adolescent Attitudes and Behaviour," *Institute for Social Science Research Quarterly* 1, 4–7.

Blythe, B.J., Gilchrist, L.D., and Schinke, S.P. (1981) "Pregnancy-Prevention Groups for Adolescents," *Social Work* 26: 503–5.

Bonilla, J. (2001) *A Demographic Profile of Latinas in the U.S.*, Washington, DC: The Population Resource Center.

Bowdler, J. (2004) *Latina Housing and Homeownership. Statistical Brief*, Washington, DC: National Council of La Raza.

Boyer, D. and Fineman, D. (1992) "Sexual Abuse as a Factor in Adolescent Pregnancy and Child Maltreatment," *Family Planning Perspectives* 24(1), 4–13.

Brener, N., Lowery, R., Kann, L., Kolby, L., Lehnherr, J., Janssen, R., and Jaffe, H. (2002) "Trends in Sexual Risk Behaviours Among High School Students – United States, 1991–2001," *Morbidity and Mortality Monthly Report* 51, 856–9.

Brindis, C.D. (1997) "Adolescent Pregnancy Prevention for Hispanic Youth," *The Prevention Researcher* 4, 8–10.

Brown, R.R., Wyn, R., Yu, H., Valenzuela, A., and Dong, L. (1998) "Access to Health Insurance and Health Care for Mexican American Children in Immigrant Families," in *Crossings: Mexican Immigration in Interdisciplinary Perspectives* (ed. M.M. Suarez-Orozco), Cambridge, MA: David Rockefeller Centre for Latin American Studies, Harvard University, pp. 227–47.

Buriel, R. (1984) "Integration with Traditional Mexican-American Cultural and Sociocultural Adjustment," in *Chicano Psychology* (eds J.L. Martinez, Jr. and R.H. Mendoza), Orlando: Academic Press.

Campbell, K. and Kaplan, C. (1997) "The Relationship between Acculturation and Cigarette Smoking Beliefs of Hispanic Women," *Journal of Health Behaviour* 21(1), 12–20.

Cass, C. (1994) "In Teen-age Pregnancy, it isn't Race, it's Poverty," *St. Louis Post-Dispatch*, December 1, 1994.

Centers for Disease Control and Prevention (1999) *Sexually Transmitted Disease Surveillance, 1998*, Atlanta: Centers for Disease Control and Prevention.

Chavez, L.R. (2004) "A Glass Half Empty: Latina Reproduction and Public Discourse," *Human Organization* 63, 173–88.

Clancy, M., Orszag, P., and Sherraden, M. (2004) *College Savings Plans: A Platform for Inclusive Saving Policy?*, St. Louis: Washington University, Center for Social Development.

Conrad, C. (1996) "Is Pregnancy a Rational Choice for Poor Teenagers?," *Wall Street Journal,* January 18, 1996.

Darabi, K.F. and Ortiz, V. (1987) "Childbearing Among Young Latino Women in the United States," *American Journal of Public Health* 77(10), 25–8.

Darroch, J. and Landry, J. (1999) "Age Differences between Sexual Partners in the United States," *Family Planning Perspectives* 31, 160–8.

Day, J.C. (1996) "Population Projections of the United States by Age, Sex, Race, and Latina Origin: 1995 to 2050," *Current Population Reports*, 25–1130.

de Anda, D. (1985) "The Latina Adolescent Mother: Assessing Risk in Relation to Stress and Social Support," in *Stress and Latina Mental Health: Relating Research to Service Delivery* (eds L. Vega and M. Miranda), Rockville, MD: National Institute of Mental Health, pp. 267–89.

de Anda, D., Becerra, R., and Fielder, E. (1988) "Sexuality, Pregnancy, and Motherhood among Mexican-American Adolescents," *Journal of Adolescent Research* 3, 403–11.

de Anda, D., Becerra, R.M., and Fielder, E. (1990) "In Their Own Words: The Life Experiences of Mexican-American and White Pregnant Adolescents and Adolescent Mothers," *Child and Adolescent Social Work* 7, 301–18.

Dickson, M.C. (2001) *Latina Teen Pregnancy: Problem and Prevention*, Washington, DC: Population Resource Center.

Driscoll, A., Biggs, M., Brindis, C., and Yankah, E. (2001) "Adolescent Latino Reproductive Health: A Review of the Literature," *Hispanic Journal of Behavioural Sciences*, 23, 253–326.

DuRant, R.H., Pendergrast, R. and Seymore, C. (1990) "Sexual Behavior Among Latina Female Adolescents in the United States," *Pediatrics* 85, 1051–8.

East, P. and Felice, M. (1996) *Adolescent Pregnancy and Parenting*, Mahwah, NJ: Lawrence Erlbaum Associates.

Erickson, P.I. (1998) *Latina Adolescent Childbearing in East Los Angeles*, Austin: University of Texas Press.

Erickson, P.I., and Kaplan, C.P. (1998) "Latinos and Abortion," in *The New Civil War: the Psychology, Culture, and Politics of Abortion* (eds L.J. Beckman and S.M. Harvey), Washington, DC: American Psychological Association.

Fix, M. and Passel, J. (2002) "Assessing Welfare Reform's Immigrant Provisions," in *Welfare Reform: The Next Act* (eds A. Weil and K. Finnegold), Washington, DC: Urban Institute Press, pp. 179–202.

Flores, E., Eyre, S.L., and Millstein, S.G. (1998) "Sociocultural Beliefs Related to Sex Among Mexican American Adolescents," *Hispanic Journal of Behavioural Sciences* 20, 60–82.

Ford, K. (1990) "Duration of Residence in the United States and the Fertility of U.S. Immigrants," *International Migration Review* 24, 34–68.

Franklin, C. and Corcoran, J. (1999). "Preventing Adolescent Pregnancy: a Review of Programs and Practices," *Social Work* 45, 40–52.

Friedrich, A., and Rodriguez, E. (2001) "Financial Insecurity Amid Growing Wealth: Why Healthier Savings is Essential to Latino Prosperity," *National Council of La Raza (NCLR) Issue Brief* 5, 1–18.

Fuligni, A.J. and Hardway, C. (2004) "Preparing Diverse Adolescents for the Transition to Adulthood," *Future of Children: Children of Immigrant Families* 14, 2.

Furstenberg, F.F. and Crawford, A.G. (1978) "Family Support: Helping Teenage Mothers to Cope," *Family Planning Perspectives* 10, 322–33.

Geronimus, A.T. (2003) "Damned if You Do: Culture, Identity, Privilege, and Teenage Childbearing in the United States," *Social Science and Medicine* 57, 881–93.

Giachello, A. (1994) "Maternal/perinatal health," in *Latino health in the U.S.: A growing challenge* (eds C.W. Molina & M. Aguirre-Molina). Washington, DC: American Public Health Association.

Gilbert, M.J. (1987) "Alcohol Consumption Patterns in Immigrant and Later Generation Mexican American Women," *Hispanic Journal of Behavioural Sciences* 9: 299–313.

Gillock, K.L. and Reyes, O. (1999) "Stress, Support, and Academic Performance of Urban, Low-income, Mexican-American Adolescents," *Journal of Youth and Adolescences* 28, 259–82.

Groggier, J. and Trejo, S.J. (2002) *Falling Behind or Moving Up?: the Intergenerational Progress of Mexican Americans*, Berkeley, CA: Public Policy Institute.

Guendelman, S. and Abrams, B. (1995) "Dietary Intake Among Mexican-American Women: Generational Differences and a Comparison with White non-Hispanic Women," *American Journal of Public Health* 95, 20–5.

Guendelman, S., Gould, J., Hudes, M., and Eskenazi, B. (1990) "Generational Differences in Prenatal Health Among the Mexican American Population. Findings from HHANES 1982–1984," *American Journal of Public Health* 80 (suppl.), 61–5.

Hamilton, B.E., Martin, J.A., and Sutton, P.D. (2003) "Births: Preliminary Data for 2002," *National Vital Statistics Report* 51(11).

Harris, K.M. (1998) "The Health Status and Risk Behavior of Adolescents in Immigrant Families," in *Children of Immigrants: Health, Adjustment, and Public Assistance* (ed. D.J. Hernandez), Washington, DC: Committee on the Health and Adjustment of Immigrant Children and Families, Board on Children, Youth, and Families.

Harris, M. and Franklin, C. (2003) "Effects of a Cognitive–Behavioral, School-based, Group Intervention with Mexican American Pregnant and Parenting Adolescents," *Social Work Research* 27(2), 71–83.

Haveman, R., Wolfe, B., and Wilson, K. (1997) "Childhood Poverty and Adolescent Schooling and Fertility Outcome: Reduced-form and Structural Estimates," in *Consequences of Growing up Poor* (eds G.J. Duncan and J. Brooks-Gunn), New York: Russell Sage Foundation, pp. 419–60.

Henshaw, S.K. and Kost, K. (1996) "Abortion Patients in 1994–1995: Characteristics and Contraceptive Use," *Family Planning Perspectives* 28(4), 140–7.

Hernandez, D. and Chaney, E. (eds) (1998) *From Generation to Generation: the Health and Well-being of Children in Immigrant Families*, Washington, DC: National Academy of Sciences Press.

Kahn, J.R. (1988) "Immigrant Selectivity and Fertility: Adaptation in the United States," *Social Forces* 67, 108–27.

Kalil, A., Spencer, M., Spieker, S., and Gilchrist, L. (1998) "Effects of Grandmother Coresidence and Quality of Family Relationships on Depressive Symptoms in Adolescent Mothers," *Family Relations* 47, 433–41.

Kaplan, C.P., Erickson, P.I., Stewart, S.L., and Crane, L.A. (2001) "Young Latinas and Abortion: the Role of Cultural Factors, Reproductive Behaviour, and Alternative Roles to Motherhood," *Health Care for Women International* 22, 667–89.

Kirby, D. (1997) *No Easy Answers: Research Findings on Programs to Reduce Teen Pregnancy*, Washington, DC: National Campaign to Prevent Teen Pregnancy.

Kirby, D. (1999) "Reducing Adolescent Pregnancy: Approaches that Work," *Contemporary Paediatrics* 16(1), 83–94.

Kirby, D. (2001) "Emerging Answers: Research Findings on Programs to Reduce Teen Pregnancy - Summary." The National Campaign to Prevent Teen Pregnancy. (Available online at http://www.teenpregnancy.org/resources/data/pdf/emeranswsum.pdf).

Klepinger, D.H., Lundberg, S., and Plotnick, R.D. (1995) "Adolescent Fertility and the Educational Attainment of Young Women," *Family Planning Perspectives* 27(1), 23–8.

Kullgren, J. (2003) "Restrictions on Undocumented Immigrants' Access to Health Services: the Public Health Implications of Welfare Reform," *American Journal of Public Health* 93, 1630–4.

Lesser, J., Tello, J., Koniak-Griffin, D., Kappos, B., and Rhys, M. (2001) "Young Latino Fathers' Perceptions of Paternal role and Risk for HIV/AIDS," *Latina Journal of Behavioural Sciences* 23, 327–43.

Luker, K. (1991) "Dubious Conceptions: the Controversy over Teen Pregnancy," *American Prospect* 5: 73–83.

Marsiglio, W. (1993) *Fatherhood: Contemporary theory, Research, and Social Policy.* Thousand Oaks, CA: Sage.

Marín, G., Peréz-Stable, E.J. and Marín, B.V. (1989) "Cigarette Smoking Among San Francisco Hispanics: the Role of Acculturation and Gender," *American Journal of Public Health* 79: 196–9.

Marín, B.V., Tschann, J.M., Gomez, C.A., and Kegeles, S.M. (1993) "Acculturation and gender differences in sexual attitudes and behaviours: A comparison of Hispanic and non-Hispanic White unmarried adults." *American Journal of Public Health*, 83(12), 1759–1761.

Martin, J.A., Hamilton, B.E., Sutton, P.D., Ventura, S.J., Menacker, F., and Munson, M.L. (2005) "Births: Final Data for 2003" *National Vital Statistics Reports* 54(2).

Maynard, R. (1996) *Kids Having Kids: A Robin Hood Foundation Special Report on the Costs of Adolescent Childbearing,* New York: The Robin Hood Foundation.

Meza, F. (2000) "Latino Health Profile," *Latino Medicine, 1997* (available online at http://www.latinomed.com/resources/latino_profile.html).

National Research Council (2006) *Multiple Origins, Uncertain Destinies: Hispanics and the American Future* Washington, DC: The National Academies Press.

Nguyen, J.D., Carson, M.L., Parris, K.M., and Place, P. (2003) "A Comparison Pilot Study of Public Health Field Nursing Home Visitation Program Interventions for Pregnant Hispanic Adolescents," *Public Health Nursing* 20, 412–48.

O'Connor, M.L. (1999) "Academically Oriented Teenage Women have Reduced Pregnancy Risk," *Family Planning Perspectives* 31(2), 105–6.

Ozawa, M.N. (1999) "The Economic Well-being of Elderly People and Children in a Changing Society," *Social Work* 44(1), 9–19.

Pabon, E. (1998) "Hispanic Adolescent Delinquency and the Family: a Discussion of Sociocultural Influences," *Adolescence* 33, 941–55.

Padilla, A.M. and Baird, T. L. (1991) "Mexican-American adolescent sexuality and sexual knowledge: An exploratory study." *Hispanic Journal of Behavioral Sciences,* 13, 95–104.

Padilla, A.M. and O'Grady, K.E. (1987) "Sexuality Among Mexican Americans: a Case of Sexual Stereotyping," *Journal of Personality and Social Psychology* 52, 5–10.

Pedraza-Bailey, S. (1985) *Political and Economic Migrants in America: Cubans and Mexicans,* Austin: University of Texas Press.

Portes, A. and Rumbaut, R. (2001) *Legacies: The Story of the Immigrant Second Generation,* Berkeley: University of California Press.

Portes, A. and Zhou, M. (1993) "The New Second Generation: Segmented Assimilation and its Variants," *Annals of the American Academy of Political and Social Science* 530, 74–96.

Remez, L. (1991) "Rates of Adolescent Pregnancy and Childbearing among Mexico-born Mexican Americans," *Family Planning Perspectives* 23(2), 88–9.

Reynoso, T.C., Felice, M.E., and Shragg, G.P. (1993) "Does American Acculturation Affect Outcome of Mexican-American Teenage Pregnancy?," *Journal of Adolescent Health* 14, 257–61.

Romo, H.D. and Falbo, T. (1996) *Latino High School Graduation: Defying the Odds*, Austin: University of Texas Press.

Rumbaut, R.G. (1997) "Assimilation and its Discontents: Between Rhetoric and Reality," *International Migration Review* 31, 923–60.

Scott, G. and Ni, H. (2004) "Access to Health Care Among Hispanic/Latino Children: United States, 1998–2001," *Advance Data from Vital and Health Statistics* 344, 1–24.

Scott, C.S., Shifman, L., Orr, L. Owen, R.G., and Fawcett, N. (1988) "Latina and Black American Adolescents' Beliefs Relating to Sexuality and Contraception," *Adolescence* 23, 667–88.

Scribner, R. and Dwyer, J. (1989) "Acculturation and Low Birth Weight Among Latinos in the Hispanic HANES," *American Journal of Public Health* 79, 1263–7.

Sherraden, M.S. and Barrera, R.E. (1996) "Healthy Babies Against the Odds: Maternal Support and Cultural Influences Among Mexican Immigrants," *Families in Society* 77, 298–313.

Sherraden, M.S. and Barrera, R.E. (1997a) "Family Support and Birth Outcomes Among Second-generation Mexican Immigrants," *Social Service Review*, 71(4), 607–33.

Sherraden, M.S. and Barrera, R.E. (1997b) "Culturally-Protective Health Practices: Everyday Pregnancy Care Among Mexican Immigrant Women," *Journal of Multicultural Social Work* 6(1/2), 93–116.

Stephen, E.H. and Bean, F.D. (1992) "Assimilation, disruption and the fertility of Mexican origin women in the United States." *International Migration Review* 92(1), 67–88.

Suro, R. (1998) "Generational Chasm Leads to Cultural Turmoil for Young Mexicans in the U.S.," *New York Times*, January 20, 1998, p. A11.

Sutton, P.D. and Matthews, T.J. (2004) "Trends in Characteristics of Births by State: United States, 1990, 1995, and 2000–2002," *National Vital Statistics* 5(19).

Sylvester, K. (1996) "Punish the Predators: It's Time to Get Tough with Men who Prey on Young Women," *The New Democrat*, May/June, pp. 22–3.

Tello, J. (2000) *A Reflection on Latino Fathers: Sustainability and Survival Through Welfare to Work*, Los Angeles: National Urban League.

Thierren, M. and Ramirez, R. (2001) *The Hispanic Population in the United States: Population Characteristics*, Washington, DC: US Census Bureau.

Thomas, E., Jr. (1996) "Is Pregnancy a Rational Choice for Poor Teenagers?," *Wall Street Journal*, January 18, 1996, p. B1.

Torres, A. and Singh, S. (1986) "Contraceptive Practice Among Hispanic Adolescents," *Family Planning Perspectives* 18, 193–4.

Trent, K. and Harlan, S. (1994) "Teenage Mothers in Nuclear and Extended Households," *Journal of Family Issue* 15, 309–37.

Treviño, R.P., Treviño, F. Medina R., Ramirez, G., and Ramirez, R. (1996) "Health Care Access Among Mexican Americans with Different Health Insurance Coverage," *Journal of Health Care for the Poor and Underserved* 7, 112–21.

Trueba, E.T. (1998) "The Education of Mexican Immigrant Children," on *Crossings: Mexican Immigration in Interdisciplinary Perspectives* (ed. M.M. Suarez-Orozco), Cambridge, MA: David Rockefeller Centre for Latin American Studies, Harvard University, pp. 227–47.

Unger, D. and Cooley, M. (1992) "Partner and Grandmother Contact in Black and White Teen Parent Families," *Journal of Adolescent Health Care* 13, 546–52.

Urban Institute (2004) *Two-thirds of Uninsured Children in Fair or Poor Health are Latina*, Washington, DC: Urban Institute.

Urrutia, M. (2004) "Health, in *State of Latina America 2004: Latino Perspectives on the American Agenda*, Washington, DC: National Council of La Raza, pp. 37–42.

US Census Bureau (1999) *The Hispanic Population in the United States*, Washington, DC: US Census Bureau (available online at http://www.census.gov/prod/2000pubs/p20-527.pdf).

US Census Bureau (2000) "Table 24: Projections of Resident Population, by Age, Sex, and Race, 2000 to 2025," in *Statistical Abstract of the United States, 1999*, Washington, DC: US Census Bureau.

US Census Bureau (2001a) "Table 8.1: Population by Sex, Age, Foreign Born Status, Latina Origin, and Race: March 2000," Washington, DC: US Census Bureau.

US Census Bureau (2001b) "Table 1: Total Population by Age, Race, and Hispanic or Latino Origin for the United States, 2000," Washington, DC: US Bureau of the Census (available online at http://www.census.gov/population/cen2000/phc-t9/tab01.xls; retrieved August 17, 2004).

US Census Bureau (2003) *Current Population Report, Children with Health Insurance: 2001*, Washington, DC: US Department of Commerce.

US Department of Justice (2003) *Sexual Assault of Young Children as Reported to Law Enforcement: Victim, Incident, and Offender Characteristics,"* Washington, DC: US Department of Justice (available online at http://www.ojp.usdoj.gov/bjs/abstract/saycrle.htm; retrieved August 17, 2004).

US Immigration and Naturalization Service (INS) (2002) *Illegal Alien Population Report*, Washington, DC: INS (available online at http://permanent.access.gpo.gov/lps18167/www.ins.gov/graphics/aboutins/statistics/illegalalien/illegal.pdf; retrieved August 17, 2004).

Vélez-Ibáñez, C.G. (2004) "Regions of Refuge in the United States: Issues Problems, and Concerns for the Future of Mexican-origin Populations in the United States," *Human Organization* 63(1), 1–20.

Wakschlag, L., Chase-Lansdale, P., and Brooks-Gunn, J. (1996) "Not just 'Ghosts in the Nursery': Contemporaneous Intergenerational Relationships and Parenting in Young African American Families," *Child Development* 67, 2131–47.

Warren, C.W., Santelli, J.S., Everett, S.A., Kann, L., Collins, J.L., Cassell, C., Morris, L., and Kolbe, L.J. (1998) "Sexual Behaviour Among U.S. High School Students, 1990–1995," *Family Planning Perspectives* 30(4), 170–4.

Weigers, M.E., and Sherraden, M.S. (2001) "A Critical Examination of Acculturation: The Impact of Health Behaviors, Social Support, and Economic Resources on Birthweight among Women of Mexican Descent," *International Migration Review* 35(3), 804–39.

Wertheimer, R. and Papillo, A.R. (2004) "An Update on State Policy Initiatives to Reduce Teen and Adult Nonmarital Childbearing," *New Federalism, Series A, No. A-66*, Washington, DC: The Urban Institute.

Zambrana, R.E., Dorrington, C., and Hayes-Bautista, D. (1995) "Family and Child Health: a Neglected Vision," in *Understanding Latino Families: Scholarship, Policy, and Practice* (ed. R.E. Zambrana), Thousand Oaks, CA: Sage, pp. 157–76.

Zayas, L. Schinke, S.P., and Casereno, D. (1987) "Hispanic Adolescent Fathers: At Risk and Underresearched," *Children and Youth Services Review* 9, 235–48.

Zedlewski, S. (2002) "Left Behind or Staying Away? Eligible Parents who Remain off TANF," Washington, DC: Urban Institute (available online at http://www.urban.org/url.cfm?ID=310571; retrieved August 17, 2004).

Chapter 4

In a class of their own?

The education of pregnant schoolgirls and schoolgirl mothers

Nona Dawson

The government's Teenage Pregnancy Strategy states that the aim of the national campaign is 'to halve the rate of conception among under 20 year olds in England by 2010 and to reduce the risk of long term social exclusion for teenage parents and their children by getting more parents into education, training and employment'.

This chapter will consider the commitment in the UK to provide education for pregnant schoolgirls and schoolgirl mothers.

The education of school-aged mothers

In the UK, it is a legal requirement that mothers aged less than 16 years are required, like their non-pregnant and non-parenting peers, to receive education (DfES 2001). This group of pupils is small and averages about one or two girls per secondary school each academic year (Dawson *et al.* 2004), although in reality some schools rarely have pregnant pupils and others have more than two per year. Local education authorities (LEAs) are obliged to ensure that under-16-year-olds in their area receive education.

> Each local education authority shall make arrangements for the provision of suitable education at school or otherwise than at school for those children of compulsory school age who, by reason of illness, exclusion from school or otherwise, may not for any period receive suitable education unless such arrangements are made for them.
>
> (Section 19, Education Act 1996)

LEAs have the power to provide suitable education or otherwise also to young people over the compulsory school age but under the age of 18 years. Additionally, OFSTED (Office for Standards in Education) states that all children, including pregnant schoolgirls and schoolgirl mothers, should have access, entitlement and an equal opportunity to the National Curriculum.

Unfortunately, the experience of pregnant schoolgirls and school-aged mothers does not always live up to this demand. Under-16-year olds who become pregnant and continue with their pregnancy to motherhood characteristically will not have experienced a particularly fruitful time at school before the pregnancy. Once a school knows that a girl is pregnant and is going to become a mother, decisions need to be made about the rest of her education. Typically she will not stay at school. A growing number of authorities, particularly those with a large number of young mothers, provide off-site educational establishments, some with child care provision. Another alternative is home tuition.

Education continuing in school

Currently, a small number of young mothers are able to continue their education within mainstream schools. However, this is unusual. Indeed, some schools use health and safety reasons as an excuse to remove pregnant young women (Dawson *et al.* 2004).

> Schools must develop and communicate clear health and safety policies for pregnant young women. They should be encouraged to undertake risk assessments for pregnant pupils, as they should for members of staff.
>
> (Dawson *et al.* 2004).

> It is the aim of the current government to ensure that young mothers do return to mainstream school once they have had their child. We believe they should wherever possible participate in the school full time.
>
> (Estelle Morris MP, 1999)

This view was shared in a government-sponsored report of more than 20 years ago from the National Council for One Parent Families, which states that:

> The policies of Local Education Authorities and schools should be to encourage a girl to continue her education at school.
>
> (Miles *et al.* 1979: 26)

However, the Department for Education and Employment (DfEE) considers full-time education at school, a further education college or suitable unit as options (Department for Education and Employment 1999).

This notion is fraught with difficulties. Certainly, in terms of equal opportunity to the National Curriculum, school is the place to be. However, young mothers are not only schoolgirls, they are also mothers, and they therefore have special needs in terms of support to enable them to grow up to be a good enough parent. It is also typically the case that school-aged mothers have not had a particularly productive school experience before pregnancy and returning to school is not a favoured option. If schools are to provide for young mothers there will be a need for extra resources in terms of child care, special provision for ante- and post-natal care as well as the specialist advice already existing in many of the excellent off-site centres in the UK.

Circular 10/99 (DfES 1999) makes clear that pregnancy is not a reason for exclusion from school. Health and safety should not be used as a reason to prevent a pregnant pupil attending school. The school's aim should be to keep the pregnant pupil or school-aged mother in learning. This means keeping the pupil on the school roll, even if she may not be able to attend for a period of time; keeping up to date with her progress; and working with the LEA to find a suitable time to reintegrate her into the school. If, exceptionally, a head teacher considers that the school is no longer a suitable environment for the education of a pregnant pupil or school-aged mother, the pupil, her parents, the LEA and the pupil's Connexions[1] or Sure Start Plus[2] personal adviser (if she has one) should be involved in deciding the most suitable provision for her (Department for Education and Skills 2001).

Home tuition

LEAs are responsible for making arrangements for the provision of suitable education otherwise than at school for pupils of compulsory school age who may not for any period of time receive suitable education unless such arrangements are made for them (DfES 2003). Suitable education is defined as 'efficient education suitable to the age, ability, aptitude and to any special educational needs the child (or young person) may have' (Department for Education and Employment 1999). This includes pregnant schoolgirls and school-aged mothers. This could be through home tuition, a pupil referral unit or further education college (DfEE web site). The DfEE states that individual tuition at home is not usually appropriate, although it may sometimes be the only short-term option (DfEE 11/99). For some young mothers in the UK it is the only option. The number of school-aged mothers and the financial support for specialist education varies throughout the UK.

Home tuition provided by education authorities varies in the number of hours available and the level of contact with a young mother's school. In the mid-1990s the average number of hours of home tuition provided for school-aged mothers was 5 in England and Wales and 8 in local authority areas in Scotland and Northern Ireland (Dawson 1997). Needless to say, this small amount of time, and lack of access to specialist equipment, in for example science laboratories, is a critical factor in a young mother's equal opportunity to a full education. There is no doubt that home tutors are valuable for young mothers, particularly in terms of support; however, this cannot be described as a complete education. This is compounded by the experience of isolation a young mother feels when she is not with other young people during her education, although the DfEE emphasises the need for collaboration between home tutor and a young mother's school or suitable pupil referral unit (PRU).

One of the factors in the varying experience of education for school-aged mothers in the UK is finance. Some education authorities are very rural and young mothers are spread throughout the authority area. In such cases, it is obviously not financially viable to set up several special centres or for pupils to travel to one central centre. Thus, if returning to school is not an option, as is often the case, home tuition may be the only remaining alternative. Of course, in largely urban authority areas, where the majority of young mothers are typically to be found, the setting up of specialist provision is more financially viable and can be supported.

Special centre provision

Special centre provision has grown in the UK. In England, for example, there are approximately 60 off-site educational units for school-aged mothers. These vary in the extent of curriculum provided, whether there is child care support on site and whether there is access to other agencies such as those which provide health care and careers advice. In special centres that provide both education and support for motherhood, pupils' attendance records often reach 100 per cent, and girls are able to sit national examinations. Inevitably, this type of centre is most likely to be found in areas where it makes financial sense for the LEA to provide it, and in areas where the LEA is committed to providing as broad an education as possible for pupils not in mainstream school. PRUs first took their place in England in 1994. The DfEE is quite clear about their role:

> The PRU curriculum should be balanced and broadly based . . . Teaching should cover at least the core subjects of mathematics, English and science. It should also include elements of spiritual, moral, cultural and social development and social education programmes, access to both aesthetic and practical experiences, humanities, some opportunities to engage in planned physical activities and the chance to acquire relevant skills.
>
> (Department for Education 1994)

There are several key differences between PRUs and schools (Department for Education and Employment 1999):

- The management committee of PRUs, which may cover two or more PRUs, can include members from a wide range of backgrounds, including head teachers from maintained schools, LEA officers, parents and representatives of charitable organisations, the careers service, the police, etc.
- Pupils attending PRUs may continue to be registered at a mainstream school, i.e. dual registration.
- Requirements regarding staffing and the duties of LEAs and teachers in charge differ, e.g. the teacher in charge, while considered the teacher, may not be formally employed as a head teacher, and staff should be given time to plan for individual pupils' re-entry into education or employment and to build relationships with pupils.
- The PRU does not have to provide the full National Curriculum but it should offer a balanced and broadly based curriculum that promotes spiritual, moral,

cultural and physical development and prepares pupils for the opportunities, responsibilities and experiences of adult life.

• Premises requirements are less stringent, with PRUs not having to provide a head teacher's room, playing fields or staff accommodation for teachers to use for both work and social purposes.

There is a variety in the quality of educational and child care provision in the current PRUs and other off-site provision. Some PRUs include child care provision, others accept schoolgirls only until the child is born and others have no child care provision.

To young women who have not enjoyed or attended school regularly, the unit offers a more adult environment where they are on first-name terms with the teachers and there are no unnecessary rules. Far from being irresponsible, these young women are crying out for some independence and responsibility, which ordinary schools are not prepared to give them (Warr 1996: 7–8).

PRUs are open for OFSTED inspection, and a number of English PRUs specifically set up for young mothers have been inspected. OFSTED inspects PRUs using the framework of inspection for schools, adapted for PRUs.

Schofield (1994) identifies two questions to be considered in service provision for school-aged mothers. First, how can specialist provision be offered to meet the specific needs of these girls while at the same time helping them to lead as normal life as possible, avoiding in particular stigma and isolation? Second, how can channels be provided for young mothers themselves to influence the nature of services and to be empowered to make choices?

As Schofield points out, there is a concern that attending off-site units will isolate a schoolgirl from her peers and make her seem different. In fact, there is little empirical evidence to support this. As has been stated above, many pupils, including those who had poor attendance when at a mainstream school, achieve 100 per cent attendance at specialist centres for young mothers and their babies. Although the off-site centres are not required to offer the full National Curriculum, there are excellent examples in the country where full educational provision is made for young mothers alongside good professional support for parenthood. This type of off-site provision has grown in the UK, and in the past has been welcomed by education authorities and central government. However, within the current drive for social inclusion, the move is to have school-aged mothers remain at school. This notion of inclusion needs much more thought.

Child care

Child care is crucial if young mothers are to be able to complete their education. Grandmothers can no longer be relied upon for child care as often they will be working. Most schools do not have crèches, and home tuition alongside the baby is unsatisfactory in educational terms. Many pupils value being able to attend an educational establishment that also provides child care nearby for their young child. Additionally, teenage mothers often come from troubled and disrupted families.

Along with experiencing education the young mother is also able to care for and feed her child, and learn the important lessons of child development. Often the school-aged mother's child will be very young – a baby or young toddler – so this opportunity to be with her child contributes to the vital stage of bonding and learning to be a parent. Young mothers are caught in the prevailing tension of encouraging mothers to be trained and to go out to work and to be part of the current parenting campaign and learn to be good parents.

One of Warr's (1996: 14) recommendations for practice includes:

> Child care should be funded, for young women at school and within units. Young women who return to school should not be dependent on female family members for child care, nor should they be prevented from returning to school because of lack of child care. Child care is also necessary within units, to ensure that the young women are able to concentrate on their studies.

The type of child care on offer to young mothers varies: in special units, on-site child care may be provided by trained nursery nurses; or their local authority may fund a child minder; or they may take part in a government initiative such as Sure Start Plus. However, child care can be a sensitive issue for young mothers. For example, Dawson and Meadows (2001) found that young mothers taking part in a training programme in Northern Ireland (Youth Action in Belfast) did not want their young child to be cared for by a child minder. They wanted more family involvement. In this case, the initiative of which they were a part arranged for money to be paid to a relative to look after the children while the mothers were attending class if they so wished. Other research (e.g. Dawson *et al.* 2004) has found that young mothers as a whole do not favour child minders, possibly because they are concerned that their baby will become attached to another woman.

By failing to provide child care the government is increasing and not decreasing dependence on the state and the feminisation of poverty (Warr 1996: 18).

Provision of education for young mothers in the UK

As part of a study of education and employment opportunities for young mothers in Europe, a survey of educational facilities for school-aged mothers in each authority in the UK was carried out by Dawson and Meadows (2001). Table 4.1 shows the number of education authorities which responded in each country of the UK. The overall response averaged not much more than half. This is disappointing, as inevitably some of the data will not reflect the whole experience of the UK. The mid-1990s survey (Dawson 1997) elicited a much higher response (between 80 per cent and 100 per cent from each country) and therefore resulted in a more reliable set of data. The response rate in the 1994 survey was 84 per cent

Table 4.1 Response to survey

Country	Total number of education authorities	Number which responded	Percentage
England	152	81	53
Wales	22	14	67
Scotland	32	21	66
Northern Ireland	5	3	60
Total	211	119	56

Table 4.2 Education provision for pregnant schoolgirls and schoolgirl mothers in the countries of the UK (% of authorities)

	England	Wales	Scotland	Northern Ireland	UK
Home tuition	52	39	45	67	47
Full-time school	36	23	50	67	38
Part-time school	25	15	60	0	30
PRU/special centre	64	31	30	0	53
Ad hoc provision	8	0	20	0	9

in England and Wales and 100 per cent in Scotland and Northern Ireland. At that time the question of the education of school-aged mothers was beginning to be considered and the local authorities valued the questionnaire as a way of helping them sort out their own position.

The authorities were asked about what educational arrangements they provided for pregnant schoolgirls and schoolgirl mothers. It was possible to select more than one type. For example, in one authority both home tuition and a PRU may be provided. Table 4.2 shows the spread of provision across authorities in the UK. When educational provision in individual countries is examined it can be seen that home tuition and full-time education are more common in Northern Ireland than elsewhere in the UK. The most common form of provision in Wales is home tuition whereas part-time schooling is more common in Scotland and PRUs or special centres are more common in England.

Figure 4.1 summarises the findings for the UK as a whole and shows that, overall, the most commonly reported form of education for young mothers was a special off-site centre (PRU), followed by home tuition and then full-time or part-time schooling. This is because PRUs are most common in England, the largest country of the UK.

In contrast, the study conducted in the mid-1990s found that the most common form of education for pregnant schoolgirls and schoolgirl mothers in the UK was home tuition (Dawson 1997). Thus, it is the case that the UK has become much more aware from government level down of the needs of teenage mothers.

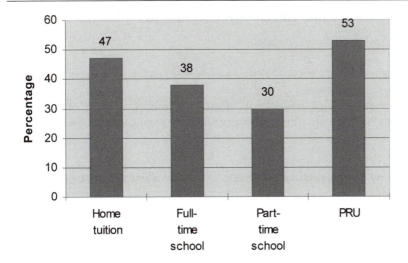

Figure 4.1 Types of educational provision for pregnant schoolgirls and schoolgirl mothers in the UK.

Views regarding the education of school-aged mothers and their possible return to mainstream schooling

In this survey (Dawson 1997), directors of education or their nominees were asked for their views regarding the education of school-aged mothers and their possible return to mainstream schooling. The main themes that emerged from this were associated with child care, mothers' reluctance to return to school, schools' reluctance to integrate young mothers, peer pressure, mothers' previous experience of schooling and the different psychological views of themselves held by young mothers. These issues will now be expanded upon.

Reluctance of young mothers to return to school after having a baby

Typical comments in this area were:

*   Pupils should stay in school and follow a revised curriculum. Once the child is born, this then becomes a difficult issue as the mother is often reluctant to return to school. They wish to remain at home with the new baby.
*   Often there is nobody to look after the child and an inability to return to school as the pupil has moved on both emotionally and physically. In any case, pupils are often reluctant to leave their baby with someone else.

Reluctance of some schools to reintegrate young mothers

The following points were made:

- The constraints are only that mainstream schools are reluctant to integrate schoolgirl mothers.
- The attitudes of school staff. Especially school uniform rules are the constraints along with youngsters who are accommodated and constantly moving homes.

Effect of peer pressure on young mothers' desire to return to school

The following comments fell into this category:

- In practice, return to mainstream education can be difficult. Constraining factors include peer pressure and criticism.
- Some young mothers also feel that the reaction of their peers may be unfavourable.

Poor attendance at school before their pregnancy

Typical comments were:

- Often the girls have been non-school attenders at their previous mainstream school and are reluctant to return to what did not work for them before.
- Returning to school is generally more successful if a pupil was a good attender prior to becoming pregnant.

Young mothers feel more grown-up than their peers

Typical comments were:

- The feeling of being a schoolgirl is no longer appropriate when they are mums.

Child care

Typical comments regarding this aspect were:

- Lack of suitable child care is often a problem for a young mother considering a return to school.
- Child care problems: there are no crèches available in schools.
- However, school is only possible if the girl makes her own child care arrangements. In practice, this rarely happens.

Many respondents expressed a concern about the lack of child care facilities for a young mother and how this would affect her move into further education and training and employment. This view applied to all the countries in the UK.

There is an urgent need for financial support for pupils going on to further education and training to enable them to access child care. Nursery fees are prohibitive and help is patchy and often restricted to looked-after young people.

The major factor is child care. Social services offer a sponsored child minder – the young women want nurseries. The other issue then is the funding for the child care, which varies from case to case. The Benefits Agency sometimes helps, but again there is a lack of co-ordination of resources.

Opportunities are totally non-existent without good, relevant child care.

Others involved with the young mother and her child

Another concern was related to the people associated with the young mother, her partner and parents in particular, and how these people may be involved with the child. It was recognised that partners may often be unemployed.

If the live-in partner is also unemployed there is often no work ethos. Effort needs to be put into whatever family unit has been created to encourage a cohesive work package for all carers, taking account of the needs of the baby/toddler.

Grandparents are recognised as important in supporting their daughter and grandchild.

The pressure placed on grandparents, particularly in child care and financial terms, is often very high.

Equal access to education

Some respondents were aware that young mothers' opportunity for education had been very variable in the past and were keen to work to change this.

Over the years teenage mothers have suffered discrimination because many of them have had no access to full-time education and subsequently employment. This authority now provides full-time education for these students along with a comprehensive careers education programme, which has led to employment or further education.

Perceived psychological characteristics of young mothers

Young mothers were identified as a group who are disadvantaged in terms of their psychological characteristics, particularly in terms of self-esteem, self-confidence and aspirations.

> The underlying problems within our schools are very low self-esteem, low confidence and extremely limited aspirations for the future. We, of course, try to tackle these throughout the whole curriculum and in the methods and styles in which the students are taught. To develop our provision this year we have introduced CLAIT level 1 and a NAMCW child care course to try to provide the students with skills which not only develop them personally but also improve their employability and raise expectations for the future.

Wanting to be a mum

It was recognised that the majority of the young mothers have very young children, usually not yet of school age. For the mothers of very young babies, access to child care is difficult. Some respondents pointed out that some young mothers want to be a mother first, and then later to consider further education and/or employment.

> Ensure that continuity of advice is maintained. The mum may be reluctant to part from her baby in the first year, but if contact is maintained then after 12 months the novelty may have worn off a little and, as toddlerhood approaches, the mum may be more receptive to having independent aspects to her life so long as adequate child care is available.

> We have students keen to go on into further education but who unable to participate as their babies are too young for crèches and they have to miss a year.

> I often feel that everything that is on offer for these mums is badly timed. For many, the help is just what is needed, but for many more the case is that they have no interest in their education at that point. Lots of people's time and money is spent trying to help them gain qualifications at a time when they just want to be a mum. Many of them develop very good avoidance strategies. Then when they are keen to be trained and get a qualification as an adult they do not have the resources.

It was emphasised that when working with young mothers both their academic position and their place as young mothers with young children need to be taken into account.

I am impressed by the level of attainment by young mothers who attend our provision. I am also impressed by their level of maturity. Girls respond well to being treated as responsible adults. I feel our provision is successful because it integrates education/unit care and support to be a parent.

Social exclusion

A number of authorities cited the Social Exclusion Unit (SEU) report recommendations regarding education. This was aimed at England only; however the National Assembly of Wales is to examine this, and the relevant bodies in Northern Ireland and Scotland are also examining the position and needs of teenage parents.

Some respondents clearly felt that teenage parents constitute an excluded group and that this has an impact on their experience of school education, further education/training and opportunities for employment. The fact that many young parents come from disadvantaged homes was also raised.

Over the years teenage mothers have suffered discrimination because many of them have had no access to full-time education and subsequently employment.

Prior to the SEU government report, very little support for post-16 mums existed. We are hopeful that this report will change the climate of thinking. Our experts in this area feel that the whole cycle of social deprivation has to be broken to free up all types of opportunities including employment for these girls. There remain concerns about under-16s being even more at a disadvantage due to benefits paid via their own parents.

Better sex education for boys as well as girls in school but an overall acknowledgement of the links between economic/social class and early pregnancy would move the debate forward.

It was also clear to some authorities that young mothers belong to a disadvantaged group in UK society and that their experience of poverty would inevitably have an impact on their opportunity for education and employment.

The main problem faced by girls and their parents is poverty.

There was a concern that the guidance relating to the education of teenage mothers in comparison with excluded pupils was generally not clear.

The guidance regarding the education of teenage mothers is less clear and directive than the guidance regarding excluded pupils. By the year 2002 all

LEAs must provide full-time educational opportunities for excluded pupils. Because teenage mothers are supported in a variety of ways in the UK, e.g. by PRUs, home teaching, special groups, etc., the provision may be less specific. Some LEAs are creating two-tier provision, i.e. full-time for excluded pupils while pregnant or sick pupils may receive only a few hours education per week, e.g. 5 or 8. In other LEAs pregnant pupils/young mothers do receive full-time provision. National consistency is needed for this group of pupils and equal opportunity for access to full-time provision for all pupils educated outside school.

Conclusion

Teenage pregnancy and motherhood is of current concern to the UK. The present government has identified this concern in a way that no other government has. In response to the SEU's report (Social Exclusion Unit 1999), it has set up the Teenage Pregnancy Unit in England. Meanwhile, in the other countries of the UK the issue of teenage pregnancy is being seriously considered.

The government's aims are to reduce the pregnancy rate among the under-18s by 50 per cent by the year 2010 and to eliminate social exclusion of young mothers and their children. To this end the government is sponsoring work in two areas – prevention of pregnancy and reduction in early sexual experiences, and support for young mothers and their children, particularly in terms of encouraging mothers' employment.

With regard to the education of school-aged mothers, it is clear that there is a tension between government plans to have girls return to mainstream school and the views and experience of those working with very young mothers. It is generally considered a bad idea to send girls back to school and it is believed that provision of academic education combined with support to become a parent is a much better arrangement. Some of the better PRUs do precisely this. However, in one region in the UK – Fife, Scotland, all 19 schools have agreed that young mothers may continue with their education at school.

The main focus on employment training for young mothers that has emerged is concerned with how young women view themselves and how this affects their choices. Much good work has been done to build self-confidence, and this would seem to be a key feature of any good employment training support for young mothers.

The existence of a conflict between wanting to care for one's small child and to be employed has emerged. This is a concern and it would be regrettable if the proposed changes to social security payments, particularly ONE,[3] were to affect a young mother caring for her baby.

The government has announced two concerns. First, young parents and their children are often socially excluded, and this needs to be addressed. Second, the quality of parenting needs to be improved, with the aim of affecting the behaviour of children who are a potential threat to the communities in which they live. There has been a push to increase the availability of parenting classes to help young parents bring up their children, although such classes seem to be aimed only at young parents judged to be disadvantaged.

There is clearly a potential paradox between, on the one hand, encouraging young mothers to join the workforce, and on the other hand, encouraging parents to spend time with their children.

It is clear that for the UK to support young mothers in their development as full and mature members of the workforce, and good enough parents of their children, the following points need to be borne in mind:

- A range of educational provision to suit the individual needs of a young school-aged mother and her child needs to be available.
- Support for school-aged mothers comes from providing them not only with equal access to the full mainstream curriculum but with the chance to learn how to mother, as well as emotional and social support.
- Access to good child care for all teenage mothers is crucial.
- Credible accredited courses that lead to further education and/or decent jobs are essential.
- Listening to the voices of young mothers themselves is fundamental to an understanding of the lives and future aspirations of teenage mothers.

Notes

1 Connexions has been set up in England and offers guidance and support for young people up to the age of 19 years.
2 Sure Start is aimed at giving children a 'sure start' in life. It is targetted at children under 4 years, and their families, in areas of need. Sure Start Plus is aimed at the children of young mothers under 18 years.
3 This approach aims to bring together the Employment Service, Benefits Agency and other welfare providers at a single point of contact (DfES 1998). The ONE service came into full operation in April 2000. ONE means that all benefit claimants of working age, including young mothers, will be compelled to attend a work-related interview as part of the claims process.

References

Dawson, N. (1997) 'The Provision of Education and Employment Opportunities for Pregnant Schoolgirls and Schoolgirl Mothers: a Crossnational Comparison within the UK', *Children and Society* 11, 242–51.

Dawson, N. and Meadows, S. (eds) (2001) *Education and Occupational Training for Teenage Mothers in Europe: the UK National Report.* End of grant report to the EU Leonardo da Vinci Programme.

Dawson, N., Hosie, A., Meadows, S., Selman, P. and Speak, S. (2004) *The Education of Pregnant Young Women and Young Mothers in England*, London: Department of Health.

Department for Education (1994) The *Education by LEAs of Children Otherwise than at School* (Circular 11/94), London: Department for Education.

Department for Education and Employment (1999) *Social Inclusion: Pupil Support* (Circular 11/99), London: DfEE.

Department for Education and Skills (2001) *Guidance on the Education of School Age Parents*, London, DfES (available at http://www.dfes.gov.uk/schoolageparents/).

Miles, M. (1979) Joint working party on Pregnant Schoolgirls and Schoolgirl Mothers. Pregnant at School. London: National Council for One Parent Families.

Schofield, G. (1994) *The Youngest Mothers: the Experience of Pregnancy and Motherhood Among Young Women of School Age.* Aldershot: Avebury.

Social Exclusion Unit (1999) *Teenage Pregnancy: Report by the Social Exclusion Unit*, London: Stationery Office

Warr, J. (1996) *The Education of School-aged Mothers: Experiences, Aspirations and Practice*, Oxford: Oxford Brookes University.

Chapter 5

Teenage pregnancy and social exclusion

An exploration of disengagement and re-engagement from the education system

Alison Hosie and Peter Selman

Introduction

This chapter explores the roots of the government's Teenage Pregnancy Strategy and its decision to refer the issue of teenage pregnancy to the newly formed Social Exclusion Unit (SEU). The solution to social exclusion for young parents and their children is seen as education and training, raising questions about the competing discourses on social exclusion. This is explored using a typology suggested by Ruth Levitas (1998), together with a brief consideration of the relationship between poverty, deprivation and high teenage conception and birth rates.

The second part of this chapter concentrates on the government strategy to reduce the risk of social exclusion, looking in detail at one specific policy aimed at reintegrating school-aged mothers into education. This is examined with reference to the authors' monitoring of the Department for Education and Skills (DfES) Standards Fund Teenage Pregnancy Grant (Selman *et al.* 2001), with particular reference to those mothers who had disengaged from education before they conceived.

The competing discourses on social exclusion

The term social exclusion is a relatively new one, the origins of which are said to lie in French policy, in which context it 'was used to refer to a disparate group of people living on the margins of society' (Percy-Smith 2000: 1). Some sceptics now see it as an acceptable New Labour term for poverty, just as health inequalities have been replaced by health variations.

There is a need to recognise that its meaning and the meaning of the apparent solution, i.e. social *inclusion*, is not uncontested. Levitas (1998) suggests there are at least three differing discourses around social exclusion. All have had some influence on New Labour thinking. Each implies different definitions of the problem and a different approach to the causes of high teenage pregnancy rates, and hence different policy solutions towards reducing the likelihood of long-term social exclusion. The definitions are:

MUD – moral underclass discourse.

SID – social integrationist discourse: inclusion is primarily viewed in terms of labour market attachment.

RED – redistributionist discourse: primarily concerned with poverty.

MUD is most clearly seen in the works of Charles Murray and the underclass debate (Murray 1990, 1994). In the USA this became entangled with the welfare debate (Luker 1996; Selman 2003a,b). This approach suggests a moral crisis in which action is needed not so much because teenage pregnancy is a problem for mother and/or child, but as part of a war against a major threat to civilisation. This approach characterised the philosophy of the Conservative administrations of the 1980s and early 1990s and is seen in Mrs Thatcher's later comments in respect of children born into single-parent families, for example:

> We took the wrong steps many years ago when . . . there were only a few such children . . . We wanted to do our best for them. Our best was to see that the young mother had a flat of her own . . . and also had an income to look after the child.
>
> (*Daily Express*, November 21 1998)

She conceded that this had been wrong and that, 'In tackling the situation in that way we were unwittingly multiplying the number of people who had illegitimate children' (ibid.).

SID represents an important shift away from this approach and towards a more humane version of welfare into work as developed under New Labour. It can imply, however, that we have in a sense brought this upon ourselves by allowing young mothers to draw benefit and enter social housing without any obligations in respect of education and training. The model approximates most closely the approach found in the government Teenage Pregnancy Strategy discussed below.

RED envisages the roots of social exclusion as more structural, taking the view that the low aspirations that lead to high rates of teenage motherhood are inevitable in a divided and unequal society. Further to this, solutions cannot be sought in better sex education or contraception alone (although this is important as a right) but must also involve a reduction in inequalities.

Luker's (1996) account of the politics of teenage pregnancy in the USA demonstrates clearly the dominance of MUD in the 1990s but calls for an approach that would be close to RED:

> Society should worry not about some epidemic of 'teenage pregnancy' but about the hopeless, discouraged and empty lives that early childbearing denote. Teenagers and their children desperately need a better future, one with brighter opportunities and greater rewards.
>
> (Luker 1996: 192)

The reality of potential social exclusion for young mothers is clearly shown in the gloomy picture emerging in a paper by John Hobcraft and Kathleen Kiernan (2001). Their study used data from the National Child Development Study (1958 birth cohort) to examine outcomes at age 33 for several domains of adult social exclusion in respect of those having their first child before age 23. The indices of adult deprivation included being a lone mother, living in social housing, qualifying for welfare benefits, having no qualifications, having a low household income, having no telephone, being in ill-health, smoking and having a high malaise and low life satisfaction.

Early motherhood was shown to be associated with most of these indicators, even after controls on childhood poverty and other background factors. This effect was noticeable for those giving birth before the age of 23, although greater for those having their first child as a teenager. Moreover, the impact of early (pre-23) motherhood was greater than that of childhood poverty with deferred childbearing. The worst outcomes were for teenage mothers with experience of childhood poverty.

A social exclusion focus also raises questions about the well-established relationship between poverty and teenage pregnancy (Smith 1993; Babb 1994; Botting 1998; Selman 2003b). It is important to remember the context of all this, the fact that UK birth and conception rates for teenagers are much higher than in the rest of Europe, although similar to those in other Anglo-Saxon countries and lower than in the USA (Singh and Darroch 2000; United Nations Children's Fund 2001). UK and US rates rose in the 1980s, a period of widening inequalities in both countries, at a time when rates in mainland Europe fell. Therefore, initially both countries have the task of getting back to where they were in the 1970s before going on to match the reductions in Europe (Selman 1996; Selman and Glendinning 1996).

The Social Exclusion Unit (SEU) report

The SEU published its report *Teenage Pregnancy* in June 1999. The report includes a detailed analysis of the current situation and highlights two policy goals:

- Reducing the rate of teenage conceptions (46.6 per 1,000 women aged 15–17 in 1998), with the specific aim of halving the rate of conceptions among under-18s by 2010, with an interim target of a 15 per cent reduction by 2004 (to 39.6 per 1,000) and establishing a downward trend in under-16 conceptions.
- Getting more teenage parents into education, training or employment to reduce their risk of long-term social exclusion, measured by an increase in sustained participation by teenage parents in education, employment or training.

Both goals are of particular importance for the minority of teenage women who conceive under the age of 16 and for whom pregnancy often leads to a disruption of education or arises in the context of prior disengagement from schooling, including formal exclusion from school (Osler 2000).

Given the evidence that a high proportion of under-18 conceptions are unplanned (Social Exclusion Unit 1999: 28), few would argue with the notion of it being a good thing to reduce these. However, specific targets raise a number of problems; for example, if the rate is not halved by 2010 will this be taken as evidence of the failure of the strategy, even if young people have benefited from access to improved sex education and contraception?

The Teenage Pregnancy Strategy was seen initially as a success, with a decline in the under-18 conception rate from 46.6 in 1998 to 42.3 per 1,000 in 2001. However, the rate rose to 42.6 in 2002. The provisional figure for 2004 is 41.5 – a reduction of 11 per cent rather than the 15 per cent target (to 39.6).

Education and young motherhood

For some time, the link between low educational aspirations and achievement and higher rates of teenage pregnancy has been acknowledged (Morrison 1985; Kraft et al. 1990; Moore et al. 1995; Stevens-Simon and Lowly 1995; Luker 1996; Turner 2001). However, it is often assumed that pregnancy is the reason that young women drop out of school and fail to finish their education. Recent research (Selman et al. 2001; Hosie 2002, 2003; Dawson and Hosie 2005) highlights that often this relationship is reversed and that many young women have either been officially excluded from school or have effectively disengaged themselves from education prior to pregnancy.

The Standards Fund Grant for teenage pregnancy

The introduction of the Standards Fund Grant in September 2000 was a key support initiative by New Labour to help reintegrate young mothers back into school in England. Prior to the existence of the grant, pregnant young women and young mothers of school age had a limited range of approaches available to them with regard to their continued education (Selman et al. 2001). Whilst some Local Education Authorites provided access to full- or part-time specialist units[1] for pregnant young women and young mothers of school age, others offered only the choice of remaining in mainstream school or accessing home tuition.

The grant enabled most LEAs involved[2] to have a dedicated reintegration officer (or equivalent[3]) whose remit was to liaise with schools, to raise awareness around the issue of teenage pregnancy and education, to establish procedures for pregnant young women and young mothers of school age, to collect baseline data, to overcome barriers to reintegration, to improve the attendance of pregnant young women and young mothers of school age in education and to provide general support for these young women.

Issues of concern prior to the Standards Fund Grant

Prior to introduction of the Standards Fund Grant, the level of help available to pregnant young women and young mothers of school age depended to a great degree on what provision already existed within an LEA and the level of priority accorded teenage pregnancy within that LEA.[4]

A range of concerns about the practice of dealing with the educational needs of pregnant young women and young mothers were raised by the newly appointed reintegration officers in each LEA at the start of the research. It became apparent that LEAs generally had very little information about the numbers of pregnant young women and young mothers of school age in their area, and had little knowledge about their educational activities or needs. Once the reintegration officers started to compile such data, it became increasingly apparent that young women entitled to home tuition commonly were not receiving it because schools were unaware of the correct procedure, failed to fill in the relevant request forms or attempted to hide the fact that a pupil was pregnant by failing to inform the appropriate education welfare officer (EWO).

The data also revealed that a significant proportion of these women had effectively disengaged themselves from school or were erratic attendees prior to pregnancy. Without adequate follow-up on non-attendance, therefore, many of the LEAs did not respond to their needs because they were unaware that the need existed. In some areas, there was evidence of schools removing pregnant young women from their rolls, enforcing extended maternity leave and refusing to admit year 11 mothers who had missed a substantial amount of year 10. There was also evidence that some schools were falsifying attendance records. For example, one young woman was marked down as being on an 'outward bound course' by her school, when the reintegration officer knew that she had in fact been in labour at the time.

There was also evidence that, even although schools are not legally able to exclude on the basis of pregnancy, some pregnant young women were told that they could stay only as long as their pregnancy bump was not visible. The reason cited was the adverse effect that the presence of a pregnant pupil might have on younger vulnerable pupils or the school ethos. Other pupils were publicly humiliated, their pregnancy used as a warning to others, as one pregnant young woman described:

> He told me to leave. Said he didn't want me causing any problems and disrupting everyone else's education . . . he then held a school assembly and announced the situation to the whole school in a 'let this be a warning to you all . . .' manner.

Pregnant young women were often informed that they could not remain in school due to concerns over health and safety. This breaches sex discrimination legislation, but the young women in question were not aware of their rights at the time. One young woman explained how, on informing her school of her pregnancy, she was told not to return to school:

> They just said that if I get hurt then it's on their backs and basically they didn't want it. I was annoyed because I couldn't do my GCSEs. I got my social worker to go up a few times, to try and ask them why, but they just told him the same thing they told me.

Some of the issues raised by the young women highlighted problems within the education system that led to their initial disaffection from school prior to pregnancy. The most disturbing aspect was how often this story was repeated. The factors that most often initiated a career of disengagement were lack of interest in particular lessons, being forced by the National Curriculum to study subjects that they did not enjoy, being constantly treated like a child or failing to receive respect from teachers and bullying from pupils and staff.

A striking pattern for many of the young women involved in the study was an average to good attendance during the transition from primary to secondary in year 7, signs of unrest and initial disengagement by the end of year 8, a high level of disengagement by year 9 and presenting as pregnant by year 10.

It is important for reintegration officers to recognise that reintegration into mainstream schooling is not necessarily the best or most appropriate option for these young women. A young woman who has disengaged herself from school prior to pregnancy is unlikely to want to return to mainstream education directly, if at all. For her to do so may place her educationally at a disadvantage in relation to her peers, as one young mother stated:

> I think they could have done so much more to help . . . One teacher, when I went back to school, made me feel really bad for having the baby; he called me stupid. And then they put me back a year; they just decided. I sort of felt like everyone was making my decisions for me. I wanted to carry on in the year I was in. I really hated it; they put me back with students younger than me and, with me being in the situation I was, just made fun of me all the time. I left after one month.

Prior to the existence of the grant, a young woman who presented to a school as pregnant would often be faced with a range of practices that impacted negatively on her desire to remain within education, and this was the reason for the greatest level of discontent amongst the experiences of the young women interviewed by Selman *et al*. (2001). In particular, negative staff attitudes towards pregnant young women and young mothers, with a common prevailing assumption that their lives and education were now over, did little to enthuse young women to continue their education. More often, it confirmed in their own minds that these assumptions that they were continually faced with in other social contexts, particularly from the media, were true.

Many young women felt that as soon as they announced their pregnancy at school they no longer had control over any aspect of their educational career. Someone else now held ownership over decisions and choices about what was best for them. This often resulted in the rejection of an established positive practice because it was not the young woman's decision and therefore resented. One example of such a case is the flexible or part-time timetable. If this was offered as a choice to a young woman it was often appreciated and accepted; however, when it was a decision made for a young woman it was more often than not resented and/or rejected.

In a number of cases, schools would not enter pregnant pupils for some or all of their GCSEs; this was particularly the case for young women with a history of disengagement. Reintegration officers noted many such cases and believed that schools had undertaken such practice because of the pressures on them to present well in league tables. Schools apparently felt that pregnant young women and young mothers generally would not do well because of their maternity absence or prior disengagement from school.

Young women also commented that they were often made to feel guilty and shameful about their pregnant status, often being located in a separate classroom to study so as not to encourage similar behaviour amongst other pupils. Many young women noted that when they returned to school there was no appreciation from staff of the difficulties they faced in combining motherhood and school, whilst trying to do their best at both.

Many young women continuing their education in mainstream schools raised a variety of practical issues that either prevented them from attending or seriously risked the health of themselves and their unborn child if they did. Young women talked frequently about the inflexibility of some schools over school uniform so that pupils were not allowed to attend unless they were wearing standard uniform. In many cases, shortage of money prevented the young women from replacing their clothes as their bodies changed during pregnancy. Also, not being allowed to wear sensible shoes (such as trainers) made it physically difficult for them to move about, especially in the later stages of pregnancy.

Of particular concern were schools that would not allow anyone, including pregnant young women, to bring water into the classroom. This can have serious consequences, as one reintegration officer noted:

> I've had a couple, no, three girls in hospital now, with serious kidney problems. And I think it's because they are not able to drink enough and use the loo when they like. At the hospital they told me it was a common problem if you don't get plenty of fluids when you're pregnant.

Although the majority of negative practices prior to the grant occurred within the mainstream system, other types of educational provision were not without their problems. A criticism levelled at specialist units by government in the past has been that, unlike mainstream education, specialist units do not offer the full

National Curriculum and therefore put attendees at an educational disadvantage. This is in fact true in only a minority of cases, although in some units particular subjects may be taught only by teachers who are not specialists in a subject. Some young women, while saying that 'they did their best', cited the lack of specialist area help as a barrier to continuation of a subject or a reason for failing to achieve a good grade.

An issue frequently raised in areas with long-established specialist units was that many schools would refer any pregnant pupil automatically, without considering each individual case. Reintegration officers believed that, although some schools genuinely believed that these specialist centres could offer better support, in many cases referral was perceived as an easy way of concealing the pregnancy within their school. This meant that some young women who would have benefited from remaining in mainstream education, particularly if their preferred subjects were not catered for in their local unit, would often be encouraged to move to a unit even if it left them educationally disadvantaged.

With regard to home tuition, the main criticism repeatedly raised, if a young woman had been fortunate enough to receive any (in one LEA as many as 50 per cent of pregnant young women prior to the grant were not receiving their entitled home tuition), was the low level of educational provision and support that it provided. Those who do benefit from this provision on average receive only 3 to 5 hours' tuition per week (5 hours being the national average for England; Dawson 1997). Many young women stated that this limited time left them very behind with their work, or able to focus only on a small number of subjects in order to obtain decent grades in their GCSEs.

Some women receiving home tuition said that they felt very isolated because their tutor was someone with whom they had no prior relationship; in addition, many had no continued contact with their school during the maternity period. This made reintegration into school post birth considerably harder and often unsuccessful. Furthermore, in a number of cases home tuition was found to be very basic, with the tutor assuming that the pregnant young woman would not be interested in her education. This often resulted in disengagement with this form of education as well, as one young mother highlights below:

> It was only 5 hours and it was a waste of time; all I did was copy out of books. She was a specialist in maths and, I'm not being funny, but . . . I was more intelligent than her. She sat there; I was 15 year old then and she was sitting there having me learning my two and three times table. I think she thought that because I was stupid enough to get pregnant at that age that I was stupid full stop and that I wouldn't be interested in doing schoolwork.

The impact of reintegration officers

The research findings suggest that a dedicated reintegration officer can help pregnant young women and young mothers of school age to continue with their education, whether in mainstream schooling, college or specialist units or with home tuition. Many of the interviewees responded positively to their reintegration officer and showed a great deal of desire to succeed, in part because they wanted to be able to provide for their child. However, there was also evidence that an increased desire to succeed was being fostered because of the fact that someone had, often for the first time in many of these young women's lives, shown an interest in their welfare and cared what happened to them.

The area where there appears to have been the greatest impact in this way was with mothers who had disengaged from school before pregnancy, and had remained disengaged with little effort from the LEA or school to re-engage them, prior to the introduction of the grant. As one young mother described:

> I did not enjoy school, I'd stopped going. Then a specialist learning mentor[3] told me about (FE college) and I went from about my 30th week and then came straight back once the baby was born . . . I'd rather be there than going to school. I like the things that I do there . . . If I had not been contacted and encouraged by them I probably wouldn't have gone back to education. The programme is much better, there's less pressure and you get to talk with people who 'understand' . . . They're nicer, they help, both staff and other girls . . . When I first went, I knew it was going to work.

Since the arrival of the reintegration officers, schoolteachers also noted that their job was becoming easier because they had a named person that they could contact as soon as they found out that a young woman was pregnant. As a result, in most areas, there was a notable increase in the speed at which pregnant young women were being identified by LEAs and consulted about their educational needs. Many schools also noted that the work that reintegration officers had done in schools had been invaluable in changing the attitudes of both staff and other pupils towards teenage parents.

An early observation by many reintegration officers was that, if young mothers are to be expected to engage with education, particularly those who were previously disengaged, provision has to be flexible. That recognition was confirmed by the research of Selman *et al.* (2001), which highlighted that there is no single form of education or educational alternative that suits all young women. However, there was ample evidence of positive practice that could be extrapolated from one alternative setting and applied within different educational settings, including mainstream school.

Changing educational practice

What became apparent as the research developed were the overwhelmingly positive experiences that young women, especially those who had previously disengaged, were having within alternative provisions such as specialist units, further education colleges or city learning centres, in comparison with those in mainstream school or receiving home tuition. For many, the most positive element that encouraged re-engagement in education simply was the fact that the alternative was not school. For an equally large portion of young women, however, the principal benefit of alternative education was the supportive educational atmosphere that they encountered, which they had never experienced within mainstream schooling. Many noted that what they liked best about the alternatives was that they felt respected and were treated like adults; they could be educated at the same time as enjoying being mothers and in many cases be educated alongside their babies; they were able to undertake more flexible timetables; there was more one-on-one teaching; and they had the ability to play an active role in decisions about their education.

During the course of this research there were noted improvements within many of the LEAs with regard to the educational alternatives that were developed as a result of the grant. There were also improvements in the attitude and flexibility of schools towards alternative arrangements to enable pregnant young women and young mothers of school age to remain in school, or combine attendance at school and alternatives.

Whilst positive changes in practice were by no means universal across all schools or in every LEA, there was evidence of the reversal of many of the negative practices highlighted above. Many young women noted particular improvements amongst the attitudes of teachers and fellow pupils, following re-education about pregnancy at school undertaken at the school level by reintegration officers.

Further improvements included more women stating that they had been actively consulted about their educational needs and futures, including being asked if they wanted part-time timetables; being provided with 'rest room' facilities if required; flexibility over school uniform or funds to update their uniform as required; being provided with extra help and support to help catch up if required; and the acknowledgement that it was the young woman's, and not the school's, decision when she should go on maternity leave.

Within specialist provisions, a great deal of positive practice already existed prior to the introduction of the grant. For the most part the introduction of the grant enabled a more coordinated approach to this form of provision, including quicker referrals, the provision of transport for young women to encourage attendance and increased nursery provision within units.

From the young women's perspective, the most positive aspect of attending specialist provisions was the fact that they did not have to attend full time, as expected in most types of mainstream provisions, and were often offered part-time timetables if a full timetable was too much to cope with. Some stated that, whilst they recognised the value of continuing their education during the pregnancy, often it had been too difficult at school, particularly as the pregnancy became more advanced. To such women the unit offered continued engagement with an educational environment throughout the later stages of pregnancy without making excessive demands on them as they prepared for motherhood. Equally, for many new young mothers, attending a specialist provision post birth enabled a continued connection with education at a point when they were needing time to adjust to motherhood.

Many young women valued being educated alongside other women who were 'in the same boat' as themselves and who knew what they were going through. It was common for young women to talk about the transition to motherhood leaving them feeling 'older' or 'different' in some way from their peers at school and, helpful as many of their friends were, they simply 'didn't understand' what they were going through.

The young women also noted the support of the teachers within the specialist units in their preparation for motherhood. Many talked of their appreciation on gaining knowledge about becoming a mother and how to cope with everything from changing nappies, feeding, bathing, to dealing with stress, without feeling like they were being patronised or were bad mothers because someone had to provide that information, as one mother noted:

> It was really helpful what we got told about feeding and knowing what different cries could mean, stuff like that. Cause I was really worried and I was worried what people would think if I didn't know, an' just assume I was thick cause I was a stupid young girl who got pregnant, you know? But the teacher told us about what she did when she had her first kid which made us all laugh and see that most mas don't have a clue the first time, whatever age they are.

Despite the various problematic issues raised above in relation to home tuition, it remains an important option for three key reasons. First, even if a young woman wants to return to school after the birth of her child, she may not want to do so immediately, preferring time to bond with her baby before returning to school. This point raised an interesting question of the drive to encourage young mothers of school age to return to education quickly.

Much criticism is often levelled against mothers who work rather than 'choosing' to raise their child at home. However, a younger mother is expected to resume her educational status swiftly, demoting her role as a mother to a secondary position and something she does after school. Many professionals had serious contention with this point and felt that home tuition offered a valuable educational provision where there were no alternatives to which a young mother could bring her child to be educated.

Second, home tuition enables education to be continued throughout the maternity period, minimising any falling behind with study, and is particularly valuable when combined with continued interest from the school over the pupil's welfare, including providing work to be done at home.

Third, despite the intention to stay at school or attend alternative provision during pregnancy and to return to that provision post birth, for some young women ill health results in a change of plans. For a small number of young women morning sickness can be so severe that attending anything other than home tuition is just not feasible. Equally, post birth, especially if the birth has been particularly difficult or involved a caesarean section, a speedy return to education other than through home tuition is not easily achieved. Thus, home tuition remains an important option that must be available in every LEA.

Finally, in counties where the size or distribution of the population makes other non-mainstream provisions impracticable, home tuition remains an important educational option, and often the only alternative to mainstream schooling. In this case, reintegration officers have to develop ways of working with the education system to minimise the problems of home tuition, such as limited tutor time available and isolation from friends and school. For example, one reintegration officer initiated a system of grouped home tuition for pregnant young women and young mothers in her LEA. As a result, the total number of hours of tuition provided each week was greatly increased, and the young women received the 'peer support' so valued within alternative settings.

One initiative that was uncovered during the research was the use of a further education college as an alternative venue to mainstream school. To make this option feasible, grant money was used to procure a working area for the young women and to convert an adjacent room into a baby room (in many colleges on-site crèches would take only children over 18 months old). This arrangement meant that young women could return to education very quickly after birth and have their child located close to them as they worked.

Initially young mothers attending the college studied not academic GCSE and GNVQ courses, but alternative courses, including preparation for motherhood. However, the workers on this initiative started to notice an unexpected phenomenon, which they came to refer to as *education by stealth*, and it had two key components. The first was that many activities that the initiative incorporated involved the subtle development of skills such as literacy, numeracy and IT. In designing their own baby books, for example, most of the work was undertaken using computer programs such as Word, PowerPoint and design packages. Therefore, even although the activity itself was not considered 'academic', it was fostering marketable, transferable skills for these young women.

The second aspect was in relation to the location of the initiative. The further education college introduced these young women to the concept that mainstream school was not the only venue where they could receive an education. As the coordinator noted:

> If they had rejected school, why not try a slightly more adult environment [further education college] where they wouldn't stick out like a sore thumb, because there would be other young mothers there, 17, 18, 19 and where you could say, 'life isn't over, education isn't over', college is a realistic proposition. It was a way forward that had never occurred to them before, it raised their aspirations, raised their self-esteem visibly.

Having the initiative located in the college, therefore, gave the young women the option to explore other courses they might want to study in the future. Early evidence showed that a large proportion of young women who had attended the initiative at the college were currently or were planning to undertake courses the following academic year at that college.

The need for choice in educational provision for young mothers

One of the areas studied looked at the impact of the main strategies for reintegration, either to encourage continuation in mainstream schooling or to use part-time specialist units (Selman *et al.* 2001). Attendance prior to pregnancy was much better amongst those continuing in mainstream education (91 per cent good or excellent) than in those attending specialist provisions (30 per cent good or excellent). All but one of the 11 young women who continued in mainstream schooling maintained their good/excellent attendance during pregnancy. For those in specialist provisions, 48 per cent showed a marked improvement, mostly from poor or average to good or excellent, and only two (7 per cent) had worse attendance.

It would seem, therefore, that young women with a good attendance record can maintain this through and after pregnancy in mainstream schooling, but for poor attenders improvement in attendance is more likely to be achieved by specialist provision. This reinforces the point made earlier that many school-aged mothers become disengaged before pregnancy and, for them, pregnancy can actually be a way back into education. The problems surrounding social exclusion again seem to have more to do with the circumstances leading to early pregnancy and motherhood than with the fact of being a young mother.

Child care

Any discussion of how to facilitate and encourage young mothers to either continue their engagement or re-engage with education would not be complete without consideration of the issue of child care. This research revealed that child care is a major issue for all young women returning to education after they had had their baby in all 6 areas included in the study, although not always for the reasons that policy-makers might expect, such as lack of funding or availability.[5]

The grant made money available for child care, and in most areas there were child care places available that could be purchased for the young mothers. One of the key problems was that suitable child care was often located too far from the school or college to make it worthwhile making the round trip. In some cases mothers had to leave home before 7 o'clock in the morning to enable them to take their child to crèche or nursery and still reach school on time, a journey that would take its toll on even the most dedicated pupil.

A further issue in the case of reintegration into mainstream school was that some mothers did not want to be away from their child for an entire school day – a problem not encountered by those being educated within a specialist provision that incorporated child care. The tension aroused between the expectation that these young women were to be pupils first and mothers second was too much for some, whose reintegration failed purely because they missed their child too much. The fact that young mothers could go with their child to continue their education, often the child being located in a crèche room next door was, therefore, perceived as one of the greatest benefits of being educated within specialist provisions.

Perhaps one of the most difficult child care issues to overcome was that of trust. A large proportion of young mothers stated that they simply did not trust or want paid child care and would much prefer that family, friends or partners watched their child while they attended school and would not want to go if this was not a viable option. A common explanation provided for this was the adverse publicity in the media, especially over nannies, had undermined confidence, with the result that many young women simply did not trust anyone they did not know to look after their child.

In addition, many young mothers wanted their child to go to a nursery to get the benefit of socialising with other children in a nursery environment, a benefit that they did not think nannies would provide, or because they did not want another adult to form a one-on-one relationship with their child, especially as the reason for being denied this right was to go to school.

Some positive findings in respect of child care provision did, however, emerge and could be applied elsewhere. The use of grant money to develop a baby room at a further education college not only enabled young mothers to return to education very quickly, but also allowed the mothers to learn to trust 'paid' child care. Many of the pregnant young women at this college initiative held grave reservations about 'paid' child care but used the baby room because all the young women on the project did so. The baby room was therefore aiding in normalising the use of at least one form of child care that did not involve family.

Further to this, reintegration officers who were having great difficulty in finding child care that was both suitable and available developed a system of encouraging family members to become qualified. This had the dual benefit that the mother was happy that her child was being looked after by family and therefore was able to focus at school and that child care was not achieved at the expense of a family member's job or ability to look for work.

Conclusions and policy recommendations

The success of the government's Teenage Pregnancy Strategy will depend on whether it can achieve the twin aims of reducing under-18 conception rates and reducing the risk of long-term social exclusion for those young women who do become pregnant and choose to keep their babies. There is a danger that this second goal may be neglected in the pursuit of the clear targets for reducing conception rates by 2010.

This chapter has presented research on one strand of the initiative to reduce social exclusion by means of encouraging more teenage parents into education. Findings on the funding of reintegration officers through the Standards Fund Grant suggest that there is much to be gained by the appointment in LEAs of someone with the central task of maximising the continuation in education of pregnant young women and young mothers of school age. However, the success of such a strategy also depends on the availability of a range of alternatives to a return to mainstream education and the availability and affordability of suitable child care that is acceptable to these young women.

Many of those interviewed had disengaged from education prior to pregnancy, and for these young mothers reintegration into schools, and particularly into the school they had already left or been excluded from, was often unattractive. The availability of a specialist unit or a further education college as a point of re-entry offered a genuine opportunity to rethink engagement with education in the light of their changed circumstances and responsibilities.

Low educational aspirations and lack of self-esteem are key factors in pre-16 pregnancy in England. These can be compounded by a lack of support for pregnant young women and young mothers of school age. Flexible reintegration policies offer hope that teenage pregnancy need not mean an end to education. On the contrary, for many of the young women interviewed, pregnancy and mother-hood were key factors in initiating a return to education, often after long periods of disengagement.

At present, most of these initiatives are located within local authorities with the highest under-18 conception rates. As a consequence, a majority of pregnant young women and young mothers in England continue to have limited opportunities to re-enter education and remain dependent on whatever pattern of provision happens to have been developed in the area in which they live. As a result of the findings of this research, it is recommended that the role of reintegration officer be extended to many more LEAs as an important first step in ensuring that the educational needs of all young mothers, especially those who become pregnant under 16, are made a priority (Hosie 2003).

From 2003 the Standards Fund Teenage Pregnancy Grant was subsumed into the new Vulnerable Children Grant (Department for Education and Skills 2004),[6] which means that there is potential for every LEA in the country to utilise this fund to break down barriers in relation to teenage pregnancy and education. The money, however, is no longer ring fenced, leading the Teenage Pregnancy Unit in London to express concern that LEAs should continue to develop work with teenage mothers and that LEAs new to this money should seriously consider the positive benefits of following what other LEAs have achieved so far with this funding (see Hosie 2003).

The shift of funding from the new grant has, however, placed young mothers in a problem category along with drug users, asylum seekers and others, a fact compounded by the Department for Education and Skills web site, which includes the words 'sick children'. Jones (2004) has pointed out that the label of vulnerable implies a 'generalised individual deficit' and, in the case of young mothers, would seem to define them as failed parents. She points out that this is reminiscent of the comments of Bauman (2000, cited in Jones 2004) that:

> Definitions of the members of the 'underclass', poverty-stricken people, single mothers, school drop-outs, drug addicts and criminals on parole, stand side by side and are no longer easy to set apart. What unites them and justifies piling them together is that all of them, for whatever reason, are a 'burden on society'. We would all be better off and happier if they somehow miraculously disappeared.

If young mothers are to be seen as part of this burden there is a real danger that, in Levitas' terminology, their social exclusion will be seen from a MUD rather than a SID perspective and that the goal of reducing the number of conceptions will be prioritised over the provision of support and issues of prior disengagement from the education system will continue to be ignored.

Acknowledgements

This chapter draws on two previous (unpublished) papers presented by the authors at conferences in Chicago (Hosie 2002) and Sheffield (Selman 2001).

Notes

1 Although a range of out-of-education sites are available for young people in England any reference in this chapter to specialist units is to provisions specifically developed for the education of pregnant young women and young mothers.
2 The Standards Fund Grant provided additional finance for 48 LEAs in areas with high under-18 conception rates, to enhance provision for 'reintegration' of pregnant young women and young mothers of school age into the education system. The grant was subsequently made available in another 41 LEAs in 2001.
3 In this chapter we refer often to the reintegration officer. In a number of LEAs the person undertaking what we would define as the reintegration officer's role does not always have this title. In some areas this person is called a specialist learning mentor, teenage pregnancy inclusion officer, officer with responsibility for pregnant teenagers in school and so on. Therefore, when reference is made throughout to the reintegration officer, take this to mean reintegration officer or equivalent.
4 Selman et al. (2001) assessed the impact of various educational alternatives on the education of young pregnant women in six LEAs using baseline data on their school attendance and achievements from before the project began. Qualitative data were also collected through in-depth semistructured interviews with 48 pregnant young women and young mothers of statutory school age (14–16 years) as well as schoolteachers and reintegration officers in each of the LEAs under study.
5 The availability of child care has been improved by the introduction of Care to Learn in 2003 and its extention to young women of school age from August 2004 (Dawson and Hosie 2005: 202–3).
6 The National Foundation for Education Research has recently published an evaluation of the first two years of the Vulnerable Children Grant (Kendall et al. 2006),

which found that the grant had not been used to support young parents in eight of the 50 LEAs studied but that in nine areas there had been new developments, mainly '. . . new appointments of reintegration officers and key worker roles'. The Vulnerable Children Grant is to be subject to further change from 2006 to 2007, when it will become part of a new unhypothecated Children's Services grant (LASSL[2004]4).

References

Babb, P. (1994) 'Teenage Conceptions and Fertility in England and Wales, 1971–1991', *Population Trends* 74, 12–17.

Bauman, Z. (2000) *The Individualized Society*, Cambridge: Polity Press.

Botting, B. (1998) 'Teenage Mothers and the Health of their Children', *Population Trends* 93, 19–28.

Dawson, N. (1997) 'The Provision of Education and Opportunities for Future Employment for Pregnant Schoolgirls and Schoolgirl Mothers in the UK', *Children and Society* 11, 252–63.

Dawson, N. and Hosie A. (2005) *The Education of Pregnant Young Women and Young Mothers in England*, Final Report to Teenage Pregnancy Unit, Bristol: Universities of Bristol and Newcastle Upon Tyne (available online at www.renewal.net/Documents/RNET/Research/Edpregnantyoung.pdf).

Department for Education and Skills (2004) *Vulnerable Children Grant: Guidance for Financial Year 2004–05*, London: DfES (available at http://www.dfes.gov.uk/sickchildren/vcgc.shtml; accessed 21 September 2004).

Hobcraft, J. and Kiernan, K. (2001) 'Childhood Poverty, Early Motherhood and Adult Social Exclusion', *British Journal of Sociology* 52, 495–517.

Hosie, A. (2002) 'Teenage Pregnancy in Young Women of School Age: an Exploration of Disengagement from the Education System, PPaper presented to the Society for the Study of Social Problems, Chicago, 15–17 August 2002.

Hosie, A. (2003) *Re-engagement and Re-integration of Pregnant Young Women and Young Mothers of School Age*, Briefing Paper for Teenage Pregnancy Unit (available at http://www.info.doh.gov.uk/tpu/tpu.nsf).

Jones, S. (2004) 'Supporting SID – the Role of the "Vulnerable" in EU and UK Social Policy', Paper presented at the Annual Conference of the Social Policy Association, Nottingham, 13–15 July 2004.

Kendall, S., Johnson, A., Gulliver, C., Martin, K. and Kinder, K. (2006) *Evaluation of the Vulnerable Children Grant*, Research Report no 592, London: DfES: avialable at www.DfES.gov.uk/sickchildren/Pdfs/RR592.pdf

Kraft, P., Træen, B. and Rise, J. (1990) 'AIDS og Prevensjon – Øket Bruk av Kondom ved Første Samleie Blant NORSK ungdom [The HIV Epidemic and Changes in the Use of Contraception among Norwegian Adolescents]', *Tidsskr Nor Laegeforen* 110, 1490–2.

Levitas, R. (1998) *The Inclusive Society? Social Exclusion and New Labour*, Basingstoke: Macmillan.

Luker, K. (1996) *Dubious Conceptions: the Politics of Teenage Pregnancy*, London: Harvard University Press.

Moore, K.A., Miller, B.C., Glei, D. and Morrison, D.R. (1995) *Adolescent Sex, Contraception and Childbearing: A Review of Recent Research*, Washington, DC: Child Trends.

Morrison, D.M. (1985) 'Adolescent Contraception Behaviour: a Review', *Psychological Bulletin* 98, 538–68.

Murray, C. (1990) *The Emerging British Underclass*, London: IEA.

Murray, C. (1994) *Underclass: The Crisis Deepens*, London: IEA.

Osler, A., Street, C., Lall, M. and Vincent, K. (2000) *Girls and School Exclusion*, London: New Policy Institute.

Percy-Smith, J. (ed.) (2000) *Policy Responses to Social Exclusion*, Buckingham: Open University Press.

Selman, P. (1996) 'Teenage Motherhood Then and Now: a Comparison of the Pattern and Outcome of Teenage Pregnancy in England and Wales in the 1960s and 1980s', in *The Politics of the Family* (eds J. Millar and H. Jones), London: Avebury, pp. 103–28.

Selman, P. (2001) 'Teenage Pregnancy and Social Exclusion', Paper Presented at national Conference on Teenage Pregnancy in Context, University of Sheffield, November 2001.

Selman, P. (2003a) 'Scapegoating and Moral Panics: Teenage Pregnancy in Britain and the United States', in *Families and the State: Changing Relationships* (eds S. Cunningham-Burley and L. Jamieson), Basingstoke: Palgrave.

Selman, P. (2003b) 'Teenage Pregnancy, Poverty and the Welfare Debate in Europe and the United States', in *Poverty, Fertility and Family Planning* (eds M. Cosio-Zaval and E. Vilquin), Paris: CICRED and IISUNAM.

Selman, P. and Glendinning C. (1996) 'Teenage Pregnancy: do Social Policies make a Difference?', in *Children in Families: Research and Policy* (eds J. Brannen and M. O'Brien), London: Falmer Press, pp. 202–18.

Selman, P., Richardson, D., Hosie, A. and Speak, S. (2001) *Monitoring of the DfES Standards Fund Teenage Pregnancy Grant*, Final Report to DfES, Newcastle upon Tyne: Department of Sociology and Social Policy, University of Newcastle.

Singh, S. and Darroch, J.E. (2000) 'Adolescent Pregnancy and Childbearing: Levels and Trends in Developed Countries', *Family Planning Perspectives* 32(1): 14–23.

Smith, T. (1993) 'Influence of Socioeconomic Factors on Attaining Targets for Reducing Teenage Pregnancies', *British Medical Journal* 306, 1232–5.

Social Exclusion Unit (1999) *Teenage Pregnancy, Cm 4342*, London: HMSO.

Stevens-Simon, C. and Lowy, R. (1995), 'Teenage Childbearing – An Adaptive Strategy for the Socio-economically Disadvantaged or a Strategy for Adapting to Socio-economic Disadvantage?', *Archives of Paediatrics and Adolescence Medicine* 149, 912–15.

Turner, K.M. (2001) 'Predictable Pathways? An Exploration of Young Women's Perceptions of Teenage Pregnancy and Early Motherhood', unpublished doctoral thesis, University of Stirling.

United Nations Children's Fund (UNICEF) (2001) *A League Table of Teenage Births in Rich Nations*, Innocenti Report Card no. 3, Florence: UNICEF Innocenti Research Centre.

Chapter 6

Sexual health and unwanted pregnancy among adolescents

Implications for sex education in Hong Kong

Billy C. O. Ho and Dennis S. W. Wong

Introduction

In recent decades, the rapid rise in sexual activity in young people has aroused public concern. The sexual health of adolescents in Hong Kong is threatened by increasingly open, liberal and permissive attitudes to sexual matters. More alarmingly, unsafe sex and risk-taking sexual behaviour is increasingly common among Hong Kong adolescents. Consequently, the rates of unwanted pregnancy and sexually transmitted infections (STIs) and the potential risk of HIV infection have been on the increase in recent years. This chapter highlights the changes in sexual attitude and behaviour among adolescents that endanger their sexual health. It also discusses the development of sex education and strategies to safeguard the sexual health of adolescents in Hong Kong.

Adolescent sexuality in Hong Kong: a trend analysis in figures, 1981–2001

Sexuality is a broad term that may include different dimensions, such as sexual knowledge, values, attitudes and behaviours (Hofferth and Hayes 1987). In Hong Kong, a number of recent studies on adolescent sexuality have revealed that the sexual attitudes and behaviours of teenagers are becoming much more liberal and permissive than in the past. However, the level of sexual knowledge and sexual health awareness is still far from satisfactory (Family Planning Association 1983, 1986, 1994a,b, 1996a, 2001; Breakthrough 1994; Boys' and Girls' Club Association of Hong Kong 1996; Lam 1997). Being unequipped with the knowledge and means for protection, the sexual health of adolescents will be threatened by earlier and more frequent engagement in sexual contacts.

We have reviewed the major studies conducted from 1981 to 2001 by different youth organisations in Hong Kong. These studies focused on different aspects of adolescent sexuality, such as the onset of puberty, dating and sexual experience, premarital sex, condom use and participation in commercial sex. Most of the data used in the trend analysis were extracted from the Hong Kong Family Planning Association youth sexuality surveys, which have been conducted every 5 years since 1981. These surveys provide the most reliable figures on the sexual behaviour of adolescents and young people in Hong Kong. Other studies of youth sexuality carried out among different youth groups in recent years, such as marginal youths, school youths and unattached youths, were also examined to substantiate the analysis.

1   *Onset of puberty*. The onset of puberty is commonly marked by the onset of first menstruation for girls and onset of first nocturnal emission for boys. In 1996, the mean age at first menstruation was 12.3 years, not dissimilar to the figures of 12.6, 12.3 and 12.4 for 1981, 1986 and 1991 respectively. Likewise, age at first nocturnal emission is quite similar in the four surveys from 1981 to 1996, with the mean age of onset generally stable at about 13.6 years (Family Planning Association 1996b).

2   *Dating and sexual experience*. The in-school survey results of 1986, 1996 and 2001 show an increasing trend of sexual activity. The proportion of boys aged 14–17 who reported dating increased from 42.0 per cent in 1986 to 51.9 per cent in 1996, and reached 57.0 per cent in 2001. A similar trend is noted among girls, with an increase from 42.5 per cent in 1986 to 52.0 per cent in 1996, then to 57.4 per cent in 2001. Regarding experience of sexual intercourse, the boys' figure increased from 1.2 per cent in 1991 to 8.7 per cent in 2001 and the girls' figure rose from 0.2 per cent to 5.2 per cent over the same period (Family Planning Association 2001: 97).

3   *Premarital sex*. A study by the Family Planning Association (2001: 103) reveals a rising trend in premarital sex among both young men and young women aged 18–27 over the past two decades. Among those who had premarital sex, about 25 per cent of men and 20 per cent of women did not use contraception. More than one-third of the respondents used withdrawal/coitus interruptus, which has been proven to be an unreliable method of contraception. The prevalence of unsafe sexual behaviour among young people has gradually become the paramount concern of HIV/AIDS and sex educators.

4   *Condom use*. Recent research findings have shown that adolescents are becoming more and more sexually active and increasingly permissive and liberal in their sexual attitudes. Whether they practise safer sex, such as consistently using condoms, has become the paramount concern of health and sex educators. According to a study of marginal youth (Ho and Pun 1997), only 17.1 per cent of sexually experienced respondents were consistent condom users. One-third had never used condoms. Only 41.3 per cent had used condoms in their last sexual encounter. Those using condoms had done so for contraceptive purposes rather than for protection against sexually transmitted infections (ibid.). Other psychosocial factors that discourage adolescents and young people from using condoms include fear of rejection by partner, reduced sensitivity, lack of preparation, fear of being found distrustful and low self-efficacy on condom use.

5   *Engagement in commercial sex*. Another risk factor for STIs/HIV transmission is the extent of engagement in commercial sex. According to a survey of school leavers conducted by the Family Planning Association, the percentage

of males who had visited prostitutes increased from 11.7 per cent in 1991 to 13.9 per cent in 1996 (Family Planning Association 1994b, 1996b). Another local study on marginal youth revealed that 19.9 per cent of the male respondents had previously paid for sex (Ho and Pun 1997). The increasing trend of engaging in commercial sex has exposed adolescents to STIs/HIV infection.

To recapitulate, the trend analysis on different aspects of youth sexuality in Hong Kong from 1981 to 2001 significantly indicates that Hong Kong young people are becoming sexually active at an earlier age. Sexual attitudes are more permissive and liberal. Dating is not uncommon; and more and more adolescents have engaged in intimate behaviour while dating, such as petting, kissing and sexual intercourse. Furthermore, Hong Kong adolescents change their sexual partners quite often before entering into a stable relationship. They are more promiscuous and carefree with sex than in the past, as reflected by their high sexual partner exchange rate and low frequency of consistent condom use. Adolescents are at risk from their increasing sexual liberality while paying little heed to safer sex.

Unwanted pregnancy

There is no official reporting system to record unwanted pregnancies among the youth population of Hong Kong, so it is impossible to determine the rate of unwanted pregnancies. Nevertheless, service statistics for youth health care centres (open to those under the age of 18, the legal age of marriage in Hong Kong), operated by the Hong Kong Family Planning Association, reveal an alarming trend in adolescent pregnancy. Youth health care centres have the specific aim of managing sexual health problems, such as termination of pregnancy, and providing contraceptive and sexuality counselling for adolescents in Hong Kong. As shown in Table 6.1, the number of new clients seeking services from the youth health care centres is growing steadily. The majority of clients are female. The major services sought are termination of pregnancy and emergency contraception. In 1992, 1,073 young persons sought termination of pregnancy. By 2001, the figure had doubled to 2,451. Similarly, 584 persons sought emergency contraception (including post-coital contraceptive services) in 1992. By 2001, the figure was 1,128.

These figures reflect only young, unmarried girls seeking services through the official channel. It is believed that a further large number of adolescent girls undergo illegal abortion locally or in Shenzhen, a special economic zone in the south coastal area of mainland China. Qualitative studies on teenage pregnancy demonstrate that it is more convenient and cheaper to have an abortion in Shenzhen (Hong Kong Federation Youth Groups 1995a). However, the number of illegal abortions conducted locally or on the mainland each year is unknown. Were these figures available, they might demonstrate an even more alarming scenario.

A local youth organisation in Hong Kong conducted an exploratory and qualitative study looking at teenagers who had become pregnant under the age of 18

Table 6.1   Service statistics of youth health care centres of Family Planning Association (1992, 1997a, 2001)

	1992	1997	2001
Total no. of new clients	2,067	4,442	6,230
10 years and below	3	6	2
11–15 years	218	172	149
16–20 years	1,097	2,005	2,819
21–25 years	747	2,251	3,259
26 years and above	2	8	1
Major service sought			
Termination of pregnancy	1,073	1,565	2,451
Emergency contraception	584[a]	1,335	1,128
Contraceptive counselling	214	421	485
Pregnancy counselling		159	285
Sexuality counselling		46	8
Gender			
Female	2,037	4,424	6,221
Male	30	18	9

Source: Statistics on characteristics of new clients from various annual reports of the Family Planning Association (1992, 1997b, 2001).

Note
a   In this year, the figure represents post-coital contraception (PCC).

(Hong Kong Federation of Youth Groups 1995b). This is the only in-depth study on teenage pregnancy in Hong Kong. The study shed light on underlying attitudes towards sex and contraception as well as the decision-making process regarding abortion. A total of 25 girls were interviewed. They were referred by the Social Welfare Department and other non-governmental organisations. The respondents' profiles are as follows:

- At the time of interview, 12 of the 25 girls were continuing with the pregnancy or had already given birth; 13 had had an abortion or were planning to.
- Most of the girls had become pregnant at the age of 14. Two girls were 13 when they became pregnant.
- Most of the girls were pregnant for the first time.
- As having sexual intercourse with a girl under the age of 16 is a criminal offence, it was the case that 76 per cent of the girls' boyfriends had committed this offence.
- Over half of the girls were students when their pregnancies were confirmed.

The study also explored respondents' attitude towards sex and contraception. Almost half of the respondents had their first sexual experience at the age of 14; and the sexual activity usually took place in their boyfriend's home. One-fifth of the girls had had two or more sexual partners in the 3 months before pregnancy. During this period, most of them had sexual intercourse more than five times. Three-quarters claimed that they had never had intercourse against their will. All of the girls had heard of at least one method of contraception, but less than half had ever used any. Some of the young women had adopted the relatively unreliable rhythm method. Their knowledge of sex was piecemeal because it seemed that they were not well informed and they did not really understand the importance of contraception. In sum, there were observable discrepancies in sexual knowledge and behaviour. On the one hand, they were sexually active but, on the other, they were relatively ignorant about sex and contraception. There were also gender role conflicts. Although the young women had sex willingly, they seemed to be too embarrassed to discuss contraception with their boyfriends. This mismatch of behaviour and knowledge is of concern.

The study also analysed the teenage girls' attitudes to and abilities in problem-solving. It was found that most girls chose to have an abortion in Hong Kong. They did not want their lives encumbered by a baby. About half of the girls made the decision to terminate the pregnancy within 2 weeks of its confirmation. How-ever, four girls could not make up their minds or disagreed with their boyfriends about a decision. In these cases, the 24th week passed without a decision, making it too late for a legal abortion. In dealing with their pregnancies, the girls seemed to be motivated by self-centredness and what they themselves wanted. Most of them had discussed the decision with others, although one-fifth had never in-volved a third person. Most of the girls had a say in the decision, and about half were the sole decision-makers. Their major concern was the change in their future lifestyle rather than moral or social issues. To summarise, the study found that the pregnant girls had actively participated in the decision-making process, and might even make the decision alone. Their parents were often notified some time after the confirmation of pregnancy. Expectations of parents were of straightforward practical help. Some parents were not informed at all.

The psychosocial impacts of unwanted pregnancy and abortion on adolescents' development are immense. Undergoing abortion may be a traumatic event. Physi-cally, the girls may risk infertility, especially in the case of illegal abortion. Psy-chologically, they may suffer from post-traumatic stress syndrome, which may manifest in feelings of guilt about killing their babies, fear of having sex and fear of developing heterosexual relationships in the future. Socially, the girls who chose not to have an abortion may bear the stigma of being unmarried moth-ers, and their schooling and living activities will be affected. Obviously, teenage pregnancy is a growing problem, as are related sexual health problems such as prostitution, promiscuity and STIs/HIV infections. The unintentional pregnancies examined in the previous study came about through failure of contraception or ignorance of fertility and contraceptive methods, all of which seriously hampered the sexual development and health of the young girls.

Sexually transmitted infections (STIs)

Sexually transmitted infections are not notifiable diseases under Hong Kong law. However, statistics released by the Social Hygiene Service of the Department of Health (Table 6.2) show that the total number of STIs almost doubled between

1992 and 1999. According to an epidemiological survey of STIs/HIV carried out by the Department of Health in early 1997 (Department of Health 1998), roughly 80 per cent of cases of STIs were treated in the private sector (e.g. by private practitioners, herbalists, unregistered doctors and/or by self-treatment) and 20 per cent in the public sector, i.e. by the Social Hygiene Service. Thus, the statistics presented below reflect only the tip of an iceberg rather than the whole picture.

The number of cases of syphilis infection almost trebled between 1992 and 1999, from 421 to 1,110 (Department of Health 2000: Figure 3). This increase may be due to an increase in participation by Hong Kong citizens in commercial sexual activities in mainland China[1] and South-East Asia. The government has re-corded an increasing trend of overseas sources of STIs, with nearly 70 per cent of new infections linked to the mainland. Surveillance studies show that 30 per cent of males attending the Social Hygiene Service in 1996, and 33 per cent of those attending in 1997, had never used a condom with non-regular sexual partners (predominantly prostitutes) (Department of Health 1998).

Table 6.2 shows that the number of STIs in the under-20 age group increased from 488 in 1992 to 877 in 1999, reflecting a drastic upsurge of STIs among adolescents. A report from the Department of Health (2000: 9) also noted:

> Young people constitute an increasing percentage of patients infected with sexually transmitted diseases (i.e. STI). Most of the clients of Social Hygiene Service are in the age range 20–40. The proportion in the year 1999 was 58 per cent. Attitudes and practices of young people are matters of concern. Some early teenagers may not consider multiple sex partners as harmful. The added complication of unsafe sex is unwanted pregnancy, the prevalence of which in teenagers would reflect another type of risk to the population. Access to the internet is creating another conducive environment to high-risk sexual behaviours.

As reflected in the above review, young people in Hong Kong participate widely in unsafe sex either locally or by crossing the border from Hong Kong to mainland China. All these sexual risk-taking behaviours suggest that adolescents may be subject to a higher risk of STIs.

Table 6.2 Number of people presenting to the Social Hygiene Service for the treatment of STIs[a]

Year	Age under 20	All ages
1992	488	13,257
1995	477	18,115
1999	877	24,389

Source: Department of Health (1995, 1996, 2000).

Note

a 'STIs' (sexually transmitted infections) include syphilis, gonorrhoea, non-gonococcal genital infection, genital wart and herpes genitalis.

HIV infection

HIV has spread to every part of the world since its identification in the USA in 1981, and Hong Kong is no exception. Although the number of HIV infections in Hong Kong is not high compared with that in other Asian countries, the rate of HIV infection has been increasing steadily in the past two decades, and there are currently around 200 new cases of HIV infection each year.

In 2003, the latest year for which data are available, a total of 229 HIV cases were reported to the Department of Health, compared with 189 in 1998, a rise of 21 per cent. In 2003 the cumulative total of HIV infections since 1984 stood at 2,244, of which 36 were in children under the age of 14. Compared with the cumulative figure of 25 children by the end of 1996, this represents a 44 per cent increase in 7 years (Department of Health 1997, 2003). Although the majority of HIV-infected children are haemophiliacs who were infected via infusion of contaminated blood or blood products before 1985, when the blood screening and effective inactivation of HIV in blood products was introduced, the increase between 1996 and 2003 suggests that more and more young people are acquiring HIV infection by other means.

Sexual transmission resulting from unprotected sex continues to be the most important mode of HIV transmission, accounting for 70 per cent of newly reported cases. The Department of Health monitors the HIV/AIDS situation through a voluntary reporting system. The first cases of HIV and AIDS were reported in 1984 and 1985 respectively. In 2003, 56 cases of AIDS were reported to the Department of Health. This number has been largely stable since 1997, a phenomenon that is attributable to the introduction of effective HAART (highly active antiretroviral treatment) for HIV patients. However, it is estimated that over 3,000 persons are living with HIV/AIDS in Hong Kong. The high HIV rates in neighbouring cities, extensive human mobility across borders and the practice of risky behaviours are crucial factors that may lead to an epidemic of infection (Department of Health 2004).

Trend analysis suggests that heterosexual transmission is now the major route of HIV infection in Hong Kong. Thus, the promotion of safer sex practices through extensive HIV/AIDS education programmes has become a major concern for local authorities in an attempt to curb the spread of HIV. According to the epidemiological data on HIV infection in Hong Kong, the majority of HIV-infected persons are men between 30 and 39 years old and women aged 20–29. The prevalence of HIV infection in the adolescent age group (under 20) is low compared with that in the adult population: at the end of December 2003, only 64 HIV-infected persons were aged under 20 (Department of Health 2003: Chart 4.2). As a result of the epidemiological data, adolescents have been treated as a low-risk population in the local AIDS awareness programme. However, as demonstrated and discussed earlier, Hong Kong adolescents are increasingly participating in high-risk sexual behaviours. One reason for this discrepancy is that HIV has not yet taken root in the adolescent community. If the virus penetrates this homogeneous community, the rate of HIV infection will increase greatly.

Sex education for adolescents in Hong Kong

As discussed previously, young people in Hong Kong have become increasingly open and liberal towards sex. The sexual health of adolescents is declining as unwanted pregnancy and STI rates increase. Although the reported number of HIV infections among adolescents seems small, high-risk sexual behaviours exist at certain levels. The potential risk for HIV spread in the youth population should not be overlooked. There is no denying that sex education for adolescents is of paramount importance.

Sex education for adolescents in Hong Kong is delivered through formal and informal channels. Within the formal channel, sex education is provided from pre-primary to primary and secondary schools, but only on a voluntary basis. In 1976, the Education Department published its first guidelines on sex education in schools. This provided useful references for both primary and secondary schools to design their own sex education curriculum in response to the needs of their students. Since then, the Education Department (1994, 1997) has revised its guidelines in response to the changing social and sexual culture prevailing in society. Consequently, the Education Department published revised guidelines on sex education in secondary schools in 1986 and further revised guidelines in 1997. These guidelines have become the blueprint for schools to establish their principles and policies in sex education, to set up approaches to sex education and to design ways and means of implementing sex education programmes. However, these guidelines are not compulsory, and the school authority has full discretion in designing the content of sex education for students.

Many schools adopted the cross-curricular approach, supplemented by extra-curricular activities, in delivering sex education. Some subjects within the formal school curriculum, such as health science, general studies, liberal studies, general science and religious studies, include topics such as puberty, the reproductive system, interpersonal relationships, marriage and family, and sexual values (Table 6.3). Teaching of these subjects is further enhanced by educational videos on sex education produced by the Education Department. Alternatively, some schools invite outside organisations such as the Family Planning Association and youth services welfare organisations to deliver sex education talks or workshops to their students during school assemblies or specially arranged classes.

Within the informal channel, different community organisations are involved in providing sex education to the community at large. These organisations include the Family Planning Association, the Hong Kong Sex Education Association, AIDS-specific non-governmental organisations and youth services welfare organisations. Together these organisations have published numerous teaching materials on sex education, including manuals, books, pamphlets, videos, video compact discs and comic books, all of which are free of charge. In addition, upon invitation, they also deliver sex education activities in the form of talks, seminars, interactive workshops or arts performances to school students.

Mass media, television broadcasts in particular, are a popular means of delivering sex education in Hong Kong. Radio Television Hong Kong (RTHK) produced its first sex education programme in 1987. To date, RTHK has produced around 10 such programmes, the contents of which vary widely. They have included questions and answers on sexual issues and problems encountered by different age groups (Radio Television Hong Kong1999). Telephone helplines were available after the broadcasts to answer queries. These sex education television series have promoted sex education and sexual health in Hong Kong for over 10 years and have achieved a great degree of success: some programmes have won local and international awards.

What's wrong with sex education for young people in Hong Kong?

As described above, sex education for young people in Hong Kong has been implemented for over 20 years through formal and informal channels. As reflected in a number of youth sexuality studies, young people nowadays are becoming more sexually active, liberal and permissive than in the past. A number of high-risk behaviours, such as engaging in sex with multiple partners, unprotected sex, sex with prostitutes and an unrealistic optimism towards STIs/HIV infection, have been identified. However, the level of understanding about sexual health has fallen (Family Planning Association 1997b). What has happened to sex education in the past two decades? What is going wrong? To answer these questions, we need an in-depth reflection on past efforts.

First, sex education for youth in Hong Kong is highly restrained by the prevailing conservative and suppressive sexual culture among the adult world, including parents, school principals, government authorities and teachers. Sex remains a taboo in our society, and open discussions on anything related to sex are often discouraged. The implementation of sex education programmes is hampered by many moral considerations. These considerations include: When is the appropriate time for sex education? What should be the breadth and depth of its content? How explicit should it be? There is no denying that sex education may arouse young people's curiosity about sex, which in turn may trigger premarital sex and promote promiscuity.

Within this conceptual framework, an abstinence-led approach with a strong emphasis on sexual morality is widely adopted in school sex education programmes. However, such an approach is not responsive to the perceived needs of adolescents today. Instead, a learner-centred approach to sex education should be considered. This approach allows adolescents to assert their own principles on a range of sexual matters. It also encourages adolescents to make responsible decisions that are well informed.

For the past decade, sex education in Hong Kong has been considered a means of protecting adolescents against the undesirable influences of indecent and pornographic media and materials. The content of sex education has been a reaction to the prevailing pornographic culture in society, a countermeasure to the distorted and exaggerated images portrayed in pornography. In addition,

Table 6.3 Primary and secondary school subjects incorporating elements of sex education

	Chinese	English	General studies	Integrated science	Integrated science (revised)	Biology	Human biology	Social studies	Home economics	Religious studies/ethics	Liberal studies
Human sexuality								✓			
Reproductive system and physiology			✓	✓	✓	✓	✓	✓	✓		
Puberty			✓	✓	✓	✓	✓	✓	✓		✓
Self-image and self-concept	✓	✓	✓		✓			✓		✓	✓
Sexual identity and orientation								✓			
Emotions		✓	✓					✓			✓
Handling sexual drives								✓			✓
Body privacy					✓			✓			✓
Sexual habits and behaviour			✓					✓			
Sexually transmitted diseases			✓		✓		✓	✓		✓	
Contraception					✓	✓	✓	✓	✓		✓
Unwanted pregnancy			✓		✓		✓	✓	✓	✓	✓
Body care			✓					✓			
Basic values	✓	✓	✓					✓		✓	
Personal skills	✓	✓	✓					✓		✓	
Friendship	✓	✓	✓					✓		✓	
Dating, love and infatuation		✓						✓			
Sexual harassment, abuse and violence			✓					✓			
Incest											

Meaning of family	✓	✓				✓	✓	
Independence of family members and intergenerational relationships	✓	✓			✓	✓	✓	✓
Family conflicts and resolution					✓	✓	✓	
Changing patterns of family					✓	✓	✓	✓
Coping with changes in the family					✓	✓	✓	✓
Factors to consider in starting a family					✓	✓	✓	✓
Marriage and lifetime commitments			✓		✓	✓	✓	✓
Parenting			✓	✓	✓	✓	✓	✓
Social and cultural influences of sex			✓		✓	✓	✓	
Gender role	✓		✓		✓	✓		
Sex and mass media					✓	✓	✓	✓ ✓
Sex and the law								
Sex, morality and ethics						✓		

Sources: Curriculum Development Council (1997a,b).

sex education has been viewed as a social control measure to uphold the sexual morality of adolescents, and the focus of sex education has tended to be remedial as it is always problem based. The result of such influences has been that the content of sex education is fragmented and incomprehensive, with an excessive emphasis on adolescents' physical development, conventional sexual values and countering measures to undesirable influences. Other areas of life education, such as interpersonal relationships, self-esteem and assertion, self-protection, sexual communication and negotiation, are seldom considered.

Who is the most appropriate agent to be responsible for the implementation and coordination of sex education for teenagers in Hong Kong? Naturally, the family environment would be a convenient place for sex education. However, very often, parents claim to have limited knowledge and experience in delivering sex education to their children and tend to entrust the responsibility to schools. The Education Department has always taken a neutral stand, providing schools with guidelines on sex education and resource materials but not laying down rules. School authorities have full discretion over the allocation of teaching time and the content of sex education for their students. However, because of the full formal curriculum and heavy teaching responsibilities, most school authorities find it difficult to make time available for sex education. In addition, because of the conservative attitude of parents to sex education and the unavailability of qualified teachers, most school authorities prefer to avoid discussing the sensitive subject of sex education. And, because of limited resources, it is difficult for community organisations to cater for the huge needs and demands for sex education in the community at large. Thus, it is clear that currently no organisation has a distinct role in implementing and coordinating sex education programmes in Hong Kong. Failure to take responsibility for the sex education of adolescents is a common problem in Hong Kong.

Finally, another source of resistance to sex education comes from the schoolteachers and social workers who are given the task of delivering sex education to students. Neither group receives any formal tuition in sex education during their professional training in Hong Kong. Therefore, they are not equipped with the necessary knowledge and skills to deliver sex education. How can this reluctance and negative social pressure be overcome to enable them to talk about sex with adolescents? Obviously, a joint initiative involving school principals, teachers, social workers and parents is required for the implementation of a comprehensive and effective sex education curriculum for adolescents in Hong Kong.

Dilemmas encountered in delivering sex education for young people

Sex educators in Hong Kong need to resolve several dilemmas regarding the delivery of sex education. Most often, sex educators have to decide on the right time and right topics for sex education for adolescents. They worry that what they have taught may go beyond the developmental stage of adolescents and will trigger their curiosity about sex. They need to resolve this dilemma and reconcile themselves with the concept that sex education does not necessarily promote sexual activity.

In addition, sex educators often face the dilemma of whether upholding sexual morality compromises the reality of the enhancement of the sexual health of young people. Confronted by the changing sexuality of youth should we put more effort into restoring the traditional sexual values such as avoiding premarital sex and condemning promiscuity? Alternatively, in order to protect the sexual health of young people, should sex educators stress the importance of safer sex, such as condom use? Sometimes, sex educators who adopt the public health approach are criticised by conservatives for being immoral and destroying traditional sexual values. What is the baseline from which to educate? Commonly, sex educators feel they are touching the invisible edge.

As we have discussed, sex is still a taboo in Hong Kong society. It is considered private, and something that should not be talked about and discussed socially and openly. Sex educators have to face both internal and external resistance to the delivery of sex education to adolescents. The internal resistance comes from within the sex educators themselves, who must reconcile their own sexual values and attitudes towards sex education. In addition, they have to overcome external resistance from the adult world, including parents, school authorities and society, that views sex education as a kind of social control for upholding sexual morality. Should sex educators be restrained by social expectations? Or, rather, should they change or cultivate a more permissive social environment for comprehensive sex education for adolescents?

Setting an agenda on sex education for young people in Hong Kong

In view of evolving youth sexuality and its undesirable impacts on the sexual health of adolescents, a new challenge for educators and policy-makers is to design high-quality sex and HIV education programmes for children and young people. As adolescents are less health-conscious than adults, their perceived susceptibility to any disease is low. To them, the costs of adopting healthy behaviours are measured not just in terms of physical well-being but also in terms of a whole set of interpersonal, social and cultural values. To promote sexual health behaviours, we need to pay attention to what adolescents regard as important (Ho and Pun 1997).

Since the major resistance to sex education stems from the worries of adults, including school principals, parents, teachers and even social workers, there is a need to cultivate a more liberal and supportive social environment for the implementation of comprehensive sex education programmes that are tailored to the needs of adolescents. Adolescents themselves should become the subjects of sex education rather than regarded as passive recipients. The developmental characteristics of adolescents at different stages of schooling from pre-primary to senior secondary should be addressed in the design of sex education, as shown by the following quote.

> Acknowledging the needs and characteristics of adolescents nowadays, sex education no longer serves the social control function of reinforcing the traditional values on sex and suppressing the sexual desire. The whole society should recognize the ultimate goal of sex education for adolescents is to educate them to experience personal fulfilment, well being and enjoyment through a growing awareness of their sexuality and a developing regard for interpersonal responsibility. The society also has to realize that sex education is a lifelong process of acquiring information and forming attitudes, beliefs and values about our sexual identity, relationships and intimacy. It addresses the physiological, psychological, socio-cultural and ethical aspects of sexuality; covers the domains of knowledge values and attitudes, and skills; and encompasses a number of key concepts and topics that need to be acquired by adolescents.
>
> (Education Department 1997)

To meet the increasing need for sex education for adolescents, sex education should be started at home by parents, continued at schools by teachers and supplemented by community efforts. These should become the three fundamental pillars and intervention opportunities for the implementation of sex education for adolescents in Hong Kong. Accordingly, relevant parties should collaborate with each other to provide a supportive environment for the development of sex education.

Regarding the content of sex education, the Education Department has suggested the following:

> In regard to the content of sex education, a well-balanced sex education program includes accurate knowledge about sexuality, attitudes towards sex, marriage and the family, and decision-making and communication skills and a consistent system of positive values and responsible behaviour. Besides, the content of the sex education for adolescents should be comprehensive. It should touch on the physiological, psychological, socio-cultural and ethical aspects of human sexuality. The interrelationship of these four aspects of sexuality would shape an individual's sexual ideology and sexual behaviours. Thus, all of them share the same significance and should be taught with equal weights.
>
> (Education Department 1997)

Sex education should focus not only on the enhancement of knowledge at a cognitive level, but also on the development of positive sexual values and attitudes and the acquisition of appropriate skills in making sexual decisions, sexual communication and negotiation, and problem-solving for sex-related problems. The following five areas should be included in the content of sex education:

- human development;
- health and behaviour;
- interpersonal relationships;
- marriage and family; and
- society and culture.

The detailed description and design of each area should be closely interwoven with the physical, psychological, socio-cultural and ethical aspects of sex education as mentioned previously. In addition, the teaching of these five areas should address not only the knowledge but also values and skills (Education Department 1997).

HIV/AIDS education should be an integral part of sexual health education. It is best started before the onset of puberty and does not encourage increased sexual activity (UNAIDS 1997). Considering the key features of changing youth sexuality and the primary aim of improving the sexual health of adolescents, the education programmes should be behaviour specific, with a clear statement of the risks of unprotected sex and methods of avoiding it. A range of interactive activities, such as role-playing, discussion and creative art, should be employed to motivate the participants to reduce their sexual risks. The programme design should focus on teaching adolescents ways of counteracting undesirable influences from peer groups or mass media. In addition, the programmes should include activities that allow participants to observe others, and rehearse themselves, in order to develop sexual communication skills including negotiation and assertion skills about safer sex. The ultimate goal is to yield greater effectiveness in achieving delays in the initiation of sexual intercourse and the practice of protected sex.

Other than curriculum design, the most important factor for the success of sex education for adolescents is the availability of qualified and committed sex educators, teachers and social workers to implement the programmes. Specialised training in sex education for young people should be given to youth workers and teachers with the support of teaching resources and materials. It is also cardinally important to cultivate a more permissive and liberal social climate for sex education among the helping professionals in order to alleviate their internal resistance and dilemmas in delivering sex education for adolescents.

Conclusion

A trend analysis of youth sexuality reveals that Hong Kong adolescents are becoming increasingly sexually active. Premarital sex is not uncommon, and sexual activity begins at an earlier age than in the past. Adolescents change their sexual partners much more often prior to entering a stable relationship, and their rate of consistent condom use is unsatisfactory. The sexual health of young people nowadays is threatened by their habits of changing sexual partners and practising unprotected sex. Unwanted pregnancies, STIs and HIV infection rates will increase if no effective measures are taken to address the situation.

Psychological barriers, exaggerated worries and resistance from the adult world have also stimulated debates on the appropriate time, place and content of sex education for adolescents in Hong Kong. The dilemma of upholding sexual morality versus promoting the sexual health of young people will be a key conflict faced by school principals, parents and sex educators in designing the future direction and content of sex education. Vigorous debate on these controversial issues will continue. However, under the influences of mass media, the early onset of puberty and the transition of the sexual climate from conservative to more permissive, we may need to consider the adoption of a more realistic and practical approach to delivering sex education to adolescents. Sex education should be more comprehensive and specific to the developmental stage of young people. It should be started as early as possible in the family by parents, continued at schools and supplemented by community efforts. The principles, objectives and content of sex education should be observed in the design and implementation of effective sex education for adolescents in Hong Kong in the years to come.

Note

1   In July, 2004, the Joint United Nations Program on HIV/AIDS (UNAIDS) estimated that there were 840,000 people living with HIV/AIDS in China. Experts believe that many AIDS cases go unreported, especially in rural areas, where there is a lack of testing equipment, trained staff, voluntary testing and counselling services.

References

Boys' and Girls' Club Association of Hong Kong (1996) *Research Report on Youth Sexual Attitude and Behaviours: Roles of the Family* (in Chinese), Hong Kong: Boys' and Girls' Club Association of Hong Kong.

Breakthrough (1994) *Research Report on Sex Role, Attitude and Behaviours of Hong Kong Youth* (in Chinese), Hong Kong: Breakthrough.

Curriculum Development Council (1997a) *Guidelines on Sex Education in Schools*, Hong Kong: Education Department.

Curriculum Development Council (1997b) *Guidelines on Sex Education in Schools (Teachers' Manual)*, Hong Kong: Education Department.

Department of Health (1995) *Hong Kong STD/HIV Update*, Vol. 1, No. 1, pp. 1–8, Hong Kong, Department of Health.

Department of Health (1996) *Hong Kong STD/HIV Update*, Vol. 2, No. 1, pp. 1–8, Hong Kong, Department of Health.

Department of Health (1997) *Hong Kong STD/HIV Update*, Vol. 3, No. 1, pp. 1–8, Hong Kong, Department of Health.

Department of Health (1998) *Hong Kong STD/HIV Update*, Vol. 4, No. 1, pp. 1–8, Hong Kong, Department of Health.

Department of Health (2000) *Hong Kong STD/HIV Update*, Vol. 6, No. 3, pp.1–12, Hong Kong, Department of Health.

Department of Health (2003) *Hong Kong STD/HIV Update*, Vol. 9, No. 4, pp. 1–45, Hong Kong, Department of Health.

Department of Health (2004) 'AIDS Situation in 2003', extracted from press release section (available at http://www.info.gov.hk/aids/english/press/press.htm).

Education Department (1994) *Report of the Survey on the Implementation of Sex Education in Secondary Schools 1993/94*, Hong Kong: government printer.

Education Department (1997) *Guidelines on Sex Education in School*, Hong Kong: government printer.

Family Planning Association (1983) *A Study of Hong Kong School Youth 1981*, Hong Kong: Family Planning Association.

Family Planning Association (1986) *Working Report on Adolescent Sexuality Study 1986*, Hong Kong: Family Planning Association.

Family Planning Association (1992) *Annual Report (1991–1992)*, Hong Kong: Family Planning Association.

Family Planning Association (1994a) *Report on the Youth Sexuality Study 1991*, Hong Kong: Family Planning Association.

Family Planning Association (1994b) *Annual Reports (1994–1995)*, Hong Kong: Family Planning Association.

Family Planning Association (1996a) *Seminar Report on the Needs and Implementation of Sex Education for Children in Hong Kong* (in Chinese), Hong Kong: Family Planning Association.

Family Planning Association (1996b) *Report on the Youth Sexuality Study 1996*, Hong Kong: Family Planning Association.

Family Planning Association (1997a) *Seminar Report on Youth Sexuality Study 1996* (in Chinese), Hong Kong: Family Planning Association.

Family Planning Association (1997b) *Annual Report (1996–1997)*, Hong Kong: Family Planning Association.

Family Planning Association (2001) *Annual Report 2000–2001*, Hong Kong: Family Planning Association.

Hofferth, S. and Hayes, C. (1987) *Risking the Future*, Vol. 2, Washington, DC: National Academy Press.

Ho, B. and Pun, S.H. (1997) *Study on the Knowledge of and Attitude towards AIDS-related Issues among Marginal Youth in Hong Kong*, Hong Kong: Commission on Youth.

Hong Kong Federation of Youth Groups (1995a) *News Bulletin of HKFYG*, Issue 38 (in Chinese), Hong Kong: Hong Kong Federation of Youth Groups .

Hong Kong Federation of Youth Groups (1995b) *Teenage Pregnancy: Service and Policy Options*, Hong Kong: Hong Kong Federation of Youth Groups.

Lam, M.P. (1997) *A Study on the Knowledge, Attitudes and Behaviours of Secondary School Pupils Relating to Sex*, Hong Kong: government printer.

Radio Television Hong Kong (1999) *Sex Education on TV – A Complimentary VCD Introducing Sex Education Programs of RTHK*, Hong Kong: RTHK.

UNAIDS (1997) *Impact of HIV and Sexual Health Education on the Sexual Behaviour of Young People: a Review Update*, Geneva: UNAIDS.

Chapter 7

Sisters doing it for themselves

Young mothers as peer educators[1] in school-based sex education

Judi Kidger

> This is possibly one way to actually get to young people, to give them more knowledge and information about sex, contraception, the realities of having a child at a young age, the difficulties, the housing the money . . .
>
> Rosie, young mother working as peer educator

> We can't forget we're working with young mums as well, so that's quite an important thing, so who's getting more out of it really? It's difficult to tell isn't it, is it the people who do peer education or the people they're talking to?
>
> Yvonne, peer education project coordinator

As a group, young mothers are traditionally the objects of other people's concerns, debates and interventions, the characters in other people's stories. This chapter outlines a study of four projects that contravene this norm, in that they involve young mothers as agents, delivering sex education to other young people, and through so doing, giving their own accounts of teenage pregnancy and parenthood. Although such projects are unusual in this agential, empowered role that the young mothers play, they have been rising in popularity in Britain; during 2000 and 2001 when the research was conducted, at least 15 examples existed. This is due at least in part to their perceived relevance to the two prongs of the Teenage Pregnancy Strategy for England (Social Exclusion Unit 1999), that is lowering the rates of teenage pregnancy and supporting teenage mothers. As the above quote from a young mother involved in one of the projects indicates, the projects are based on the rationale that young people do not have enough knowledge regarding 'the realities' of having a child young to make the best decisions regarding pregnancy and parenthood, an assumption shared by policy-makers:

> The reality of bringing up a child, often alone and usually on a low income, is not being brought home to teenagers and they are often quite unprepared for it. They do not know how easy it is to get pregnant, and how hard it is to be a parent.
>
> (Social Exclusion Unit 1999: 7)

The implication in such an assertion is that if young people *did* have this information they would be less likely to become teenage parents, and in this sense the projects can be seen as contributing to the Teenage Pregnancy Strategy's aim of reducing the overall incidence of teenage pregnancy and parenthood.

Further, as the project coordinator quoted at the start of the chapter indicates, the projects also have the potential to be beneficial to the young mothers themselves, which relates to the second aim of the strategy, that is supporting teenage mothers. It is certainly the case that evidence from other peer education projects and other schemes in which young people volunteer shows that such participation increases individuals' self-esteem, confidence, skills and ability to instigate positive change (Phelps *et al.* 1994; Roker *et al.* 1999; Institute for Volunteering Research 2002). These benefits are likely to be particularly important for young mothers, who occupy a relatively vulnerable, powerless position in society, and tend to experience a range of social and economic difficulties (Phoenix 1991a; Dawson 1997; Allen and Bourke Dowling 1998; Kidger 1998). This vulnerability is often exacerbated by the dominant accounts of teenage pregnancy and parenthood within political, media and often academic arenas that position it as a negative, risky event, and teenage mothers themselves as sexually deviant young women, bad mothers and problematic citizens. Within this socio-moral climate, having the opportunity provided by these projects to tell their own stories therefore potentially provides a valuable route by which young mothers might construct more positive public identities for themselves.

Although previous research has highlighted various benefits enjoyed by peer educators and young people who volunteer, what is less clear is how these factors relate to the British government's more specific concern to reduce what it sees as the risk of long-term social exclusion that young mothers face. Social exclusion has emerged as a key concept in political, academic and popular rhetoric in recent years at national, European and global levels (e.g. Rodgers *et al.* 1995; Commission of the European Communities 2000; Social Exclusion Unit 2001), despite it having a vague and contested definition (Silver 1995; Levitas 1998). The way in which the term is deployed by New Labour emphasises its economic dimension, and specifically equates social inclusion with paid work (Levitas 1998), something that is clear from the wording of the strategy's second aim (www.dfes.gov.uk/teenagepregnancy/):

> Increase the participation of teenage mothers in education, training or work to 60 per cent by 2010 to reduce the risk of long term social exclusion.

However, this rather narrow definition ignores the multifaceted nature of social exclusion, and in particular downplays the importance of social cohesion and belongingness, aspects of social inclusion which may be equally, if not more, important to young mothers themselves (Kidger 2004). Involvement in projects such as those studied here, in which members work together in bringing about change in their communities, might be considered more relevant to and more likely to impact on these *social* aspects of exclusion.

Despite the apparent potential of sex education interventions delivered by young mothers to be of benefit to everyone involved, there has been very little research investigating their impact. In fact, only one piece of research has been conducted, and that was a qualitative evaluation of a pilot project, in which three groups of young mothers delivered sessions to youth clubs and schools (Fox *et al.* 1993). Although this research revealed that the young people receiving the education were very positive about the experience, it did not in fact explore whether and in what ways they felt it might impact upon their future behaviour, or indeed the extent to which it had contributed to their knowledge and attitudes in this area. The report also addressed the question of how far the young mothers themselves benefited, and found that they experienced an increase in knowledge, confidence and skills, the achievement of a different, more positive status, and the acquisition of new ideas and motivation for future training and paid work, all of which relate to various facets of social exclusion.

The research on which this chapter draws therefore sets out to build on these findings, by asking two questions in relation to projects involving young mothers as peer educators. The first was how far the projects are a useful sex education intervention, in particular what contribution they make to pupils' knowledge and attitudes regarding sex, contraception and parenthood, and to their understanding of the consequences of their decisions in these areas. The second concerned the extent to which the young mothers themselves benefit from taking part, and specifically how far any benefits relate to their experiences of social exclusion/inclusion. In the next section, I will introduce the four projects that took part in the research and briefly outline the study itself, before going on to explore what the findings showed with regard to these questions.

Researching young mothers as sex educators

All four projects that participated in the study were based in England. Three of them developed out of and recruited from support groups for young mothers, were funded by local youth and community services and were managed by youth workers. The fourth project was the only one to exist purely as a sex education project, and was funded by a combination of the government's Teenage Pregnancy Unit and charitable sources. In this case, members were recruited from local antenatal and post-natal support groups, and a trained youth worker coordinated their activities. Each year, the projects approached the secondary schools in their area and offered to deliver sex education lessons to pupils aged 14–16 years (years 10 and 11) as part of the wider sex education curriculum, using a variety of techniques including a video made by project members, activities devised by members and the project coordinator, recounting their own stories, and holding question and answer sessions.

Each of the four projects had as its primary aim not a reduction in teenage pregnancy per se, but rather assisting pupils in making 'informed choices' regarding sex, contraception and parenthood, based on the uncensored, personalised stories about 'the realities' of teenage parenthood that the project members were uniquely able to provide:

> It's about young parents sharing their experiences, which will lead to better ability of young people to make informed choices.
>
> > Karen, project coordinator

This notion of 'informed choice' fitted the empowering ethos evident in the projects and the way they were run, which reflects the dominant approach to youth and community work that has emerged in Britain in recent years (Kiely and Curran 2000; Wade *et al.* 2001). However, outcomes such as increasing 'informed choice' and empowering young people are difficult to define, identify and measure, and I therefore designed a multi-method approach, in order to explore these more qualitative, experiential notions prioritised by the projects themselves, as well as gathering measurable outcomes in the form of knowledge and attitude change.

The former set of outcomes was explored through pupil focus groups, and a total of 11 groups (15 boys and 34 girls) were held in five schools following pupils' attendance in the lessons. The purpose of these focus groups was to establish what pupils felt they had gained from the sessions, in particular to explore the pupils' own perceptions of the significance (or not) of the sessions for their own lives, and to see how these matched the projects' aims of increasing their informed choices. The pupils were interviewed in pairs or small groups rather than individually as it was felt they might be more comfortable with peers present, rather than in a one-to-one situation with an older stranger, as has been documented in other research (Madriz 2000; David *et al.* 2001).

In addition, semistructured interviews were conducted with 14 young mothers acting as peer educators. These interviews were conducted individually as the aim was to explore each individual's personal story and experience as a peer educator in depth. The interviews covered the interviewees' opinions of the benefits of the lessons for the pupils, as well as asking them about their own experiences as young mothers, and the effect that participation in the projects has had on that. The young mothers interviewed ranged in age from 17 to 25 years, reflecting the age range of each project, and their ages at conception ranged from 15 to 23 years. Although this meant that they had not all been teenagers when they conceived, research suggests that young mothers in their early 20s encounter similar difficulties to those in their teens (Hobcraft and Kiernan 2001), therefore their experiences were still considered relevant for this study.

Finally, in order to gain a broader sense of pupils' knowledge and attitudes regarding sex, contraception and parenthood, and how far these had changed following the lessons, questionnaires were collected from 240 pupils (100 male, 140 female) in three of the five schools.[2] These included a mixture of multiple-choice questions, tick boxes and short written answers. Although a comparison group would have been necessary to ensure that any change was due to the lessons and not another factor, finding a group of pupils that had covered a sufficiently similar sex education curriculum apart from that one lesson over the same time frame proved impossible due to the vast differences in content, timing and methods of sex education provided by schools in England today (Ofsted 2002). Given this lack of comparison schools, all findings from the quantitative data concerning change need to be interpreted with caution, as the possibility cannot be ruled out that they had been caused by something other than the session with the young mothers.

All the interview data were analysed qualitatively, following an abductive strategy (Blaikie 1993). This involved a two-way analysis, in which themes were identified from the data and used to build up theory, and previously held and developing theories were tested against the data in order to be refined and expanded in an ongoing cyclical process. The questionnaire data were coded, entered into the SPSS computer package and then analysed using Wilcoxon's signed-rank test to measure change between the two time points and the chi-square test (allowing up to 20 per cent of the expected frequencies to fall below 5) and odds ratio scores to compare differences by school and gender.

'It could happen to anyone' – new responses to old messages

As already noted, the projects' aim of improving pupils' ability to make informed choices is based on the assumption that pupils have gaps in their knowledge about teenage pregnancy and parenthood. To some extent the questionnaire data challenged this belief, as the pupils already had a high level of knowledge before the lessons had taken place. Where there were gaps in their knowledge, for example fewer than half of the pupils knew that oral contraception could be prescribed to girls under the age of 16 without parental consent, an improvement was visible following the lessons, suggesting that the lessons did provide some new information.

However, the overall impression, backed up by some focus group comments, was that the knowledge improvement following the lessons was quite marginal, with the lessons serving more as a confirmation of what the pupils already suspected or knew:

> I knew the stuff, but then they kind of expanded it.
>
> Year 11 female, Longfield

> You can guess, but you don't actually know 'til they come in and tell you.
>
> Year 11 male, St. Joseph's

Similarly, the questionnaires suggested that the lessons did not instigate much attitude change, in terms of the pupils' attitudes either towards teenage parenthood as a prospect in their own lives or towards teenage parents themselves. Before the lessons, the majority of pupils were clearly not planning to become teenage parents themselves and considered it disadvantageous on the whole; for example, only 9 per cent agreed that they would like a child before the age of 20, and 80 per cent felt that it would be harder to be a parent as a teenager, and these views did not change significantly. There is some anecdotal evidence of practitioner concern that these projects might actually encourage young people to become parents, but the evidence here certainly refutes that claim. Before the lessons the majority of pupils were also non-judgemental and rejected certain stereotypes regarding teen-age mothers on the whole; for example, 76 per cent disagreed with the statement that teenage mothers have only themselves to blame, and 79 per cent disagreed that teenagers get pregnant because they want a council house, and again these opinions remained in the majority following the lessons. Although such attitudes are what the projects would like to see, the fact that most pupils held them before the lessons again suggests the projects were unlikely to have much impact.

However, the focus group data provide greater evidence of a positive impact, as they reveal a subtler way in which the lessons affected the pupils. Although both the questionnaire and focus group data suggest that the pupils did not learn a great deal of factual information, or have their attitudes challenged regarding a rational decision to become a teenage parent or not, what became apparent was that imparting new information was not the only, or even most important, role that these lessons delivered by young mothers might play in the sex education curriculum. Rather, what the lessons appeared to do was encourage pupils to pay greater attention to and accept the relevance of messages they may have heard several times before, what might be considered a response at an emotional rather than an intellectual level:

> Because they're more young people, like the same age as us sort of thing, unlike with the teacher people actually sat and listened.
>
> Year 11 female, Dunsbrook

> I think we all benefited actually because most people they don't take sex that seriously, but now we've heard that it's like scary.
>
> Year 10 female, Stanford Wood

> A teacher teaches it from a sheet or just says it, that's when you don't really listen, but when you hear it from someone who has experienced it you realise it could happen to you.
>
> Year 11 female, Longfield

Previous research has emphasised the way in which young people actively and continuously co-construct their own beliefs and value systems regarding issues such as sexual activity, use or not of contraception, relationships, abortion and early parenthood (Woodcock *et al.* 1992; Hey 1997; Holland *et al.* 1998; Tabberer and Hall 2000; Thomson 2000). These 'sexual cultures' affect not only young people's choices and behaviours in these areas, but also the way in which they respond to sex education messages based on the logic of middle-class, professional adults (Ingham *et al.* 1992). Where the lessons studied here were more successful than teacher-led sessions, according to the pupils, was in their ability to speak to and challenge those beliefs. A key example of this is the belief, well documented in other research, that 'it won't happen to me':

> You just think well, me out of all these people, it's not going to be me, you know.
>
> Year 10 female, Stanford Wood

As indicated by the quote from a Longfield pupil above, and confirmed by others, this belief was transformed by the sessions into 'it could happen to anyone':

> When they came in to see us they weren't saying no, they were giving both sides of the story and it was like, it could happen to anyone.
>
> Year 11 female, St. Joseph's

The reasons the lessons delivered by the young mothers elicited this response are twofold, and are exemplified in some of the above quotes. The first reason, indicated by the Dunsbrook pupil above, is the fact that the pupils perceived the young mothers to be like themselves:

> But they could have been like me, and if I do that it's going to destroy my childhood as well as my teenagehood.
>
> Year 10 male, Stanford Wood

This view of the lessons relates to the projects' own description of themselves as peer education. In fact, despite its current, popular status in sex education programmes targeting young people in Britain (Crosier *et al.* 2002), there is much debate regarding the definition of peer education, in particular what makes someone a peer (see Kidger, 2002, for a review). On the face of it, it might be argued that these young women are in fact not peers of the pupils, given the fact that many of them were in their early 20s, and all of them had had to 'grow up' due to their new status as parents:

> As soon as I had Chloe I was like a different, grown up person. I was a mum, I had to grow up.
>
> Kathy

The reason the pupils regarded them as peers, despite these differences, appeared to be due to the more informal approach taken by the young mothers compared with teachers, their youthful manner and the fact that they did not attempt to exert authority:

They were more relaxed and a lot different to teachers, they were more similar to us 'cause they were young.

> Year 11 male, Dunsbrook

They was like really outspoken, they used slang.

> Year 11 female, Longfield

She treated us like equals, not like little kids like the teachers do.

> Year 10 female, Stanford Wood

In other words, a teaching style that stresses informality and equality can be just as important in making a lesson peer education-like in the eyes of young people as actual similarity of age or circumstance. Further, this perception of peerness directly contributed to the success of the lessons in having an impact on the pupils.

The second reason the pupils gave for the effectiveness of the lessons was their belief that they were hearing open and unbiased accounts about teenage parenthood, perhaps for the first time:

Teachers try and teach it you, um, from a teacher's point of view, they don't do it from the actual point of view, the realistic one.

> Year 10 female, Riverton

They've actually gone through it and are really speaking from experience. So it's more real and you believe it a lot more.

> Year 11 female, St. Joseph's

This notion of uncensored, 'warts and all' stories certainly fits with the projects' aim to teach young people about the realities of teenage parenthood, so they can make fully informed choices:

I don't think it's to prevent them from having children, I think it's just to make them aware of the realities of life . . . I think it works well if you're honest with them, I would say I'm not going to lecture you I'm going to tell you what it's really like.

> Marcia

However, there was some indication in the young mothers' interviews that this was not in fact what always happened, but rather that the stories the young mothers told were often shaped to be more negative:

When I go into peer education I say that I don't go out at weekends but I do, my mum has the baby every weekend so I can go out and just enjoy myself.

> Ali

I just say the complete truth about how Chloe throws paddies, all stuff like that, but I don't tell them the good bits as well, when she's laying in bed cuddling, and saying I love you.

Kathy

Such quotes suggest a process by which the young mothers collude with the dominant discourses that surround teenage pregnancy and parenthood, positioning it as problematic, rather than attempting to give an exact account of their experiences. Part of the reason for this appeared to be a genuine belief that, given the difficulties these individuals had experienced themselves in social and economic terms, other young people would be better off delaying parenthood:

Because I'd been in a bad situation when I was young, I thought if I could get across to other young teenagers not to get pregnant then it would be better all round.

Ali

Despite this selective storytelling arising from an authentic desire to do what is in the pupils' best interests, it does raise questions as to how far the pupils are being manipulated into accepting what they are hearing, based on a false premise that it is free of any agenda. Such a problem is by no means limited to these projects involving young mothers, but has been noted as a danger of peer education more widely, due to the possibility that the peer educators merely function as mouthpieces for the adult organisers (Milburn 1995; Frankham 1998). A difficult question, therefore, is whether the good that the pupils gain from the lessons, in terms of taking messages about contraception more seriously and being more aware of the consequences of their actions, outweighs the possibility that they are being misled about the nature of the stories they are hearing. The answer to that is likely to depend on one's perception of whether teenage pregnancy and parenthood should be prevented at all costs, or whether it is more important to ensure that young people are empowered to make their own choices about that, contrasting positions that touch on a wider, ongoing debate regarding the main function of sex education (Kidger 2005).

In fact, a further reason why the young mothers may have had to support the construction of teenage parenthood as negative emerged from the interviews, which did not necessarily connect to their concern to do the right thing for the pupils, and this is discussed in the next part of the chapter.

Tackling social exclusion – tales from young mothers

As indicated by Ali's comment above, all the young mothers interviewed for the study, despite coming from quite varied circumstances, had encountered various difficulties associated with their relatively early parenting status. Those difficulties mirrored findings from other research (e.g. Phoenix 1991a; Dawson 1997; Allen and Bourke Dowling 1998; Kidger 1998), and included problems completing or returning to education and employment, a lack of material resources, experiences of isolation and judgemental reactions from others. Although these areas of difficulty included the British government's main priority, that is education and employment, they were not limited to this. Rather, the exclusion experienced by the interviewees was multifaceted, and covered a range of social as well as economic factors. In examining how participation in the peer education projects might assist young mothers in achieving greater social inclusion I have therefore identified three types of social exclusion – economic, relational and moral – in an attempt to acknowledge and explore these different aspects.

Economic inclusion

Although New Labour's primary concern is assisting young mothers to return to education, training and employment, previous research has documented various structural and contextual barriers to this (Speak *et al.* 1995; Dawson 1997; Allen and Bourke Dowling 1998), which cannot be tackled through individual action but require policy intervention. Despite this, the findings from this study of peer education projects did highlight two ways in which participation in the projects could help young mothers at least indirectly to improve their circumstances in this area.

The first and most commonly mentioned benefit was the high level of personal development the interviewees gained, specifically an increase in self-confidence and self-esteem, the acquisition of important transferable skills, the opportunity to self-reflect and the motivation to engage with new activities:

> It gets you out of the house, gets your mind working again. Gets you enthusiastic, confident, makes you want to do something with the rest of your life.
>
> Jessica

> I always feel really good. When I finish a session I feel a big sense of achievement, especially if I've said everything that I wanted to.
>
> Leanne

> It's taught me to be able to mix with people easier, speak out in front of a lot of people.
>
> Bev

All of these aspects of personal development link to economic inclusion in that they provide greater confidence and motivation in identifying and accessing educational and employment opportunities. Indeed, several of the young mothers interviewed had already used these gains to access other voluntary work or training opportunities in fields such as computing, youth work, midwifery and social work. The vocationally related nature of these activities suggests that they might provide a stepping stone to paid work for those involved, something that the government itself has identified as a potential benefit of voluntary work (Chanan 1997).

The second way in which the interviewees' participation might eventually increase their economic inclusion was the fact that it improved their ability to 'sell themselves'. Because of their youth, and lack of educational and employment success, the young mothers tended to have little experience on which to draw in order to persuade employers of their abilities. These projects therefore provided a valuable addition to CVs and application forms. Indeed, the importance of this had been noted by at least two of the projects, both of which had set up formal systems of accreditation in order to recognise the work that the peer educators were doing. However, as already noted, young mothers also experience forms of exclusion which concern more social aspects of life, and I turn to these now.

Relational inclusion

Several of those interviewed for this study commented on the fact that during pregnancy and beyond they felt isolated from their friends, had no social life and had experienced limited emotional support. For these young mothers, the opportunity to meet other young women in a similar situation that the projects provided appeared highly significant, due to the emotional support, friendship and sense of social connectedness that this brought:

> Definitely being in the group, a lot of girls get out of it just having support, being able to meet up and talk about our experiences and stuff.
>
> Marcia

> It's nice just to have group, be a group and say this is our group.
>
> Leanne

The projects therefore functioned as micro-communities as well as sex education interventions, protecting members from the feelings of social isolation that they experienced elsewhere, and providing a safe environment in which they could build up a sense of collective identity and social integration. Although not emphasised within the government's approach to supporting teenage mothers, this sort of social cohesion and connectedness does underpin many theoretical accounts of social inclusion (Silver 1995), and certainly appeared to be important to the young women themselves.

As part of this community building, project members were encouraged to try out new social roles:

> We've got a committee, we set one up. The day we decided, we just chose who wanted to be what, but if anybody else wanted to join the committee we could find them a role.
>
> Christine

Indeed, as indicated in the above quote, the ethos of the projects appeared to be one of empowering the young mothers, through affording them as much input and control over the projects as possible, both during the lessons and in the more general planning and management. This resulted in the young mothers showing a deep sense of commitment to the projects, something that contributed to the final set of benefits that I discuss next.

Moral inclusion

The benefits noted above, which link to relational inclusion, are not, of course, limited to projects like these, but are likely to be a feature of support groups targeting young mothers more generally. However, what distinguishes these projects is the fact that they aim to have a positive impact on the lives of other young people. This was something that was clearly important to the interviewees:

> I feel like I'm doing something worthwhile, that I'm helping other young people.
>
> Deborah

> It's good for us as well, because we can sort of go and feel like we're doing our bit for the community.
>
> Christine

I noted earlier that projects such as these might provide the opportunity for young mothers to create more positive public identities for themselves, thereby combating the judgemental, negative stories that tend to surround teenage pregnancy and parenthood. It certainly seemed to be the case that, by believing in the value of the projects, and therefore the value of their own actions as participants, project members were able to challenge their public image as social problems, and to construct more positive self-identities as 'good' and active citizens instead:

> It gives me a bit of self-respect, you know that you're not all bad, you know when someone's putting someone else down, all single Mums blah, blah, blah. I like it, I like to know I've done something good, I've done something that's benefited someone else, that makes me feel happy.
>
> Naomi

> I thought it would be a really good thing to do, because I find it frustrating the way the government and society classes people if they have a baby young, so I was thinking just the general idea of doing something good, doing something better.
>
> Sian

Creating the potential for young mothers to be heard, and to challenge their problematic public status, has been identified as an important part of supporting them (Bullen *et al.* 2000; Schultz 2001). Indeed, Plummer (1995) argues for the key role that storytelling can play in empowering sexually deviant and/or victimised individuals and groups, through challenging the more dominant stories that exist. However, I noted earlier that several of the interviewees appeared to shape their stories to uphold the dominant accounts of teenage pregnancy and motherhood that position it as something negative and to be avoided. In other words, the process by which these young mothers created positive identities for themselves as good citizens was not by challenging dominant values, but by colluding with them:

> I hope I'm helping other people avoid the trap I got into 'cause it's too late now, I can't change what's happened now, but if I could change someone else's that they would look after themselves more, then that would be enough.
>
> Deborah

> I sort of said to them well I'd do it properly if I were you, I'd try and get yourself sorted, you know settled, get yourself married and be in a position to do it.
>
> Christine

Interviewees such as Deborah and Christine were therefore involved in a complex balancing act, in which they upheld dominant negative constructions of teenage motherhood as a 'trap' or somehow 'improper', while distancing themselves from such constructions:

> The more people say young mums are shit the more it makes me want to say look I'm not shit. I've never done drugs, I've never been arrested, my chid is tidy, he is well-behaved and I'm doing voluntary work.
>
> Deborah

In the above quote, Deborah does not challenge the immoral status conferred on those who use drugs or are arrested, or the presumed associations between young mothers and these two activities, but what she does do is emphasise that *she* is not that sort of person, noting her voluntary work as evidence of this. This process of young mothers reproducing dominant norms that position teenage motherhood as problematic while distancing themselves from such discourses is not uncommon (Phoenix 1991b; Jewell *et al.* 2000). However, the problem with it happening in such a public setting is that it may perpetuate the moral exclusion of young mothers more generally. Given this, and the tension achieving moral inclusion in this way creates between what might be in the young mothers' best interests and what might be in the pupils' best interests, as noted in the previous section, an important question remains as to whether the benefits of projects such as these outweighs the difficulties.

Conclusion

I began this chapter by suggesting that two questions need to be asked of projects involving young mothers as peer educators, and that is how far they improve young people's education about teenage pregnancy and parenthood and how far they support young mothers, particularly in terms of their experiences of social exclusion. The findings of my study revealed that both pupils and young mothers did indeed benefit from participating in such projects, the pupils because they were encouraged to recognise the implications of what they were hearing for their own lives, and the young mothers because they used the projects to develop ways of countering their own economic, relational and moral exclusion.

However, the findings also highlighted a fundamental tension within the projects, regarding what is in the pupils' best interests and what is in the young mothers' best interests, and the implications this has for the aims of the projects. If, on the one hand, the projects really are about giving pupils fully informed choices, then the young mothers should genuinely be encouraged to tell their own uncensored stories, including those aspects that challenge dominant discourses regarding teenage pregnancy and parenthood. However, it is questionable whether this is really what teachers, policy-makers and other professionals are prepared for when setting up and supporting these projects, and it certainly goes against the grain of mainstream sex education, where the messages are largely based on prevention or morality (Kidger 2005). Further, until the problem of the moral exclusion of young mothers is tackled, it would take a courageous young woman indeed to risk further stigma by publicly challenging dominant values in this area. On the other hand, if the projects are really set up with the aim of preventing teenage pregnancy and parenthood, then this needs to be made transparent; otherwise the pupils will be misled as to the nature of the message they are hearing. And if the aim of the projects is merely to replicate the dominant messages of teachers and other professionals in this way, then they lose their value in terms of providing young mothers with unique opportunities to have their *own* voices and stories heard. Whether these problems can be resolved, reflective as they are of tensions that infuse current policies regarding sex education and teenage pregnancy and parenthood, remains to be seen. However, given the potential benefits for both pupils and young mothers, it seems worth the attempt.

In the meantime, despite these problems, this study did provide some important insights regarding sex education and supporting teenage mothers that have a wider application. As far as sex education is concerned, what the lessons delivered by young mothers emphasised was the importance of educational messages engaging with the sexual cultures in which young people actively and continuously invest, if they are to understand and accept their relevance. Using peer educators and real-life stories appear to be two ways in which this can be achieved, but there may well be others. Ensuring that this message acceptance is translated into behaviour is then another question, and a matter for further research. Turning to the needs of young mothers, the projects also revealed the multiplicity of ways in which they can benefit when given the opportunity to actively address their experiences of social exclusion. Developing policy and practice that empowers young mothers as agents, and which provides them with opportunities to increase their confidence and skills, to form strong and supportive relationships, to contribute to their community and to collectively develop more positive identities, would therefore improve their own and their children's chances of enjoying a greater sense of social inclusion at all levels.

Notes

1 The projects that are the focus of this chapter describe what they do as peer education, therefore I refer to it as such. However, the definition of peer education is contested, and I discuss the extent to which this is in fact an appropriate label for these projects briefly later in the chapter.
2 Two of the five schools were not included in this phase of the research due to difficulties in arranging for lessons to be set aside for questionnaire completion – sex education tends to receive low priority in busy school timetables.

References

Allen, I. and Bourke Dowling, S. (1998) *Teenage Mothers: Decisions and Outcomes*, London: Policy Studies Institute.

Blaikie, N. (1993) *Approaches to Social Enquiry*, Cambridge: Blackwell Publishers.

Bullen, E., Kenway, J. and Hay, V. (2000) 'New Labour, Social Exclusion and Educational Risk Management: the Case of "Gymslip Mums", *British Educational Research Journal* 26, 441–56.

Chanan, G. (1997) *Active Citizenship and Community Involvement: Getting to the Roots*, Dublin: European Foundation for the Improvement of Living and Working Conditions.

Commission of the European Communities (2000) *Communication from the Commission: Building an Inclusive Europe* (available online at http://europa.eu.int).

Crosier, A., Goodrich, J., McVey, D., Forrest, S. and Dennison, C. (2002) *Involving Young People In Peer Education: a Guide to Establishing Sex and Relationships Peer Education* Projects, London: Department of Health.

David, M., Edwards, R. and Alldred, P. (2001) 'Children and School-based Research: "Informed Consent" or "Educated Consent"?', *British Educational Research Journal* 27, 347–65.

Dawson, N. (1997) 'The Provision of Education and Opportunities for Future Employment for Pregnant Schoolgirls and Schoolgirl Mothers in the UK', *Children and Society* 11, 252–63.

Fox, J., Walker, B. and Kushner, S. (1993) *'It's Not a Bed of Roses': Young Mothers' Education Project Evaluation Report*, Norwich Centre for Applied Research in Education, University of East Anglia.

Frankham, J. (1998) 'Peer Education: the Unauthorised Version', *British Educational Research Journal* 24, 179–93.

Hey, V. (1997) *The Company She Keeps: an Ethnography of Girls' Friendships*, Buckingham: Open University Press.

Hobcraft, J. and Kiernan, K. (2001) 'Childhood Poverty, Early Motherhood and Adult Social Exclusion', *British Journal of Sociology* 52, 495–517.

Holland, J., Ramazanoglu, C., Sharpe, S. and Thomson, R. (1998) *The Male in the Head: Young People, Heterosexuality and Power*, London: Tufnell Press.

Ingham, R., Woodcock, A. and Stenner, K. (1992) 'The Limitations of Rational Decision-Making Models as Applied to Young People's Sexual Behaviour', in *AIDS: Rights, Risks and Reason* (eds P. Aggleton, P. Davies and G. Hart), London: Falmer Press.

Institute for Volunteering Research (2002) *UK-Wide Evaluation of the Millennium Volunteers Programme*, Nottingham: DfES.

Jewell, D., Tacchi, J. and Donovan, J. (2000) 'Teenage Pregnancy: Whose Problem is it?', *Family Practice* 17, 522–8.

Kidger, J. (1998) 'A Study of Young Women's Health Needs and Behaviour, with Particular Regard to their Sexual Health, and the Effectiveness of a Self-help Group in Addressing such Issues' unpublished Masters dissertation, Manchester Metropolitan University.

Kidger, J. (2002) 'Young Mothers as Peer Educators in School Sex Education: a Beneficial Approach?', unpublished PhD thesis, University of Bristol.

Kidger, J. (2004) 'Including Young Mothers: Limitations to New Labour's strategy for supporting teenage parents', *Critical Social Policy* 24, 291–311.

Kidger, J. (2005) 'Stories of Redemption? Teenage Mothers as the New Sex Educators,' *Sexualities* 8, 481–96.

Kiely, E. and Curran, A. (2000) 'Community Education and Young Women – an Opportunity to Put Feminist Theory into Practice?', *Scottish Youth Issues Journal* 1, 31–50.

Levitas, R. (1998) *The Inclusive Society? Social Exclusion and New Labour*, Basingstoke: Macmillan.

Madriz, E. (2000) 'Focus Groups in Feminist Research', in *The Handbook of Qualitative Research*, 2nd edn (eds N.K. Denzin and Y.S. Lincoln), London: Sage.

Milburn, K. (1995) 'A Critical Review of Peer Education with Young People, with Special Reference to Sexual Health', *Health Education Research* 10, 407–20.

Ofsted (2002) *Sex and Relationships*, London: Ofsted.

Phelps, F.A., Mellanby, A.R., Crichton, N.J. and Tripp, J.H. (1994) 'Sex Education: the Effect of a Peer Programme on Pupils (Aged 13–14 Years) and their Peer Leaders', *Health Education Journal* 53, 127–39.

Phoenix, A. (1991a) *Young Mothers?*, Cambridge: Polity Press.

Phoenix, A. (1991b) 'Mothers Under Twenty: Outsider and Insider Views', in *Motherhood: Meanings, Practices and Ideologies* (eds A. Phoenix, A. Woollett and E. Lloyd), London: Sage, pp. 86–102.

Plummer, K. (1995) *Telling Sexual Stories*, London: Routledge.

Rodgers, G., Gore, C. and Figueiredo, J. (eds) (1995) *Social Exclusion: Rhetoric, Reality, Responses*, Geneva: ILO Publications.

Roker, D, Player, K. and Coleman, J. (1999) *Challenging the Image: Young People as Volunteers and Campaigners*, Leicester, Youth Work Press.

Schultz, K. (2001) 'Constructing Failure, Narrating Success: Rethinking the "Problem" of Teen Pregnancy', *Teachers' College Record* 103, 582–607.

Silver, H. (1995) 'Reconceputalising Social Disadvantage: 3 Paradigms of Social Exclusion', in *Social Exclusion: Rhetoric, Reality and Responses* (eds G. Rodgers, C. Gore and J. Figueirdo), Geneva: ILO Publications, pp. 283–311.

Social Exclusion Unit (1999) *Teenage Pregnancy*, London: HMSO.

Social Exclusion Unit (2001) *Preventing Social Exclusion* (available at www.cabinet-of-fice.gov.uk/seu).

Speak, S., Cameron, S., Woods, R. and Gilroy, R. (1995) *Young Single Mothers: Barriers to Independent Living*, London: Family Policy Studies Centre.

Tabberer, S. and Hall, C. (2000) *Teenage Pregnancy and Choice: Making the Decision to Have an Abortion*, Paper given to ESRC and Joseph Rowntree Foundation 'Youth Research 2000' conference, September 2000, Keele University.

Thomson, R. (2000) 'Dream On: the Logic of Sexual Practice', *Journal of Youth Studies* 3, 407–27.

Thorogood, N. (1992) 'Sex Education as Social Control', *Critical Public Health* 3(2), 43–50.

Wade, H., Lawton, A. and Stevenson, M. (2001) *Hear by Right: Setting Standards for the Active Involvement of Young People in Democracy*, Leicester: Local Government Association/National Youth Agency.

Woodcock, A.J., Stenner, K. and Ingham, R. (1992) 'Young People Talking about HIV and AIDS: Interpretations of Personal Risk of Infection', *Health Education Research, Theory and Practice* 7, 229–47.

Chapter 8

Controversial issues surrounding teen pregnancy

A feminist perspective

Nancy Shields and Lois Pierce

The social construction of teen pregnancy as a social problem

The term "teenage pregnancy" emerged in middle-class America in the 1970s (Hacking 1999). At the same time, teenage pregnancy, which had been defined as a private problem, was reconstructed as a public problem (Addelson 1999). A greater stigma became attached to teen pregnancy, especially among minorities (Addelson 1999), and the "good girl" who had made a mistake came to be viewed as promiscuous. Kelly (2000) argues that teen mothers have served as scapegoats for negative social trends (such as poverty), and have been stereotyped as "stupid sluts," rebels, the product of dysfunctional homes, irresponsible, dropouts, and neglectful mothers. Naturally, teen pregnancy occurred at a significant rate before the 1970s, but, when the way society defined teen pregnancy changed, teenagers and their families were expected to change their responses to the pregnancy. As a private problem, pregnancies were something to be ashamed of and hidden. Many teenagers simply married before the child was born, or went into seclusion while pregnant (living in a home for unmarried mothers or with a relative) and ultimately gave the child up for adoption. In more recent times, adoption has become much rarer, with only 5 percent of teenagers giving their babies up for adoption in 1992 (Custer 1993). More current statistics are not available because 1992 was the last year that systematic, national data on adoptions were collected (National Adoption Information Clearinghouse, 2005) in the USA.

The relationship between the social construction of teen pregnancy as a social problem and the actual number of teen births is an interesting one. Childbearing among teenagers between the ages of 15 and 19 actually reached an all-time high in 1957 (96 births per 1,000) and declined to an all-time low in 2003, the most recent year for which data are available (42 births per 1,000) (Boonstra 2002; National Center for Health Statistics 2004). The percentage of all live births that were to teenagers rose from 14 percent in 1960 to 19 percent in 1975 (Furstenberg 1991), during the same period that teen pregnancy was being constructed as a social problem. This increase occurred, however, not because of an increase in the birth rate, which actually declined steadily during the 1960s and 1970s, but because of the dramatic increase in the number of teenagers that occurred during that period as a result of the baby boom (the number of young women aged 15–19 increased by 52 percent between 1960 and 1975) (Furstenberg 1991). This created the impression of an epidemic of teen pregnancy among professionals working with pregnant teenagers, who suddenly saw their caseloads climb sharply.

During the same period, the "pregnancy rate" (a combination of the rate of abortion and the rate of live births) increased (Luker 1996), and the proportion of teenagers giving birth who were unmarried also increased dramatically, from 13 percent in 1950 to 79 per cent in 2000 (Boonstra 2002). However, most babies born outside marriage are actually born to older women, rather than teenagers. In 2002, the birth rate in unmarried mothers was highest among 20- to 24-year-old women (70.5 per 1,000), followed by women between the ages of 25 and 29 (61.5 per 1,000), and then teenagers aged 18 and 19 (58.6 per 1,000). Birth rates for unmarried mothers are much lower for teenagers aged 15–17 (20.8 per 1,000) (National Center for Health Statistics 2004). By the 1970s, acceptance of sex outside of marriage was widespread, and it became difficult to argue that this acceptance should apply only to adults (Luker 1996).

Luker (1996) argues that the social construction of teenage pregnancy as a social problem paralleled economic developments in the 1970s that continue to-day. It became more and more difficult to support a family on one income. The two-career marriage replaced the traditional middle-class model (with only the husband employed outside the home), and the single-parent household emerged as an alternative. From 1980 to 2003, by far the greatest increase in real median income (adjusted for inflation) occurred in married couple family households, from US$49,013 in 1980 to US$62,405 in 2003 (an increase of US$13,392) (US Census Bureau 2004a). In contrast, the increase for all households combined was US$5,871, and for households headed by men it was only US$1,075. The dramatic increase in married couple households can be attributed to the rise of two-career couples. In 2003, there were 23,209,000 married family groups with children under 15 (US Census Bureau 2004b). Of these families, slightly less than one-fourth (23 percent) had a "stay-at-home" mother, and only 0.4 percent had a "stay-at-home" father (US Census Bureau 2004b). In the 1980s, two-parent working couples, primarily highly paid blue-collar and white-collar families, became intolerant of single teen mothers on welfare (Luker 1996).

Fertility patterns also changed, with a trend toward either early or late child-bearing among women between the ages of 20 and 44. In 2002, the highest birth rate was among women aged between 25 and 29 (114 per 1,000), followed by women aged 20–24 (104 per 1,000). The birth rate in the 35–39 years age group was 41 per 1,000, and for the 40–44 year age group it was 8 per 1,000, the highest rate in over 30 years. On the other hand, the birth rate among the 30–34 year age group declined to 91.5 per 1,000. Ironically, the birth rate among teenagers between the ages of 15 and 19 declined a remarkable 30 percent between 1991 and 2003, from 61.8 per 1,000 to 42 per 1,000, during the same time that it was considered a major and growing social problem (National Center for Health Statistics 2004).

Teen mothers often live with their parent(s), and receive financial support and other resources, such as assistance with child care. Kalil and Danziger (2000) found that, in a study of teen mothers in one Michigan county, 79.3 percent were living with their mothers, and Acs and Koball (2003) found that 75 percent of a national sample of minor teen mothers were living with their parents, which places an additional financial drain on the teenager's family of origin. In contrast, two-career couples delay childbearing to a time when they are financially more secure. It is interesting to note that there has not been public concern with the high cost of late childbearing, even though these pregnancies tend to have more complications (Luker 1996).

The ideology of adolescence

During the same time that society was redefining teen pregnancy, a growing emphasis on adolescence as a special developmental period that should not include childbearing (Luker 1996) was contributing to the new definition. Teen mothers were described as "babies having babies" (Luker 1996) and as relinquishing their childhoods (Kelly 2000). MacLeod (2001) also comments on the trend toward equating childhood and adolescence, and as adolescence as a time for having fun and enjoying life. The emphasis, for an adolescent, came to rest on completing an education, preparing for a career, and delaying adult responsibility. Consistent with the new "ideology of adolescence" that called for extending the period of adolescence, the average age at first marriage increased. Between 1970 and 2000 the median age at first marriage increased from 23.2 to 27.1 for men and from 20.8 to 25.3 for women (Fields 2004). In addition, 55 percent of young adults between the ages of 18 and 24 were living with one or both parents in 2003 (Fields 2004). The average age at first birth for women increased from 21.4 in 1970 to 25.1 in 2002 (National Center for Health Statistics 2004).

In the 1970s and 1980s, it was generally believed that teen motherhood led to teenagers dropping out of school, thereby ending an important phase of adolescence. Yet the evidence does not seem to completely support this belief. Some teenagers had already dropped out of school before becoming pregnant, and those who were not doing well in school were more likely to become pregnant (Luker 1996). Further, many teenagers do complete their high-school education after becoming pregnant. One study (Kalil and Danzinger 2000) found that 84.1 percent of teenage mothers were still attending school, had graduated, or had received a General Educational Development (GED), and another study (Acs and Koball 2003) found that over 60 percent of a national sample fell into one of these three categories. Geronimus and Korenman (1990), using data from sister pairs in the National Longitudinal Survey of young women, concluded that there was no relationship between teenage childbearing and finishing high school. In fact, the more "successful" a pregnant teenager was, and the more successful she expected to be, the more likely she was, and still is, to have an abortion (Luker 1996). Those who choose abortion are more likely to come from affluent, white, two-parent families.

Among both blacks and whites, those who are discouraged and disadvantaged are more likely to become pregnant (Luker 1996).

Frequently, the label "teen pregnancy" lumps together all teenagers between 13 and 19, married and unmarried. Yet there is obviously a difference between a 19-year-old married mother and a 13-year-old unmarried mother. In fact, the vast majority of teen births are to older teens. In 2002, the birth rate among teenagers under 15 years was only 0.7 per 1,000, compared with 23.2 per 1,000 among those aged 15–17 years, and 72.8 per 1,000 in the 18–19 years group (Martin *et al.* 2003).

Ironically, during the same time period that an "ideology of adolescence'" was emerging, teenagers were being encouraged, sometimes even required, to take on adult roles. In 1965, the Twenty-sixth Amendment to the constitution was passed, lowering the voting age to 18 for federal elections and giving adolescents an adult role in the political process. Five years later it was lowered to 18 for all elections, including state elections (S. Rep. No. 26, 92nd Cong., 1st Sess., 1971; H. R. Rep. No. 37, 92nd Cong., 1st Sess., 1971). Also during the same period (1970–75), the minimum legal age for consuming alcohol was lowered to 18, 19, or 20 in 29 states. When evidence accumulated that suggested that this had resulted in more traffic accidents and fatalities among youth, 16 states restored the minimum drinking age to 21. In 1984, the federal government enacted the Uniform Drinking Age Act, which reduced federal transportation funds to states that had not restored the minimum age to 21 (American Medical Association 2005). Finally, millions of young men were taking on very adult roles by serving in the war in Vietnam during a similar time period, and many (25 percent) were required to do so by the draft. Over nine million military personnel served between August 1964 and May 1975, and the mean age was only 19. In contrast, the average age of soldiers during World War II was 26 (Vietnam Veterans of America 2005).

Who has the right to control fertility?

When society views teen pregnancies as a public problem, one that creates later problems for the mothers, their children, and society, controlling adolescent pregnancies becomes an obligation. Feminists, in their critique of teen pregnancy, question who has the right to control fertility behavior. They have argued that all women (including teenagers) have the right to make decisions about their own bodies, including the decision to have children.

Other concerns with freedom of fertility behavior specifically arise out of state attempts to prevent certain groups from bearing children. Reilly (1987) traces the history of involuntary sterilization in the USA, which emerged out of the eugenics movement in the late 1800s, flourished in the early 1900s, and persisted until the 1950s. Sterilization laws were primarily applied to criminals and so-called "mentally defective" individuals committed to state institutions and diagnosed as "unimprovable." Between 1905 and 1963, there were involuntary sterilization laws in 30 states, and over 60,000 people (both men and women) were sterilized.

Around 1930, there was a significant increase in the number of women sterilized. In addition to a concern for eliminating "genetically inferior" individuals from the population, there was also a concern that these individuals would place an economic burden on the rest of the population (similar to the argument made regarding teen mothers and welfare). During the 1960s and beyond, these eugenics programs came to be seen as extremely questionable, on both scientific and moral grounds, and were eventually repealed. More recently (Lykken 1996), an article written by a psychology professor and published in the *Chronicle of Higher Education* proposed that legislation should be passed that would require parents to be married, over 21, self-supporting, and free of criminal records and mental illness. Some have even argued for forced administration of contraception, such as the long-lasting depot contraceptive Norplant®, which can be removed only by a professional heath care worker (Kelly 2000).

The contemporary controversy revolves around an individual's right to be sterilized, and the protection of incompetent persons. Feminists have advocated that all women (including teens) should have the right to receive birth control, abortion, and sex education. However, others view teenagers, who are still developing physically and mentally, as not yet fully competent to make decisions regarding these activities.

Sex education

When teen pregnancy moved from being a private problem to a public one, responsibility for sex education was transferred from the family to schools, although there is still disagreement about what schools should include in these classes. Many families still believe that sex education should take place both at home and through sex education or family life classes at school. In spite of this, a number of studies, including one completed by the National Campaign to Prevent Teen Pregnancy (NCPTP 2004), have found that many parents assume that peers have the greatest influence on teenagers' sexual decisions, despite the fact that teenagers say that their parents have the most influence on their decisions. Many teenagers would like to be able to have more open talks with their parents, but only about 60 percent have been able to do this (ibid.). One reason may be that most parents (90 percent) are unsure about how to start the conversation and what to say (NCPTP 2004).

O'Sullivan *et al.* (2001) examined more closely what happens when mothers talk to their young daughters about sex, and found that in urban African–American and Latino families, most mothers and daughters reported discussing sexual issues. These talks often began when daughters entered puberty. However, as the NCPTP study (2004) suggests, many of these discussions were not very open. Instead, they were described as relatively antagonistic. Daughters felt as though mothers mostly wanted to know about their sexual experiences and were reluctant to share information with their mothers. Mothers, who were often ambivalent about their daughters' developing sexuality, described their fears that such discussions might encourage their daughters to become more sexually involved. On the other hand, daughters often felt mothers were only trying to scare them into not having sex.

O'Sullivan *et al.* (2001) also found that the daughters in their study often turned to others in the family or friends of the family for sexual information. Mothers most often focused on reproduction and hygiene, not issues of commitment, love, and jealousy, which interested girls the most. Although this study included urban only youth, the NCPTP study (2004) found similar concerns expressed by the teens and parents surveyed. A majority of these teens (64 percent) said that they believed that their morals and values were as important as health information in influencing sexual decisions. Both studies suggest that adolescents want faith communities and other social institutions to be more prepared to provide adolescents with information about sexuality (O'Sullivan *et al.* 2001; NCPTP 2004).

Most schools already provide information on reproduction and sexuality in middle and high school. These programs usually describe adolescent physiological development and methods of birth control. However, now, under President Bush's administration, any school that accepts government money must present abstinence as the only way to prevent pregnancy. Only the failure rates of different kinds of birth control can be presented. This approach works if a teenager is not yet sexually active. But what if an adolescent does have sex?

Critics of the "abstinence only" approach believe that it is based on assumptions that are out of date and unrealistic in our modern world (Bearman and Brückner 2001). Teenagers are bombarded with sexual images in advertising, television, movies, music, and on the Internet. In addition, Kelly (2000) has noted that the average age of puberty is now 12, down from 15 in the nineteenth century, while the average age of marriage has increased significantly for both males and females. This has resulted in a large increase in the period for which individuals are expected to abstain from sex. More important to critics is the belief that programs teaching "abstinence only" send the wrong message: sex is bad. Critics want adolescents to be aware of the risks associated with sexual activity, including unwanted pregnancies, abortion, and participating in other high-risk activities such as drinking and abuse of substances. They believe that youth need to know how to prevent pregnancy and sexually transmitted infections once they become sexually active.

Those in favour of the "abstinence only" approach believe that presenting information about contraception sends a mixed message: that you should not have premarital sex, but just in case you do . . . (Brody 2004). This, critics believe, would be similar to saying that premarital sex is acceptable. The NCPTP survey (2004) found that about 30 percent of teenagers surveyed agreed that this is a confusing message. Yet there is evidence that premarital sex is accepted among older age groups. In 2002, the number of births to unmarried women reached an all-time high – 1,365,966 – which has been attributed to the growing number of unmarried women rather than to an increase in the actual birth rate, which remained constant at 44 births per 1,000 (National Center for Health Statistics 2004).

Obviously, abstinence is the only fail-safe way to prevent pregnancy, but many question how realistic that approach may be, particularly with older adolescents. Bearman and Brückner (2001) examined the use of virginity pledges – pledging to abstain from sex prior to marriage – and whether or not they prevented sexual activity before marriage. Their findings were mixed, but, generally, virginity pledges reduced the likelihood of having sex, although the pledges work best for younger adolescents.

Bearman and Brückner (2001) also found that, once an adolescent broke a pledge, he or she was one-third as likely to use contraception as those who had not taken the pledge. However, the authors found that the effect of the pledges was largely contextual, and the pledges were most likely to work if a minority of students in a school were pledgers. The use of pledges creates a moral community in a school, but students lose interest in being a part of the community if everyone belongs.

Although nearly all teenagers (94 percent) surveyed for the NCPTP study (2004) believed that they should be strongly encouraged not to have sex until they are out of high school, and most teenagers (81 percent) believed that they should not have sex until later, the majority (57 percent) believed that, if they do become sexually active, they should have access to birth control. In fact, 81 percent of teenagers wanted more information on both abstinence and contraception.

Knowledge about birth control and sexually transmitted infections (STIs)

Knowledge about birth control and STIs is particularly important for teenagers, who are more likely than older men and women to use contraception only sporadically (Guttmacher Institute 1999). However, the proportion of teenagers using contraception (all types combined) at first intercourse (most often condoms) increased from 65 percent in 1988 to 75 percent in 1995. Use of condoms at first intercourse increased from 48 percent in 1988 to 63 per cent in 1995. In spite of the increased use of condoms, every year about 25 percent of sexually experienced teenagers acquire an STI. In some settings, up to 29 percent of sexually active teenage women have chlamydia; in some states, up to 15 percent have human papillomavirus, often the type linked to cervical cancer, and more teenage women than adult women have gonorrhea (Guttmacher Institute 1999).

Although STI rates among teenagers are still relatively high, pregnancy rates have decreased during the last 10 years (Boonstra 2002; Darroch and Singh 2004). Santelli et al. (2004) examined the role that changing sexual behaviors among high-school students played in this decline. Data from the national Youth Risk Behaviour Survey ($n = 31,058$) provided information on sexual activity and contraception use among teenagers aged 15–17 between 1991 and 2001. The researchers combined these data with information on contraceptive failure rates from the 1988 and 1995 National Survey of Family Growth and pregnancy rates from the National Vital Statistics System. They found that the pregnancy rate in the 15–17 years age group had declined by 33 percent during the 9 years covered by the studies.

Santelli *et al.* (2004) also found that the percentage of teenagers who had ever had intercourse declined by 16 percent overall and by 28 percent among blacks. The rate was unchanged in Hispanic teenagers and fell by 14 percent in white teenagers. There was no change during the study in the percentage of adolescents who had had intercourse in the previous 3 months. However, during the period studied, adolescents did change contraceptive methods, with the use of less effective methods decreasing. This resulted in a decrease of 15 percent in the contraceptive failure rate. By 2001, the percentage of adolescents using no contraception was 12 percent among blacks and whites. Among Hispanics it had decreased, but was still 20 percent. When all groups were considered, the authors attributed 53 percent of the change in the pregnancy rate to decreased sexual experience and 47 percent to change in contraceptive methods.

It appears that adolescents have been receiving both sex education messages. They are having sex less frequently, but are more likely to use effective contraception when they do have intercourse. However, in spite of the increased use of condoms, from 36 percent in 1991 to 46 percent in 2001, the relatively high rates of STIs in adolescents suggest that they may need more information on STIs, particularly how to recognize and prevent them.

Who pays for teen pregnancy?

If teenagers decide to be sexually active and then become pregnant, a major controversy is the question of who will pay for the pregnancy and who will support the teenager and her child. One source of negative attitudes arises from the idea that these teenagers and their children will become dependent on "welfare" (Luker 1996; Kelly 1999). Pregnant teenagers are seen as the undeserving poor, draining the resources of the state. They are seen as financially dependent, still in the process of completing the tasks of adolescence, and abandoned by the fathers of their children (Davies *et al.* 1999). Some people continue to argue that teenagers actually become pregnant in order to receive welfare. The available data on this issue are unclear.

In 1996, Luker (1996) discussed data that compared the USA with other industrialized nations. The results showed that the USA has one of the highest teenage birth rates yet provides less support to teen mothers. More recent data also confirm that, between the years 1970 and 2000, birth rates among teenagers aged 15–19 were higher in the USA than in Canada, Sweden, England and Wales, and France, and rates have declined less in the USA than in the other countries (Boonstra 2002). In addition, Luker (1996) argued that there is no correlation between welfare benefits and out-of-wedlock births.

In 1996, a major change in welfare policy occurred when the federal government instituted the Temporary Assistance for Needy Families (TANF) program, which required a minor teen mother to live with her parents or another responsible adult, and attend school or participate in a training program in order to receive benefits (Acs and Koball 2003). Kaestner *et al.* (2003) used data from the National Longitudinal Survey of Youth from 1997 and 1979 (before and after the TANF era) to determine whether there had been a change in the birth rate for those two cohorts. They compared unmarried teenagers age 17 and under, as only minors are eligible for TANF. They found that the birth rate for that age range actually increased from 3.5 percent in 1979 to 5.7 percent in 1997. They also found that "high-risk" teenagers (based on the mother's education and marital status) were more likely than "low-risk'" teenagers to give birth, and even found some evidence of increased fertility among girls most likely to be affected by the new welfare policy. However, the trend over the years was for an increase in the birth rate between 1981 and 1994, and then a gradual decline from 1994 to 1999 (Ventura and Bachrach 2001; Ventura *et al.* 2001).

The issue is further complicated by the availability of other forms of public assistance. For example, although the percentage of minor teen mothers receiving TANF assistance dropped from 25 percent in 1997 to 5 percent in late 1999/early 2000, almost 80 percent of those teenagers were receiving assistance such as food stamps, WIC (Special Supplemental Nutrition Program for Women, Infants and Children), and housing (Acs and Koball 2003). A slightly earlier but similar study by Kaestner and O'Neil (2002) that focused on older teenagers (aged 17 and 19) reached similar conclusions. Their analysis suggested that welfare reform had reduced the amount of welfare received, fertility rates, marriage rates, and school dropout rates among high-risk teenagers.

In fact, although it is true that half of the families on welfare at any given time began with a teenage mother, teenagers accounted for less than 10 percent of those on welfare in 1990 (Luker 1996). More recently (2004), however, the TANF program and contingency fund accounted for only 1 percent of the annual federal budget (Congressional Budget Office 2005). Furthermore, an interesting analysis of data from the National Longitudinal Survey of Youth compared women who had had their first child as a teenager before age 18 with a group of women who became pregnant but miscarried and did not give birth until about age 20 (the median age) (Hotz *et al.* 1997). The researchers found that teen mothers earned substantially more over their lifetimes than women who delayed their childbearing. They suggested that a reason for this might be that mothers typically work less when their children are young and more when their children are older. In the case of teen mothers, the period of non-employment would occur during their teens, when their participation in the labor force and their income would be low anyway. By the time their children are older and they are able to work, women who were teenage mothers are in their 20s and 30s, and their earning power is greater. Women who delay childbearing experience the opposite effect. Another explanation offered by Hotz *et al.* (1997) for this phenomenon is that teen mothers tend to come from less advantaged families, are less likely to be successful in school, and, therefore, less likely to pursue occupations that require higher education than women who delay childbearing. Women from similar disadvantaged socio-economic backgrounds are more likely to enter careers for which educational credentials are less important than on-the-job skills. Being a teen mother may prove to be more compatible with the limited career options they would have anyway.

Hotz *et al.* (1997) also addressed the cost the government bears as the result of teen pregnancies. They noted that the expenditures the government incurs on all public assistance programs (Aid to Families With Dependent Children, food stamps, Supplemental Security Income, General Assistance, and Medicaid) to aid teen mothers and their babies is offset by the federal, state, and local income and sales taxes. The authors determined the extent to which, over their lifetime, the taxes paid by teen mothers offset the public assistance they receive. The authors found that subtracting the net taxes teen mothers will pay over their lifetimes from the public assistance they receive reduces the annual cost of their public assistance to about US$665 per woman. Of course, the taxes teen mothers will pay over their lifetimes must also support a wide range of other government services that benefit them and their babies, in addition to the public assistance they received as teen mothers. The authors further noted that the net cost of public assistance (the public assistance teen mothers received less the taxes they paid) would actually increase if these teen mothers had delayed their childbearing. This result is the direct result of their previous finding that teen mothers would earn less over their lifetimes – and pay less in taxes – if they delayed their childbearing. Geronimus (1997) also notes that, although non-marital birth rates did rise in the 1960s, when Aid to Families with Dependent Children (AFDC) was relatively generous, they continued to rise during the 1970s and 1980s, when eligibility requirements became stricter and benefits decreased.

By the late 1970s, teen pregnancy was viewed as a fundamental cause of poverty (Luker 1996). Both liberals and conservatives supported the movement toward making birth control available to teenagers, from cost-saving (conservatives) and humanistic (liberals) perspectives. It was assumed that births would decrease and poverty would decline. Teen pregnancy became a "technical" problem to be solved by the state (Addelson 1999). Public support for birth control grew in the 1970s, and teenagers became eligible for birth control and then abortion in 1976 (Luker 1996), although controversy surrounds these issues even today. However, this view ignored the fact that many of the teenagers who have babies are poor to begin with. One study found that 80 percent of teenage mothers were living in poverty (or near poverty) before they became pregnant (Luker 1996). Luker (1996) has argued that if teenagers postpone pregnancy, it will only postpone the problem of poverty, i.e., age is not really the issue.

Abortion

Once an adolescent is pregnant, if she does not miscarry – 14 per cent do – her choices are to obtain an abortion or give birth. In 1996, approximately 56 percent of teenagers gave birth, and almost 40 percent (excluding those who experienced a miscarriage) had abortions (Guttmacher Institute 1999). Those who give birth are more likely to come from low-income families (83 percent) than are teenagers who have abortions (Guttmacher Institute 1994).

Abortion is a legal option for teenagers, although the law varies somewhat from state to state. In 13 states and Washington, DC, a teenager may request an abortion without her parents' knowledge. In other states, a parent must give permission or the girl must tell her parents that she is having an abortion. In some states, a judge can overrule the need for parental consent or permission (Cool Nurse 2004). In the majority of situations, teens who have abortions (61 percent) do so with the knowledge of at least one parent, and most parents support their daughter's decision to have an abortion (Guttmacher Institute 2004). By 2000, the abortion rate among pregnant teenagers had decreased to 33 percent and teenagers accounted for 19 percent of all abortions (Boonstra 2002). Unfortunately, little research has been carried out on teenagers and adoption. Custer (1993) found that abortion was a much more likely option for teens (40 percent) than adoption (5 percent).

Quality of teen parenting

A particularly sensitive issue surrounding teen parenting is the question of the quality of teen parenting. Teenage mothers are often thought of as inadequate, in part simply because many are single parents. Children of single parents are generally at a disadvantage, since they often have fewer resources available to them. However, there are currently a staggering number of single parents in the USA: 10,142,000 single mothers, and 2,260,000 single fathers (Fields 2004). A significant number of children spend at least part of their childhoods in a single-parent family, as a result of divorce, absence of a parent in the home, death of a parent, or being born to an unmarried woman. In 2003, 44 percent of single mothers had never been married, in 18 percent of cases the spouse was absent from the home, 35 percent were divorced, and 4 percent widowed. The corresponding percentages for the men were 38 percent, 15 percent, 42 percent, and 5 percent. Thus, children are almost as likely to reside in a single-parent household as the result of divorce as they are to have a mother who has never been married. Furthermore, births to older, more affluent, unmarried mothers have generally not been viewed as a social problem (Luker 1996).

Is there evidence that teenage mothers are less adequate than older mothers or that their children are disadvantaged? Some older research found that the children of teen mothers are more likely to have low birth weight, impaired cognitive development and problems in school, and some have suggested that they are more likely to be abused (Baldwin and Cain 1980; Hayes 1987; Furstenberg *et al.* 1990). The children of teenage mothers are at greater risk of living in poverty, and daughters of teenage mothers are more likely to become pregnant as teenagers (Hoggart 2003). However, when socio-economic status and other background characteristics are taken into account, many of these effects disappear (Luker 1996; Hoggart 2003). Buchholz and Korn-Burszlyn (1993) make a similar point.

A very recent study (Terry-Humen *et al.* 2005) compared 17,219 kindergarten children of mothers of various ages in terms of cognition and knowledge, language and communication, attitudes toward learning, social skills and emotional behaviour, physical well-being, and motor development before and after controlling for background characteristics. Before controlling for background characteristics, children of teenage mothers showed impaired development on many of the above measures. However, after controlling for background characteristics, many of the effects disappeared, although some did remain, such as general knowledge scores, some test and assessment scores (but only when compared with children of older mothers aged 22–29), ability to read independently, writing ability, and lower interpersonal skills. Ironically, after controlling for background characteristics, the children of the teen mothers actually scored higher than the children of older mothers on measures of social interaction, gross motor skills, and composite motor skills. Moore *et al.* (1997) found similar results in a study of sister pairs. Other more recent research has also found that, among African Americans, low birth weight and infant mortality actually increase rather than decrease with maternal age (see Geronimus, 1997, for a review of these studies). Finally, one study of 30,000 parents of abused children and children in out-of-home care in the USA did not find that adolescent parents were overrepresented (Massat 1995).

MacLeod (2001) notes that the literature in South Africa also portrays teen mothers as inadequate. She analyzed 77 South African published and unpublished research reports, theses, journal articles, and book chapters, and identified several themes that cast teen mothers as bad mothers. The first is "mothering as a dyad," which defines the mother–child dyad as having the greatest impact on the child, ignoring other contextual factors. The teenager is viewed as unable to bond with her infant and unable to meet the emotional and physical needs of her child because of her age. This theme also relates to "ideology of adolescence" because one of the reasons the teen mother is thought to be inadequate is because of her interest in adolescent activities. The second theme is "mothering as a skill" that must be learned, and once again the teenager is viewed as ill prepared. This stands in contrast to the dominant discourse of mothering as a "natural" ability. If the "natural ability" theme were applied to teenagers there would be no reason to question their mothering abilities, so that notion is often played down in relation to teen mothers. The third theme is "motherhood as a pathway to womanhood," i.e., if an adolescent is a child, and mothers are adults, then adolescents should not be mothers. Another aspect of this theme is that women are defined as adults in relation to men (to the father of the child) or as a mother, rather than some other marker, such as establishing a career. The last theme is "fathering the absent trace," which addresses the role of the father in teen parenting. While noting that any mention of the father in academic research is rare (MacLeod, 2001), here the single teen mother is viewed as inadequate because she cannot provide what a father could – a male role model for sons and qualities for achieving in the public world, such as motivation and cognitive abilities.

It is ironic that, in fact, teenage girls are responsible for a significant amount of child care in the USA, a practice considered perfectly acceptable despite the fact that some question the adequacy of teen mothers. Data from the National Longitudinal Survey of Youth in 1997 (Rothstein 2001), which questioned approximately 9,000 teenagers, provide an indication of how widespread this practice is. In 1997, 59.2 percent of girls aged 14 and 64.1 percent of 15-year-old girls reported that they had had some sort of job at some time during the period between 1994 and 1997. In addition, 49.1 percent of girls aged 14 were employed in "freelance" jobs, of which 91.4 percent were employed as babysitters. The corresponding statistics for 15-year-old girls were 45.8 percent (freelance jobs) and 91.4 percent (babysitting) respectively. Even more striking was the number of 12-year-old female babysitters. Fifty-one percent of the girls reported that they had worked when they were 12 years old, and 84.9 percent of those reported that their work activity was babysitting. These statistics would suggest that teen girls actually do get significant child care experience, even though we think of teen mothers as unprepared. This is not to say that babysitting is the same as motherhood, or entails the same responsibility or commitment. However, it does stand in contrast to the stereotype of the totally inexperienced teen mother.

A negative bias

The media, as well as academic research, have portrayed teen pregnancy almost entirely in negative terms. Are there any positive aspects? Kirkman *et al.* (2001) conducted in-depth interviews with 20 teen mothers in Australia. They found that the teen mothers were aware they were being condemned and were viewed as "ruining their lives," and they also acknowledged that there were indeed disadvantages to teen pregnancy. However, these views did not dominate their thinking about themselves or their identities. They viewed themselves as competent mothers, and emphasized positive aspects. The authors describe the teenagers' autobiographical accounts as a "consoling plot" that included the ideas that motherhood is a personally enriching experience; that younger mothers have the advantage over older mothers because they have more energy; that they will be free to pursue other activities at an earlier age when older mothers will still have young children; and that the child is valued by the family and brings it closer together.

Higginson (1998) conducted participant observation and in-depth interviews with teenagers in a teen parenting program (50 teen mothers and only three teen fathers), and found similar results. She found what she termed "competitive parenting," which involved a competitive stance compared with other teenage parents as well as older mothers. "Competitive parenting" revolved around the issues of financial independence and "hypermaterialism" regarding the child, pride in the child's cognitive and physical development, independence in accepting advice from others regarding how the child should be raised, and being superior to their own mothers and other older mothers. The teenage mothers clearly took pride in providing for and caring for their children. Jacobs (1994) also conducted an ethnographic study of 45 teenagers attending a school for teen mothers and found that many of the teenagers chose to keep their babies and raise them to their best ability out of a sense of responsibility to the child and hope for a better future for themselves and the child.

"Invisible" teen fathers

It is noteworthy that such little attention has been given to teen fathers (for full discussions on teen fathers see Chapters 9 and 10). As Thornberry *et al.* (1997: 505) comment, "The study of teen parenthood has become almost synonymous with the study of teen mothers, but relatively little research has been devoted to the study of teen fathers." There is even some confusion regarding how to define a teen father. For example, should a teen father be defined as a male of any age that gets a teenager pregnant or as a male teenager who gets a female of any age pregnant (Robinson 1988)? There has also been concern with the age differences between teen mothers and their sexual partners (Taylor *et al.* 1999), although Elo *et al.* (1999) found that age differences in general tended to follow societal norms, except in the case of very young teen mothers. The little research that exists tends to be from the perspective of the teen mother, and tends to focus on the mother's relationship (or lack of a relationship) with the father (e.g., Jacobs 1994; Davies *et al.* 1999; Myers 1999). From a feminist perspective, this uneven treatment can be interpreted as placing blame on the teen mother but not on the teen father for the pregnancy and birth. As Myers (1999) notes, there seems to be a societal expectation that the mother will be the primary caregiver and take responsibility for the child.

The research that has been conducted on teen fathers can be classified into several main themes: risk factors associated with teen fathering; the relationship between delinquency and teen fathering; the impact of teen fatherhood on outcomes such as education and income; and research on teen fathers' involvement with their children. Concerning risk factors, Hanson *et al.* (1989) found that teenage fathering was related to race (being African American), going steady, and having unusual attitudes toward parenting outside marriage. A study that used data from the Child Development Study in Great Britain (Dearden *et al.* 1994) found that boys from families that were experiencing financial hardships and had older siblings were at greater risk of teen fatherhood. They did not find that coming from a single-parent family was a risk factor. A large-scale study by Pirog-Good (1995) that was based on 6,403 males from the National Longitudinal Survey of Labour Market Experiences in 1979 found that teen fatherhood was associated with large, poor, unstable households whose members were not well educated. Xie *et al.* (2001) found that teen fatherhood was related to individual factors (such as high aggression and low academic ability) as well as characteristics involving peers (low popularity) and family (low socio-economic status).

A study by Thornberry *et al.* (1997) is significant in that their large sample contained a significant percentage of teen fathers. They used data from the longitudinal Rochester Youth Development Study to identify risk factors related to teen fathering. Their analysis focused on 615 young men who were interviewed in 1995 and 1996. The sample was considered ideal because there was such a high rate of teen fathering; 28 percent of the respondents were fathers by age 19. Using several multivariate models, they examined individual and other-domain risk factors and found that being African American or Hispanic was a highly significant predictor of teen fatherhood, but that effect was mediated by the age of the teen's parents' at first birth (younger ages increased the likelihood of teen fathering), parents' education, parents' expectations that the respondent would attend college, the respondents having sexual intercourse at or before age 16, and drug use on the part of the respondent. Parents' education had a strong and consistent impact on teen fathering that was not mediated by the other variables. Higher reading scores and parental expectations for college also had positive direct effects in reducing teen fathering. Having sexual intercourse at an early age, gang membership, chronic drug use, and chronic involvement in violent behavior also had significant, direct effects on increasing the likelihood of teen fathering. The authors also found significant cumulative effects in terms of both individual risk factors and risk factors in other domains. Some factors that were significant at the bivariate level, such as family and neighborhood poverty, did not have significant effects in the multivariate models.

Good and Pirog-Good (1989) also argue that the processes that generate crime are the same as the ones generating teen fatherhood, but they are much stronger among whites than blacks. Stouthamer-Loeber and Wei (1998) found that teen fathers, compared with non-fathers, were more than 200 times as likely to have been involved in serious delinquent acts. Other research (Nurse 2001) has focused on the impact of incarceration on the relationships between teen fathers and their children. It is interesting that hope for future success (as measured by parental encouragement to attend college and reading scores) has a parallel in the literature on teen mothers, while little attention has been paid to the relationship between female delinquency and teen pregnancy. Educational attainment (Pirog-Good 1996) and the labor market success (Futris 2001) of teen fathers also have parallels in the literature on teen mothers.

Perhaps the greatest research interest in teen fathers relates to the question of paternal involvement with the child and paternal responsibility. Wheat (2003) examined the effect of social support (primarily from the teen mother and teen father's mother) on the teen father's involvement with the child, and found that social support did increase involvement. Gavin et al. (2002) found that, among a sample of African American adolescent fathers, the father's involvement was related to the quality of the romantic relationship between the mother and the father, whether or not the father was employed, the maternal grandmother's level of education, and the quality of the father and maternal grandmother's relationship. In contrast, Christmon (1990) found that, among a sample of 43 African American teen fathers, responsibility was related to self-image and beliefs about role expectations, not social support. Rhein et al. (1997) found that paternal uninterest and age predicted involvement in child rearing in a predominantly African

American sample of 173 teen fathers. It is interesting that some of the emerging literature on teen fathers and their involvement with their children tends to take a sympathetic perspective toward teen fathers, noting that teen fathers state a desire to be involved with their children (Glickman 2000), but that there are social and structural barriers to involvement that are beyond their control (Paschal 2004).

Conclusions

Are we saying that teen pregnancy is desirable? Of course not. However, we are saying that being involved in a teen pregnancy does not make someone bad. Pregnancy– at any age – involves benefits, risks, and costs. In a perfect world, every pregnancy results from a decision by a woman and her partner that balances these benefits, costs, and risks. This is not the case for many teen pregnancies, and for pregnancies among many adults as well. We know that the vast majority of teen pregnancies and many adult pregnancies are not intended (Henshaw 1998). Although this might create an unfortunate situation in the short run, it does not necessarily mean that the outcome will be negative in the long run.

Many individuals believe that pregnancy in unmarried teenagers is immoral. Immoral is a criterion that defies objective measures. Thus, some have turned to other criteria, such as societal cost, that can be measured. We believe that those individuals have overstated both the extent of teen pregnancies and their deleterious effects. They have done this to obfuscate the fact that their objections are primarily based on moral grounds. Feminists have asserted that many of the arguments against teen pregnancy are political in nature and do not consider all perspectives, which makes them controversial. We have reviewed some of these issues from a feminist perspective. Finally, we argue that more research attention to teen fathers would provide a more complete and balanced picture of the phenomenon of teen pregnancy.

References

Acs, G. and Koball, H.L. (2003) "TANF and the Status of Teen Mothers under age 18," No. A-62 in the series *New Federalism: Issues and Options for States*, Washington, DC: Urban Institute (available at htpp://www.urban.org/urlprint.cfm?ID=8419).

Addelson, K.P. (1999) "How Should We Live? Some Reflections on Procreation," in *Teen Pregnancy and Parenting: Social and Ethical Issues* (eds J. Wong and D. Checkland), Toronto: University of Toronto Press, pp. 81–98.

American Medical Association (2005) "Minimum Legal Drinking Age" (available at http://www.ama-assn.org/ama/pub/category/13246.html; retrieved February 24, 2005).

Baldwin, W. and Cain, V.S. (1980) "The Children of Teenage Parents," *Family Planning Perspectives* 12(1), 34–43.

Bearman, P.S. and Brückner, H. (2001) "Promising the Future: Virginity Pledges and First Intercourse," *American Journal of Sociology* 106, 859–912.

Boonstra, H. (2002) "Teen Pregnancy: Trends and Lessons Learned," *Guttmacher Report on Public Policy 5*, New York: Guttmacher Institute (available from http://www.gutt-macher.org/pubs/tgr/05/01/gr050107.html; retrieved November 22, 2004).

Brody, J. (2004) "Abstinence-only: Does it Work?," *New York Times*, section F: 7, June 1, 2004.

Buchholz, E. and Korn-Bursztyn, C. (1993) "Children of Adolescent Mothers: Are they at Risk for Abuse?," *Adolescence* 28 (Summer), 316–82.

Christmon, K. (1990) "Parental Responsibility of African-American Unwed Adolescent Fathers," *Adolescence* 25, 645–53.

Congressional Budget Office (2005) "The Budget and Economic Outlook: Fiscal Years 2006 to 2015," Washington, DC: Congressional Budget Office (available at http://cbo.gov/showdoc.cfm?index=6060andsequence=2).

Cool Nurse (2004) "Teen Abortion Laws in the U.S.A." (available at http://www.coolnurse.com/abortion_laws.htm; retrieved January 22, 2005).

Custer, M. (1993) "Adoption as an Option for Unmarried Pregnant Teens," *Adolescence* 28, 890–901.

Darroch, J.E. and Singh, S. (2004) "Occasional Report: Why is Teenage Pregnancy Declining? The Roles of Abstinence, Sexual Activity and Contraceptive Use," New York: Guttmacher Institute (available from http://www.agi-usa.org/pubs/or_teen_preg_decline.html; retrieved December 31, 2004).

Davies, L., McKinnon, M., and Rains, P. (1999) "'On My Own': A New Discourse of Dependence and Independence from Teen Mothers," in *Teen Pregnancy and Parenting: Social and Ethical Issues* (eds J. Wong, and D. Checkland), Toronto: University of Toronto Press, p. 38–51.

Dearden, K., Hale, C., and Blankson, M. (1994) "Family Structure, Function, and the Early Transition to Fatherhood in Great Britain: Antecedents using Longitudinal Data," *Journal of Marriage and the Family* 56, 844–52.

Elo, I.T., King, R.B., and Furstenberg, F.F. (1999) "Adolescent Females: their Sexual Partners and the Fathers of their Children," *Journal of Marriage and the Family* 61, 74–84.

Fields, J. (2004) "U.S. Census Bureau: America's Families and Living Arrangements: 2003, Current Population Survey, Annual Social and Economic Supplement, 2003" (available at http://www.census.gov/prod/2004pubs/p20–553.pdf).

Furstenberg, F.F. (1991) "As the Pendulum Swings: Teenage Childbearing and Social Concern," *Family Relations* 40, 127–38.

Furstenberg, F., Levine, A., and Brooks-Gunn, J. (1990) "The Children of Teenage Mothers: Patterns of Early Childbearing in Two Generations," *Family Planning Perspectives* 22, 54–61.

Futris, T.G. (2001) "The Educational Trajectories of Adolescent Males who Become Fathers Compared to Those who Delay Fatherhood," *Dissertation Abstracts International, A: The Humanities and Social Sciences* 61(11), 4565-A.

Gavin, L.E., Black, M.M., Minor, S., Abel, Y., Papas, M.A., and Bentley, M.E. (2002) "Young, Disadvantaged Fathers' Involvement with their Infants: an Ecological Perspective," *Journal of Adolescent Health* 31, 266–76.

Geronimus, A.T. (1997) "Teenage Childbearing and Personal Responsibility: An Alternative View," *Political Science Quarterly*, 112(3), 405–30.

Geronimus, A.T. and Korenman, S.D. (1990) "The Socioeconomic Consequences of Teen Childbearing Reconsidered," Discussion paper 90–190, Population Studies Centre, University of Michigan.

Glickman, H. (2000). "Low-income Young Fathers: Contexts, Connections, and Self," *Dissertation Abstracts International, A: The Humanities and Social Sciences* 60(7), 2693-A.

Good, D.H. and Pirog-Good, M.A. (1989) "Models for Bivariate Count Data with an Application to Teenage Delinquency and Parenthood," *Sociological Methods and Research* 17, 409–31.

Guttmacher Institute (1994) *Sex and America's Teenagers*, New York: Guttmacher Institute, pp. 19–20.

Guttmacher Institute (1999) *Facts in Brief: Teen Sex and Pregnancy*, New York: Guttmacher Institute (available at http://www.agi-usa.org/pubs/fb_teen_sex.html; retrieved December 31, 2004).

Hacking, I. (1999) "Teenage Pregnancy: Social Construction?," in *Teen Pregnancy and Parenting: Social and Ethical Issues* (eds J. Wong and D. Checkland), Toronto: University of Toronto Press, pp. 71–80.

Hanson, S.L., Morrison, D.R., and Ginsburg, A.L. (1989) "The Antecedents of Teenage Fatherhood," *Demography* 26, 579–96.

Hayes, C.D. (ed.) (1987) *Risking the Future: Adolescent Sexuality, Pregnancy, and Childbearing,* Washington, DC: National Academy Press.

Henshaw, S.K. (1998) "Unintended Pregnancy in the Unites States," *Family Planning Perspectives* 30(1), 24–9, 46.

Higginson, J.G. (1998) "Competitive Parenting: The Culture of Teen Mothers," *Journal of Marriage and the Family* 60(1), 135–49.

Hoggart, L. (2003) "Teenage Pregnancy: the Government's Dilemma," *Capital and Class* 79, 145–65.

Hotz, V.J., McElroy, S.W., and Sanders, S.G. (1997) "The Impacts of Teenage Childbearing on the Mothers and the Consequences of those Impacts for Government," in *Kids Having Kids: Economic Costs and Social Consequences of Teen Pregnancy* (ed. R.A. Maynard), Washington, DC: The Urban Institute Press, pp. 55–94.

Jacobs, J.L. (1994) "Gender, Race, Class, and the Trend Toward Early Motherhood," *Journal of Contemporary Ethnography* 22, 442–62.

Kalil, A. and Danziger, S. (2000) "How Teen Mothers are Faring Under Welfare Reform," *Journal of Social Issues* 56, 775–98.

Kaestner, R., and O'Neill, J. (2002) "Has Welfare Reform Changed Teenage Behaviours?," Working paper 8932, Cambridge, MA: National Bureau of Economic Research (available at http://www.nber.org/papers/w8932).

Kaestner, R., Korenman, S. and O'Neill, J. (2003) "Has Welfare Reform Changed Teenage Behaviours?," *Journal of Policy Analysis and Management* 22, 225–48.

Kelly, D.M. (1999) "A Critical Feminist Perspective on Teen Pregnancy and Parenthood," in *Teen Pregnancy and Parenting: Social and Ethical Issues* (eds J. Wong and D. Checkland), Toronto: University of Toronto Press, pp. 52–70.

Kelly, D.M. (2000) *Pregnant with Meaning: Teen Mothers and the Politics of Inclusive Schooling*, New York: Peter Lang Publishing.

Kirkman, M., Harrison, L., Hillier, L., and Pyett, P. (2001) "'I Know I'm Doing a Good Job': Canonical and Autobiographical Narratives of Teenage Mothers," *Culture, Health and Sexuality* 3, 279–94.

Luker, K. (1996) *Dubious Conceptions: The Politics of Teenage Pregnancy*, Cambridge, MA: Harvard University Press.

Lykken, D.T. (1996) "Giving Children a Chance in Life," *Chronicle of Higher Education* B1–2.

MacLeod, C. (2001) "Teenage Motherhood and the Regulation of Mothering in the Scientific Literature: The South Africa Example," *Feminism and Psychology* 11, 493–510.

Massat, C.R. (1995) "Is Older Better? Adolescent Parenthood and Maltreatment", *Child Welfare* 74, 325–36.

Martin, J.A., Hamilton, B.E., Sutton, P.D., Ventura, S.J., Menacker, F., and Munson, M.L. (2003) "Births: Final Data for 2002", *National Vital Statistics Reports* 52, 1–10.

Moore, K.A., Morrison, D.R., and Greene, A.D. (1997) "Effects on the Children Born to Adolescent Mothers, in *Kids Having Kids* (ed. R. Maynard), Washington, DC: Urban Institute Press, chapter 5.

Myers, L.W. (1999) "Not our Kind of Girl: Unravelling the Myths of Black Teenage Pregnancy," *Gender and Society* 13, 420–1.

National Adoption Information Clearinghouse (2005) Voluntary Relinquishment for Adoption: Numbers and Trends (available at http://naic/acf.hhs.gov/pubs/s_place.cfm).

National Center for Health Statistics (2004) *Health, United States, 2004*, with Chartbook on Trends in the Health of Americans, Hyattsville, MD: National Center for Health Statistics.

NCPTP (National Campaign to Prevent Teen Pregnancy) (2004) "With One Voice 2004: America's Adults and Teens Sound Off About Teen Pregnancy," Washington, DC: NCTP (available at http://www.teenpregnancy.org/resources/data; retrieved December 30, 2004).

Nurse, A.M. (2001) "The Structure of the Juvenile Prison: Constructing the Inmate Father," *Youth and Society* 32, 360–94.

O'Sullilvan, L., Meyer-Bahlburg, H., and Watkins, B. (2001) "Mother–Daughter Communication about Sex Among Urban African-American and Latino Families," *Journal of Adolescent Research* 16, 269–92.

Paschal, A.M. (2004) "I'm Doing What I Have to Do: African American Teens and their Experiences of Fatherhood," *Dissertation Abstracts International, A: The Humanities and Social Sciences* 64, 2663-A.

Pirog-Good, M.A. (1995) "The Family Background and Attitudes of Teen Fathers," *Youth and Society* 26, 351–76.

Pirog-Good, M.A. (1996) "The Education and Labour Market Outcomes of Adolescent Fathers," *Youth and Society* 28, 236–62.

Rhein, L.M., Ginsburg, K.R., Schwartz, D.F., Pinto-Martin, J.A., Zhao, H., Morgan, P., and Slap, G.B. (1997) "Teen Father Participation in Child Rearing: Family Perspectives," *Journal of Adolescent Health* 21, 244–52.

Reilly, P.R. (1987. Involuntary Sterilization in the United States: A Surgical Solution," *Quarterly Review of Biology* 62, 153–70.

Robinson, B. (1988) *Teenage Fathers*, Lexington, MA: DC Heath.

Rothstein, D.S. (2001) "Youth Employment in the United States," *Monthly Labour Review* August, 6–17.

Santelli, J., Abma, J., Ventura, S., Lindberg, L., Morrow, B., Anderson, J., and other members of the Unintended Pregnancy Working Group. (2004) "Can Changes in Sexual Behaviours Among High School Students Explain the Decline in Teen Pregnancy Rates in the 1990s?," *Journal of Adolescent Health* 35, 80–90.

Stouthamer-Loeber, M. and Wei, E.H. (1998) "The Precursors of Young Fatherhood and its Effect on Delinquency of Teenage Males," *Journal of Adolescent Health* 22, 56–65.

Taylor, D.J., Chavez, G.F., Adams, E.J., Chabra, A., and Shah, R.S. (1999) "Demographic Characteristics in Adult Paternity For First Births to Adolescents Under 15 Years of Age," *Journal of Adolescent Health* 24, 251–8.

Terry-Humen, E., Manlove, J., and Moore, K. (2005) *Playing Catch-up: How Children Born to Teen Mothers Fare*, Washington, DC: National Campaign to Prevent Teen Pregnancy.

Thornberry, T.P., Smith, C.A., and Howard, G.J. (1997) "Risk Factors for Teenage Fatherhood," *Journal of Marriage and the Family* 59, 505–22.

US Census Bureau (2004a) *American Community Survey*, Washington: US Census Bureau (available from http://www.census.gov/acs/www; retrieved November 30, 2004).

US Census Bureau (2004b) *Current Population Survey, Annual Social and Economic Supplements* (last revised August 2004), Washington: US Census Bureau (available from http://www.census.gov/hhes/income/histinc/h09ar.html).

Ventura, S.J. and Bachrach, C.A. (2000) "Nonmarital Childbearing in the United States, 1940–99," *National Vital Statistics Reports* 48(16), Hyattsville, MD: National Center for Health Statistics.

Ventura, S.J., Martin, J.A., Curtin, S.C., Menacker, F., and Hamilton, B.E. (2001) "Births: Final Data for 1999," *National Vital Statistics Reports* 49(1), Hyattsville, MD: National Center for Health Statistics.

Vietnam Veterans of America (2005) "Speakers Bureau Handbook" (available from http://www.njscvva/vietnam_war_statistics.htm; retrieved April 4, 2005).

Wheat, J.R. (2003) "Adolescent/Young Fathers' Involvement with their Children: The Role of Social Support," *Dissertation Abstracts International, A: The Humanities and Social Science* 64, 2274-A.

Xie, H., Cairns, B.D., and Cairns, R.B. (2001) "Predicting Teen Motherhood and Teen Fatherhood: Individual Characteristics and Peer Affiliations," *Social Development* 10, 488–511.

Chapter 9

Being there

Roles and aspirations of young single non-residential fathers

Suzanne Speak

Introduction

Thus far this book has focused primarily on young mothers. Whilst we have explored many of the difficulties young mothers face, it is important to recognise that, for every young mother, there is a father. Contrary to common perception, the men who father children with young mothers are generally only slightly older than the mothers. These young fathers, particularly young, single fathers who do not cohabit with the child's mother, have suffered what can only be described as very 'bad press' in recent years.

Throughout the 1990s there was a continuous media portrayal of young men in general, and young fathers in particular, as a group which had lost its way and role in life. As academic and media interest in issues of masculinity and how it was learned and expressed grew, the focus was increasingly on the loss of traditional male role models and the demise of the socialising nature of work (Lennon 1996; Coote 1999). Even when fathers tried to show their desire to become 'new men', support their children and engage more fully in fatherhood than previous generations of men had, their attempts were frequently portrayed by the media in negative terms.

Headlines such as 'Ex-addict gets grant to run class for fathers' (Pook 1999) or 'Do we really want a divorcee to teach us how to be fathers?' (Gallaher 1999) simply added to the demonisation of those men who do not conform to the traditional, married, male breadwinner role. The assumption behind the latter is that a divorced father cannot be a good father. One can imagine the outrage if such an assumption were to be made about divorced mothers. Within the context of this demonising of young men in general, young fathers were too often portrayed as shiftless, non-committed and unsupportive of their children.

However, a number of studies since the mid-1990s present a different picture (Speak *et al.* 1995, 1997; Rolph 1999). Drawing on the still very limited research available, this chapter aims to dispel some of the myths surrounding young single fathers, to present their aspirations for their role as a father and highlight some of the barriers that prevent many from engaging fully with their children. The voices of young fathers used to illustrate the chapter are taken predominantly from a study of 40 young single fathers in Newcastle upon Tyne (Speak *et al.* 1997).

Profiling young fathers

It should be noted that, because they are largely unmarried, and because of the way in which birth data are collected, data on young fathers remain limited. Much of what we know comes from a few, small-scale, largely qualitative studies. One of the few, and probably the best source of quantitative information is Keirnen's (1995) study of 'transitions to parenthood', which drew on the longitudinal data from the National Child Development Study (NCDS).

In the UK, more young women become mothers than young men become fathers. Just over 1 per cent of teenage men are fathers, compared with over 5 percent of teenaged women who become mothers (Burghes *et al.* 1997). This figure increases to 11 per cent among men aged between 20 and 24 years. Young fathers are generally about the same age as the mothers of their babies, despite perceptions to the contrary. In a study of school-aged mothers undertaken for the Teenage Pregnancy Unit, Selman *et al.* (2004) found the fathers of schoolgirls' babies to be only a year or so older than the mothers in almost all cases.

Young fathers, like young mothers, are most likely to be unmarried. However, birth registration data show that over 67 per cent of births outside marriage to young mothers under 20 and 77 per cent of those to mothers between 20 and 24 are jointly registered with the father. Of these births, registrations in which both parents are living at the same address, presumably cohabiting, account for 60 per cent and 72 per cent respectively (Office for National Statistics 1997). A more recent, although admittedly small-scale, study with a group of 30 young fathers noted that 50 per cent of the fathers were in an ongoing relationship with the mothers of their babies and, of those, 60 per cent had been in that relationship for over 3 years (Birbeck 2004).

Keirnan (1995) highlighted the relationship between low educational achievement of boys at ages 7 and 16 and their increased likelihood of becoming young fathers. This is supported by Burghes *et al.* (1997), drawing on the British Household Panel Survey, who noted that the younger a man is when he fathers his first child, the lower his educational qualifications are likely to be, both at that point and in later life, compared with his peers who father later.

Keirnan also noted that young fathers were more likely than older fathers to be unemployed or to be living on low incomes. They were also more likely to come from families with low socio-economic status and which had experienced financial hardship. Conversely, Birbeck (2004) found 70 per cent of his sample to be employed and 5 per cent to be at university.

Dispelling the common myths

A particularly common, but false, perception of young fathers is that they are most likely to be absent fathers, abandoning the child's mother, either during pregnancy or after the birth. Even academic researchers have encouraged this stereotype, possibly as a defence for their own failing to engage with young fathers. The following typically describes the stance taken about young fathers: 'as the last stages of teenage pregnancies echo to the sounds of slamming doors as the fathers make their dash for anonymity and freedom' (Hudson and Ineichen 1999: 66).

However, from a number of other studies it is clear that young mothers are just as likely to end a relationship as young fathers are. Indeed, in some situations, young women might feel that the father, especially if he is unemployed, has little to offer. At a meeting for a study of young mothers in Newcastle the author overheard words of wisdom from an older lone mother to a young pregnant woman who had recently split up from her baby's father: 'Shut up crying pet, he's done you a favour, if you're having a bairn, the last thing you want is a man to look after!'

Whilst age is a significant factor in a father being absent from his child, Clarke and Verropoulou (1996) noted that this likelihood does not continue if the type of parental relationship is taken into account. Married or cohabiting young fathers are considerably less likely to be absent from their children's lives than those not in any significant relationship with the mother.

Whilst the vast majority of young fathers are unmarried, this does not necessarily mean they are non-residential or uninvolved. A number of studies in recent years have shown that even very young single parents are often in a relatively long-term, continuing relationship, even if they do not marry or cohabit (Kiernan 1995; Speak et al. 1997).

However, it should be acknowledged that young cohabiting relationships are apt to break down, and many young mothers do end up living as lone mothers with their children. Nevertheless, it is wrong to assume that non-residential young fathers are necessarily unsupportive, any more than non-residential divorced or separated fathers are.

In one study of young, non-residential fathers, well over 50 per cent had contact on a weekly basis with both their child and his or her mother (Speak et al. 1997). Ten per cent had daily contact with both child and mother. Rolph (1999) found similar involvement levels in his study of young fathers in Norwich.

Roles and aspirations

Many young men do remain in close contact with their children and participate fully in their upbringing. Others sit on the sidelines, contributing occasionally, often as the mother feels appropriate. Some, of course, drift in and out of their children's lives, eventually becoming completely estranged from them. Nevertheless, increasing work with young fathers highlights the aspirations these young men have and the roles they create for themselves as fathers.

A common theme emerging from interviews with young fathers is that they hope to be 'better' fathers than they feel their own fathers were. In this context 'better' generally means more involved. Whilst a few disclose either abuse or abandonment by their own fathers, many refer to them as uninvolved or distant, as this young man noted, 'He were always around but at work or down the pub or fishing'. Many young fathers are particularly keen that their children should remember them as being active in their lives.

> I just hope when she grows up she will remember stuff we did together . . . just any stuff like going down the town and that and the pictures. So she can say 'remember when you took me to . . . whatever'.
>
> (Speak *et al.* 1997)

However, young men often find it difficult to define their role as a father. In interviews, the term 'being there' is often used to describe a vague, indefinable value that young men feel they will bring to their children's lives. As these young men explain in Speak *et al.* (1997):

> You've got to be there for them, I think . . . just be there if they need you.

> It's about being there for them. My dad were never there . . .

However, in reality, many are considerably more active and practically involved than this vague definition of their role might suggest. Despite earlier beliefs that men in general had little to offer to child development and that caring for children was 'women's work' (Lamb 1975), more recently research has shown that men can be perfectly competent carers (Cath 1989). Certainly, given the opportunity, which many are not, young fathers can demonstrate excellent parenting skills and great concern for the physical well-being of the children. Some young fathers in Speak *et al.*'s (1997) study, particularly those who had attended fathers groups or parenting classes, were openly critical of the parenting abilities of their children's mothers.

In recent years a number of parenting classes aimed specifically at young fathers have developed within youth work settings and in young offenders' institutions. Dennison and Lyon (2000) explored the role of parenting classes for young fathers in young offenders' institutions and the implications of the training for their post-release behaviour. The study highlighted that, in theory at least, the majority of fathers felt that parenting should be equally shared between both parents and that parents should be 'involved for life'. Whilst the fathers enjoyed and clearly benefited from the classes, with much of the learning and practice being retained after release, there was little evidence that the training had been beneficial in terms of offending behaviour in the short term or longer term.

For a few young men in Speak *et al.*'s study (1997), caring for their own children stimulated otherwise unrecognised interests and skills, as this young man noted.

> I remember at school, well you'd never say 'I want to work with kids'. I never really thought about it but I love kids me, always have. And now I've

got a son I think well I can do this, it would be good to do this . . . look after kids, in a nursery like. I've been thinking about taking a course.

(Speak *et al.* 1997)

Barriers to participation

Clearly, not all non-cohabiting fathers, young or otherwise, do maintain ongoing contact with their children. Millar and Bradshaw (1993) found that 35 per cent of children living with lone mothers, including divorced and separated mothers, lost contact with their fathers. For a number of reasons, contact is even more difficult to maintain between younger fathers and their children. In particular, the fact that they are generally not married to the mothers increases the likelihood of problems in maintaining contact (Bradshaw and Millar 1991; Seltzer 1995).

Legal position

One of the reasons given by young single fathers for wanting to be identified on their baby's birth certificate is the belief that, in doing so, they are claiming a legal right to be involved with that child and share decision-making about its upbringing.

She said [the young man's own mother] I got to have me name on the certificate . . . yeh birth certificate or I don't have no rights to see him . . .

(Speak *et al.* 1997)

This assumption is completely incorrect. In the UK an unmarried father, young or otherwise, has no automatic legal parental rights. Thus, he has no say in medical decisions or even adoption proceedings, or whether the child may be taken out of the country. To gain such rights he must apply for a parental responsibility order. Pickford (1999) and Speak *et al.* (1997) both identified that few young, unmarried fathers, or even those working to support them, such as youth and community workers, are aware of this tenuous legal position.

However, despite this lack of legal rights, a young father is bound by all other legal responsibility placed on any other biological father to contribute to the child's support financially. This sends out false messages to young single fathers and re-emphasises the 'provider' role at the same time as diminishing the emotional, nurturing role. Many mistake the paying of maintenance as a way to ensure rights and contact, as this young man believed.

That's what the Agency [Child Support Agency] is for, isn't it. So if you pay them, the mother's money, yeh, maintenance . . . then they can see that you both have rights to the kid. I've got to pay cause I know then she can't stop me seeing K [his child].

(Speak *et al.* 1997)

Involvement of others

Speak *et al.* (1997) noted that the attitude and involvement of others conditioned a young father's responses to fatherhood. Amongst the fathers she interviewed, one of the main barriers to them being involved was the mother's reluctance to let them. Of the 40 young men interviewed, 23 said the main reason they did not have greater involvement was because the child's mother prevented it. As the mothers were not interviewed, their reasons cannot be analysed.

However, Speak *et al.*'s earlier work (Speak *et al.* 1995) with young mothers suggests that a combination of lack of confidence in the father's ability and poor experiences, including lack of commitment and reliability, during the relationship may make a mother wary of allowing the father much involvement. Similar difficulties are experienced by divorced fathers (Simpson *et al.* 1995).

Conversely, some young mothers are only too happy to allow the father ample contact with his child, seeing it as both important for the child's development and the father's duty. In this context, some young fathers do find valuable roles for themselves in providing practical child care, as this young man explains.

> I can see him whenever I like, I always look after him a few days during the week. It's only right, he's mine too and it gives his Mam a break. This way we get to spend time together and he gets to know his Dad proper.
>
> (Speak *et al.* 1997)

However, a young father's desire and willingness to provide care can also be abused:

> If she's (the child's mother) wanting to go down town she'll phone my Mama and say about picking him up and that and I'll know when she's seeing someone, aye, got a lad like.
>
> (Speak *et al.* 1997)

It is not only mothers who can deter, or condition, a young father's involvement with his child. Both fathers and mothers frequently comment that the grandparents are unsupportive of the young father. In the case of the maternal grandparents, this may be because they feel the young father is unsuitable, particularly if the relationship between the young mother and father has broken down, or, as in the case of the young man speaking below, if the father is in jail.

> 'cause I know they're telling her not to bother with me. . .when I get out like not to let S [son] see me and that. She don't bring him now . . . It were fine before . . . now I'm not good enough . . .
>
> (Speak *et al.* 1997)

Whilst it is reasonable, even natural, for a girls' parents to try and steer her away from what they perceive to be inappropriate or destructive relationships, as Dennison and Lyon (2000) note, young offending does not necessarily make a young man a poor or uncaring father.

Conversely, some less involved young fathers are encouraged by either or both sets of the baby's grandparents to see their children. A father's own parents can play a major role in supporting him as he develops a relationship with his child. They often provide not only moral support and encouragement but all the practical child care which will give the mother confidence to allow the baby to go to the father.

> I think she knows it's OK because she knows my Mam's there and she'll help me and that.
>
> (Speak *et al.* 1997)

A young father's peers also frequently give support and encouragement to be involved. Certainly, studies of young fathers seldom show their peers to be unsupportive or discouraging. More recently, youth workers have begun to develop young fathers' groups, where young men can meet, with or without their children, to discuss fatherhood and gain confidence in parenting.

Unfortunately, not all professionals are as supportive, and too frequently those working with young mothers also deter fathers' involvement. Young fathers frequently report little support throughout the pregnancy and at the birth, and comment that they are made to feel unwelcome at antenatal and post-natal classes. Even when a young father is actively involved in his child's life, suspicion, born of the general demonising of young men, can make that involvement difficult or uncomfortable (Speak *et al.* 1995, 1997; Rolph 1999).

Whilst school-aged fathers are, admittedly, few in number, one local authority's teenage pregnancy and parenting team, which recently employed a fathers' worker, found there to be far more than expected.

Education policy around schoolgirl pregnancies has improved dramatically in recent years, particularly since the introduction of local education authority Re-integration Officers in many localities. Nevertheless, findings from a study for the Teenage Pregnancy Unit (Hosie and Speak 2004) highlighted the lack of policies to support school-aged fathers.

These very youngest fathers, still in statutory schooling, can find themselves unsupported by the education system. Hosie and Speak (ibid.) noted several occasions when schools' policies had been particularly negative towards young fathers who were trying to be supportive of their pregnant girlfriends. In some cases the policy seems to be to keep the couple apart.

Practicalities and finances

A range of financial and practical constraints serve to limit the time and nature of contact between a young father and his child. For example, contact and involvement has to take place somewhere, but young men may find themselves with limited appropriate locations to take their children. By no means all paternal grandparents welcome the child into their homes and, in some cases, limited space makes taking the child there difficult, as the following quote highlights.

> Me and my brother share a room so it's not easy so I sleep on the sofa when J stays and he sleeps in his [Moses] basket.

(Speak *et al.* 1997)

In their 1997 study of young single fathers in Newcastle, Speak *et al.* identified a link between housing policy and contact. Housing policy does not prioritise the needs of non-custodial fathers, and it requires young single people seeking housing benefit to live in houses of multiple occupation (HMOs). This means that young single fathers may not have appropriate housing to take their children to, as the following quote explains

> I could have her back at my place but I don't like . . . not overnight, I mean not at my place I mean; it's too rough for a little lass . . . aye, they're drunk, pissed and doing drugs and that and there's mostly trouble mostly every night, well at the weekends when I have her . . . It's not right for a little lass.

(Speak *et al.* 1997)

Contact arrangements may be severely hampered for single, divorced and separated fathers when they do not pay maintenance or child support (Simpson *et al.* 1994; Speak *et al.* 1995, 1997). As noted earlier, young fathers are more likely than older fathers to be unemployed. Thus, there are limits to the amount they can contribute financially to their child's support and what they can afford to do with their children when they do see them. Financial considerations affect not only a mother's willingness to allow contact but also a father's self-esteem.

> It makes you feel bad not being able to do more. Sometimes I don't like to go and collect her, in case her Mam asks me for more money or if I can't afford to treat her when I see her.

(Speak *et al.* 1997)

Nevertheless, many young fathers manage to support their children in some way. Speak *et al.* (1997) noted that most fathers in their study reported contributing something towards the child's support, although this was often in the form of gifts and treats. However, welfare benefits policy acts as a deterrent to making regular payments for some. Both mothers and fathers resented the fact that a father's child support payments instantly reduced the amount of state benefit a mother could claim. Thus, it was in the mother's interest to negotiate 'alternative' payments with the father.

Lack of support

Despite a huge increase in the number of young mothers' groups in recent years, there is a notable lack of support for young fathers. Birbeck (2004) noted that 70 per cent of the fathers he interviewed had not encountered any support services following the birth of their child. The remaining 30 per cent had only encountered mainstream medical services, such as midwives and health visitors, through the mothers of their children.

Many existing fathers' groups are aimed at older married or divorced fathers and young men comment on feeling out of place. Support groups established by youth and community workers are often the most accessible for young men.

Conclusions

For well over a decade, in trying to promote and stabilise the two-parent, nuclear family, successive governments have sent out mixed messages to young fathers. Whilst raising concern about the 'father deficit', especially in the lives of young boys, politicians have shied clear of addressing the lack of legal rights of all non-married fathers. At the same time, however, they have emphasised fathers' responsibilities for financial provision, not least through the introduction of the Child Support Agency. Young men could be forgiven for equating fatherhood solely with money, rather than nurturing.

However, despite the poor public perceptions young single fathers endure, this chapter has tried to show that they are no less able or caring than any other fathers. Like divorced or separated fathers, young single fathers can, and regularly do, demonstrate a willingness and ability to be supportive, nurturing fathers. Unfortunately, many face a range of practical, legal and emotional barriers, which serve to prevent those who want to from taking a full role in their children's lives.

References

Birbeck, S. (2004) *Lads to Dads*. Unpublished report on Young Fathers Research Project for Wardon 360. Commissioned for Worcester Sure Start.

Burghes, L., Clarke, L. and Cronin, N (1997) *Fathers and Fatherhood in Britain*, London: Family Policy Studies Centre.

Cath, S. (1989) *Fathers and their Families*, Mahwah, NJ: The Analytic Press.

Coote, A. (1999) 'Boys who Can't Grow up', *Independent on Sunday (Comment)*, 14 November 1999, p. 23.

Clarke, L. and Verropoulou, G. (1996) 'Unpublished Results of Modelling the Risk of Absent Fathers', London: Social Statistics Research Unit, City Universtiy.

Dennison, C. and Lyon, J. (2000) *Young Offenders, Fatherhood and the Impact of Parenting Training*, Brighton: Trust for the Study of Adolescence.

Gallagher, P. (1999) 'Do we Really Want to Pay a Divorcee to Teach us How to be Fathers?', *Daily Express*, 9 January 1999.

Hosie, A. and Speak, S., (2004) *The Education of Pregnant Young Women and Young Moth-*

ers in England: The Views of Pregnant Young Women and Young Mothers, Final Report to Teenage Pregnancy Unit, Vol. 3, Newcastle upon Tyne: University of Newcastle.

Hudson, F. and Ineichen, B. (1991) *Taking it Lying Down: Sexuality and Teenage Motherhood*, Basingstoke: Macmillan.

Kiernan, K. (1995) *Transitions to Parenthood: Young Mothers, Young Fathers – Associated Factors and Later Life Experiences*, London: STICERD.

Lamb, M.E. (1975) 'Fathers: Forgotten Contributors to Child Development', *Human Development* 18, 245–66.

Lennon, P. (1996) 'The Men we Used to Be', *Guardian* (Society Supplement), 6 March 1996, p. 2.

Millar, J. and Bradshaw, J. (1993) 'The Circumstances of Lone Parent Families,' *Social Security Research Handbook 1991–92*, London: HMSO.

Office for National Statistics (1997) *Birth Statistics 1995* (FMI No. 24, 1997), London: Office for National Statistics.

Pickford, R. (1999) *Fathers, Marriage and the Law*, Findings No. 989, York: Family Policy Studies Centre, Joseph Rowntree Foundation.

Pook, S. (1999) 'Ex-addict gets Grant to run Class for Fathers', *Daily Telegraph*, 5 January 1999, p. 5.

Rolph, J. (1999) *Young, Unemployed, Unmarried . . . Fathers Talking*, London: Working With Men.

Selman, P., Hosie, A., Speak, S. and Dawson, N. (2004) *The Education of Pregnant Schoolgirls and Schoolgirl Mothers in England*, Research Report, London: Teenage Pregnancy Unit.

Seltzer, J.A. (1995) 'Relationships Between Fathers and Children who Live Apart', *Journal of Marriage and the Family* 52, 79–101.

Simpson, B., McCarthy, P. and Walker, J. (1995) *Being There: Fathers after Divorce*, Newcastle upon Tyne: Relate Centre for Family Studies, University of Newcastle upon Tyne.

Speak, S., Cameron, J. and Gilroy, R. (1995) *Young Single Mothers: Barriers to Independent Living*, London: Family Policy Studies Centre.

Speak, S., Cameron, J. and Gilroy, R. (1997) *Young Single Fathers: Participation in Fatherhood – Barriers and Bridges*, London: Family Policy Studies Centre.

Chapter 10

Deconstructing patriarchy and masculinity with teen fathers

A narrative approach

David Nylund

The study of teen parenthood has become almost synonymous with the study of teen mothers, but relatively little research attention has been devoted to the study of teen fathers. Nevertheless, because it appears that becoming a teen father has negative developmental consequences for both the teen father and his children, it is an important area of inquiry. Furthermore, the information gathered on teen mothers is not necessarily applicable to adolescent fathers in that different factors may influence their parental behavior and experiences. The purpose of this chapter is to provide insight into and understanding of the experiences of teen fatherhood and to examine the barriers to effective teen father parenting. Because the voices of young male parents are not adequately represented in the discourse of social science literature and social policy, this chapter provides an account of their experiences and examines the context in which their experiences occur, from the lens of a clinical example.

Research on teen father participation in child rearing suggests that the majority of teen fathers were significantly involved in the lives of their children (Rhein *et al.* 1997; Smith *et al.* 2002; Glikman 2004). The findings in these qualitative research projects help to challenge a societal stereotype of the irresponsible young father. Yet these research projects suggest that there are particular barriers that predict parental uninvolvement, including limited income, youth immaturity, and lack of parenting skills. Paschal (2004), using the lens of social ecology and feminist theory, found that many African American young fathers who were not involved with their children subscribe to traditional ideas of masculinity. These beliefs propose that mothers are responsible for parenting and fathers, at best, help out. My clinical work with many teen fathers confirms Paschal's argument; many of my clients were underinvolved with their children due to internalizing patriarchal ideas of parenting. This chapter will illustrate how I might work with young fathers to examine their ideas of fatherhood and encourage them to become involved and interested in child rearing. First, I will lay out the theoretical foundation that informs this work, namely narrative therapy. Second, I will offer a case example as an exemplar of this work.

Narrative therapy

Narrative therapy is premised on the idea that people's lives and relationships are shaped by the stories that people tell and engage in to give meaning to their experiences (White and Epston 1990). People construct certain habits and relationships that make up ways of life by staying true to these internalized stories. A narrative therapist assists people to resolve problems by separating the problem from the person based on the perception that the person is not the problem. Once the problem is separated and externalized from the person, space is open to facilitate the experience of new stories – narratives that are more empowering and more satisfying, and give hope for better futures.

Narrative therapy provides a framework for seeing problems within a cultural, political, and socio-economic context, and allows the therapist to maintain heightened sensitivity to issues of oppression, shame, and marginalization. Hence, narrative therapists pay a great deal of attention to discourses of gender, race, class, and sexuality. A discourse, according to the French historian of thought Michel Foucault (1980), is a system of words, actions, rules, beliefs, and institutions that share common values. Particular discourses sustain particular worldviews. One might think of a discourse as a worldview in action. The dominant discourses in our society powerfully influence what gets storied and how it gets storied. Discourses tend to be invisible – taken for granted as part of the fabric of reality, such as taken for granted ideas about what it means to be a man or a woman. Locating problems in particular discourses helps us see people as separate from their problems. As a narrative therapist, I seek to identify the discourses that support problematic stories, such as traditional, patriarchal masculinity. Once a problem is linked to a problematic discourse, narrative therapists can more easily help people oppose the discourse and choose to construct their relationship in line with a different, preferred discourse.

Narrative therapists view gender (and other identity categories) as social constructions that assume different forms in different historical moments and contexts. I am particularly interested in deconstructing dominant gender discourses including hegemonic masculinity. Scholars of gender (Brod 1987; Kimmel 1994) have described at least five distinctive features of hegemonic masculinity in US culture:

1   physical force;
2   occupational achievement;
3   patriarchy;
4   frontiermanship; and
5   heterosexuality.

R.W. Connell (1990) defines hegemonic masculinity as "the culturally idealized form of masculine character" (p. 83) that emphasizes "the connecting of masculinity to toughness and competitiveness," as well as "the subordination of women," and "marginalization of gay men" (ibid.: 94). Connell also suggests that hegemonic masculinity is not a static phenomenon, but is an always contested, historically situated, social practice.

Michael Messner (1997) has a useful framework in theorizing masculinities in a US context:

- Men, as a group, enjoy institutional privileges at the expense of women, as a group.
- Men share very unequally in the fruits of male privilege/patriarchy: normative/ hegemonic masculinity (white, middle- and upper-class, heterosexual) is constructed in relation to femininities and to various subordinated masculinities (racial, sexual, class, female masculinity).
- Men can pay a price – in the form of poor health, shallow/narrow relationships, for instance – for conformity with the narrow definitions of masculinity that promise to bring them status and privilege.

Messner's thematics allow theorists and therapists to speak of masculinities in the plural and to put the relationship between gender and power at the centre of analysis. Furthermore, his conceptualization creates space to examine connections between the construction of masculinities with other social constructions, such as race, class, and sexuality.

I find the concept of hegemonic masculinities useful in my work with teen fathers. Owing to the pervasiveness of dominant gender ideologies, many of the young fathers I work with subscribe to the tenets of hegemonic masculinity. A feature of traditional ideas of manhood includes the idea that it is a woman's role to take on the majority of the parenting tasks. Through the narrative process of deconstruction, I invite young fathers to examine the negative effects of traditional masculinity and their link to parenting. I will describe some of the therapeutic strategies that unpack traditional ideas of parenting.

Since masculinity has multiple and contradictory meanings and different significance in different social contexts, young men, in addition to being influenced by patriarchal masculinity, have been influenced by social/cultural movements, including feminism. Feminist ideas about gender equality influence to some extent the ways in which young men construct their identities. Hence, contemporary masculinity for young men is informed by a competing set of ideas and discourses rather than a single set of values promoted by patriarchy. In my narrative work, I ask re-authoring questions that amplify feminist ideas about gender equality that may open up space for young men to perform an alternative masculinity and become more involved in the daily practices of parenting. I will now illustrate some of these deconstruction and re-authoring questions.

Deconstructing masculinity and fatherhood

When working with young fathers, I often began the work by asking them about their ideas of manhood such as, "What ideas do you have about what it means to be a man?" and "Where did you learn these ideas?." Frequently we talk about the sites where dominant masculinity is sustained and reproduced. Some of these sites include school, family, and the larger culture. I will often ask them questions about experiences of manhood such as (Kivel 1992):

- Have you ever worried you were not tough enough?
- Have you ever exercised to make yourself tougher?
- Were you ever told not to cry?
- Have you ever been called a wimp, a queer, or a fag?
- Have you ever been told to act like a man?
- Have you ever been hit by an older man?
- Have you ever been in a fight to prove your manhood?
- Did you ever see an adult man you looked up to hit or emotionally abuse a woman?
- Have you ever been physically injured and hid the pain or kept it to yourself?
- Have you ever stopped yourself from showing affection to, hugging, or touching another man because of how it might look?

The above questions, which can be asked in individual or a group context, facilitate a rich discussion about the negative effects of traditional masculinity, including how cultural idealized forms of manhood limit men's ability to connect to others, restrict emotional expression, and reinforce violent masculinity as a cultural norm. In addition, these questions began the process of talking about fatherhood. Many of the young men, in response to these questions, share that their father or another older man helped reinforce traditional ideas about manhood through various practices of ridicule and intimidation.

Since many young men are immersed in popular culture, I also spend a great deal of time inquiring about the movies, TV shows, books, video games, and music they consume. In a mass-mediated society, popular culture has become a primary influence on young people's identities. The media, in particular, play a pivotal role in making, shaping, and recycling specific attitudes about manhood. In his compelling video titled, *Tough Guise: Violence, Media, and the Crisis in Masculinity*, Jackson Katz (1999) argues that media images have a primary influence in reinforcing hegemonic masculinity. Katz suggests that looking critically at constructed ideals of manhood by definition diminishes the otherwise silent power these very images might wield in shaping our perceptions of manhood. Employing Katz's stance, I will ask teen fathers about the images in popular culture:

- What kinds of movies, TV shows do you watch? What kind of manhood is depicted in these shows?
- Why do so many men find these shows entertaining?
- What would it mean to you if these shows helped reinforce the idea that disrespect toward women is OK?

- Do you see many young male characters in popular culture taking care of children? Why not?
- What messages do you think popular culture sends young men about fatherhood?

Many of the young fathers I have worked with have separated or broken up with the mother of their child. After the break-up, they often become minimally involved in the daily rigors of parenting. Their child, often an infant or toddler, lives with the mother and they are at a loss as to how to stay connected to their child. Such men often had very little to do with their children as babies, as this was "women's work." Here typically the mother had coached and mentored the young father as to how to be in relationship with their child. She would also have filled in the "gaps" in his fathering and made excuses for any of his shortcomings. After separation, many fathers are unsure as to how to conduct themselves without the cues and supervision that were provided by the mother. Often, the mother and father are in conflict with each other and the father finds it difficult to negotiate and stay in dialogue with the mother. This often leads to the young father backing away from the mother and/or child and becoming inconsistently involved. Typically, the father will arrange for visits through the mother relying on her to do the majority of the work of trying to conduct the father–child relationship.

To address the issue of underinvolvement or what I call "minimal fathering," I will ask several questions about the style of fathering the young man is practicing, among them:

- Did you connect with your son mainly through your connection with his mother and your now ex-girlfriend?
- When you wanted to know what was going on in his life, did you generally go to your ex to catch up with him or find out what was happening in his life?
- Would you generally remember his birthday and have some idea of what he would want as a gift or would your ex remind you?
- In the end, would you say you were relying on your ex for your relationship with him? Would you describe her as the "conductor" of your father–son relationship, keeping it going and in harmony?
- If you were to do it all over again, would you have a first-hand/direct or a second-hand/indirect relationship with your son?
- Do you suspect that if your son had a problem, a concern, or a very deep worry, he would bring this to you, his mother, or both of you?
- What kind of father–son relationship have you been left with now that you and your ex are separated?
- Do you think she is still expecting that she should keep up her conducting of your father–son relationship? And, if so, are you happy about that, now that there is so much bitterness between you?
- Is it possible that this makes it more unlikely that you and your son will have a first-hand father–son relationship without you taking some action?

- If you were to take over the conducting of your father–son relationship, what relationship skills would be required to put you in the picture of your son's heart and soul? (These questions are inspired by my colleague, Wally McKenzie.)

By externalizing "fathering practice," I can then engage the young father in a critical inquiry from a somewhat detached position. I typically am interested in locating any such practices in discourses of gender and culture. For example, I might ask, "What is the tradition of fathering in the family you came from, the family your father came from, and the family your grandfather came from? Has a practice of fathering more or less been passed down from father to son to father to son? Are there any useful examples of fathering that you have witnessed?"

Often, young men will tell me that their fathers were absent or underinvolved in their lives. For the young men who grew up with father absence, the wish to do things differently becomes fairly strong. Glikman (2004: 199) echoes this experience in her year-long ethnographic study of low-income fathers:

> The young men [who grew up with a father absent] were clearly using their experiences with their own fathers as a sort of benchmark as they considered how they would play the father role. This may be one of the most important explanations of why, despite the economic odds, low-income young men may remain involved with their children. As one young man (who remained involved with his child over the study year) said, "I just don't want my children to grow up feeling the way I feel about my dad. That's all. So, if I have to work two jobs and go to school at the same time, and sleep only two hours a day, that's what I'll do. To be sure that they don't feel the way that I feel."

Once I have externalized and deconstructed styles of fathering, the young men I work with are in a better space to consciously choose their own preferred fathering practice. If such a practice is outside their own experience, some research into alternative fathering might have to be undertaken and the skills, ideas, and habits associated with it might have to be practiced on a trial and error basis. Alternative versions might first take some conscious shape in response to such questions as these: "Now that you have the opportunity to consciously choose your own fathering practice rather than merely following in your father's footsteps, what practice might fit with your views about father–son relationships?"

At this point in the therapy, the young father is beginning to take up a more active role in the parenting. Often, the mother, who is seeking relief from the endless demands of single parenting, is appreciative and grateful. Typically the conflict between the mother and father lessens as they negotiate a more collaborative, shared parenting arrangement. At this point, I ask re-authoring questions – questions that invite the young man to appreciate and re-work his identity that is more preferred:

- Now that you are more in the forefront of your son's life, what new possibilities do you see for your father–son relationship?
- What new relationship skills are you building?
- What are you learning about yourself that is important to know?
- Would your father have gone to therapy to address these issues? Would he have had the courage to face up to his minimal fathering and take on more responsibility of the conducting of your father–son relationship?
- What does it say about you that you have changed your style of parenting? Are you setting a new tradition in your family? What messages are you sending your son about what it means to be a man/father? Are you teaching your son some new ideas about what it means be a man?
- If you had a father such as yourself, what difference might it have made to your life?

I will now describe and discuss a case vignette to illustrate narrative work with a young father.

Mauricio's journey into active fathering

Mauricio, a 19-year-old Latino male, was referred to me by the substance abuse clinic at the outpatient mental health agency where I was working at the time. Mauricio had successfully finished a 6-month intensive group drug treatment program. Apparently, Mauricio was abusing amphetamines, which led to the break-up of his relationship with his girlfriend, Sarah. Sarah and Mauricio had been dating for 3 years and had one child, Stephen, who was 2 years old at the time I began working with Mauricio. Although Mauricio had been clean and sober for 6 months, he was feeling depressed over the break-up of his relationship with Sarah.

On inquiring about the status of his relationship with Stephen, Mauricio stated that he rarely saw his son since the break-up 8 months previously. Mauricio, who was living with his mother at the time I was seeing him, blamed Sarah for his not seeing Stephen. "She doesn't trust me with him, so I backed off," he angrily said in the first interview. I asked Mauricio what kind of relationship he wanted with Stephen. Mauricio replied, "I want to be close but I don't know how to. Plus, I am so angry at Sarah, I don't want to deal with her." He was also jealous of Sarah because she was dating another man. This led to me asking the following questions:

- With you and Sarah breaking up, did you break up with Stephen in the same way?
- Has Stephen, in any way, indicated that he wanted a break-up with you?
- Is it fair to break up with Stephen? Doesn't he deserve some warning before you cut him out of your life?

- Is your fatherhood something that endures or is it a "take it or leave it" kind of thing?
- Is your anger and jealousy at Sarah being taken out on your relationship with Stephen?

Mauricio stated that he did not want to break up with Stephen, but was unconfident about how to become close with him. In inquiring about Mauricio's relationship with his father, Mauricio painfully talked about his father's inconsistent parenting since his parents divorced when Mauricio was 7 years old. This led to the following questions:

- What kind of fatherhood theory did your dad subscribe to?
- What were his ideas about manhood?
- Did he leave the bulk of the work for your mother?
- What has single parenthood been like for your mother?
- Is your dad's version of fatherhood the kind of parenting style you want to take up?

In response to these questions, Mauricio named his father's parenting style as "hot and cold fathering." Mauricio, with difficulty, described his relationship with his father as involving bursts of intense relating followed by long periods of virtual neglect. In fact, Mauricio had not had any contact with his father for over 2 years.

Future sessions focused on the effects of "hot and cold" fathering on Mauricio's childhood. Mauricio recalled "dreaming" that his father would be more involved in his life than he actually was. Mauricio's wish for a more consistent relationship with his father understandably led to a great deal of sadness and disappointment. I asked Mauricio some questions about the impact that "dream father" thinking had on his childhood:

- To what extent did your "father dream" deceive you into believing your father was a different kind of father than the father he has been to you?
- Where did the "father dream" come from? From TV? Books? Friends? Fathers? Or someplace else?
- What things have you tried to make your "father dream" come true? With what success?
- How might you channel your "dream father" thinking into becoming a better father to Stephen?

These questions led to a discussion of where his "father dream" came from, namely popular culture. Mauricio recalled watching *The Bill Cosby Show* and dreaming that his father would be similar to the Bill Cosby character – present, available, nurturing, and involved. We also examined other role models for fatherhood in popular culture, at which point Mauricio realized that the role models were few and far between on TV and film; that popular culture reinforced the idea that parenting was mainly "women's work."

After several sessions of deconstructing ideas about fatherhood, Mauricio was clearly able to state his preference for the kind of father he would like to be. Yet, Mauricio was not sure that he had the skills and patience to become more involved with Stephen. I asked Mauricio if he knew when he started the substance abuse program that he had the skills necessary to "walk away from drugs" at which point he replied "no." I asked him several questions about the skills and competencies necessary to become sober from drugs. Mauricio realized that he was stronger and more patient than he had realized. I then asked how he might use those same skills and talents and apply them to his preferred sense of fatherhood. Next, I asked Mauricio if his idea of manhood included trying to understand the experiences of others, including Sarah. When Mauricio answered "yes," I asked him to imagine himself as Sarah, while I asked him several questions. These questions, referred to as "internalized other questions," allow the client to step into an embodied experience of the "other." I often use these questions with men to help them step into the experience of their significant others, allowing them to develop a more relational notion of self (Nylund and Corsiglia 1993). I asked him the following questions as Sarah:

- Sarah, do you feel that the bulk of parenting is on you? What is that like? Do you get any rest?
- Sarah, what's it like to experience Mauricio's jealousy? Do you feel that Mauricio is punishing you by neglecting Stephen?
- What dreams do you have for your life? Do you see parenting getting in the way of your dreams?
- What do you need from Mauricio?
- Is Mauricio taking care of his financial responsibilities with Stephen?
- What would it mean to you if Mauricio took over a bit more of the responsibility of parenting so you could get a break?

These questions enabled Mauricio to realize that he needed to get a job to support his son. Soon after, Mauricio got a job at a local department store and began paying child support. Mauricio also made it clear to me (and Sarah) that he wanted to do more than just fulfill his legal and financial requirements of parenting, that he wanted to have a father–son relationship based on a moral perspective. We had lengthy discussions about what fatherhood, based on a moral perspective, would look like. Mauricio was able to envision a style of parenting that was premised on nurturing and cultivation of a close father–son relationship.

Still, Mauricio would go through periods of resentment as a result of working long hours to pay child support in addition to spending most of his free time with Stephen. He also intimated that he was envious of his male friends who "were having a good time and had more freedom . . . sometimes I feel trapped." In response to these concerns, I asked Mauricio the following questions:

- What does being a parent at this particular time in your life offer that might not be available at other times?
- If you keep the knowledge of this advantage in your awareness, how will that make a difference?
- If you think about your whole life, are there important things that you are putting on hold? How can you keep dreams and plans of those things alive for your future?
- Which people support and find joy in your parenting at this time in your life?

These questions help to deconstruct and challenge biases against people becoming parents early in life. A number of factors are associated with this bias: ideas about lack of maturity and experience, lost opportunities to complete academic education, and low earning potential because of limited formal education recruit young people into feeling bored and trapped. Some of the biases against parenting at a young age have to do with associated problems, such as poverty and instability of relationships, that could occur at any age and may not be relevant to particular parents. Rather than conceptualizing and generalizing parenting by persons of a "younger" age as problematic, it may be more useful to identify specific problems and abilities that are unique to particular parents. In addition, although feelings of being bored and trapped can be experienced by parents of any age, young parents are more vulnerable to these feelings because they contrast with the freedom and exploration available to many of their peers. The other side of the picture, which is less often presented, is of a different life sequence in which teen parents have more energy for parenting and later go back to complete their education when they are more likely to appreciate it and are more clear about career goals.

Consequently, Mauricio, while recognizing the struggles of parenting, reconsidered the ideas of fatherhood as a "trap" and realized that being a young father may have particular advantages. We talked about his future plans to go to college and become an architect. Future sessions included one with Mauricio's mother, who offered to help Mauricio so that he could attend community college. She was willing to help because she was proud of Maurcio's attempts to become a responsible father. In addition, Sarah attended a session with Mauricio in which she expressed appreciation for Mauricio's increased involvement. (Mauricio agreed to have Stephen every other weekend and once a week, plus he was paying consistent child support.) Mauricio continued to remain drug free and was pleased with stepping into a new story of manhood and fatherhood.

Conclusion

Although teen parenting is the center of much social concern and policy debate, the focus tends to be young mothers. It continues to be the case that little research and clinical attention is paid to the experiences and stories of young fathers. More research on this topic may help us challenge societal stereotypes of the negligent and immature young father. Similarly, research needs to examine the institutional and discursive barriers that prevent young men from becoming more responsible as parents. In addition to economic issues, one considerable obstruction is the institution of patriarchy and its ally, hegemonic masculinity. Narrative therapy, with its focus on stories and culture, gender, and power, is a clinical practice that critically examines the social construction of masculinity. One feature of dominant masculinity is the old idea/discourse that parenting is "women's work." My work with Mauricio demonstrates how deconstructing ideas about manhood, motherhood, and fatherhood enabled my client to become more accountable as a father. The practices of narrative therapy can be one more tool, along with other clinical and policy interventions, to increase fathers' responsibility for their children.

References

Brod, H. (ed.) (1987) *The Making of Masculinities*, Boston: Unwin Hyman.

Connell, R.W. (1990) "An Iron Man: the Body and Some Contradictions of Hegemonic Masculinity," in *Sport, Men, and the Gender Order* (eds M.A. Messner and D.F. Sabo), Champaign, IL: Human Kinetics, pp. 83–95.

Foucault, M. (1980) *The History of Sexuality: an Introduction*, New York: Vintage.

Glikman, H. (2004) "Low-income Young Fathers: Contexts, Connections, and Self, *Social Work* 49, 195–206.

Katz, J. (1999). *Tough Guise: Violence, Media, and the Crisis in Masculinity*, Northampton, MA: Media Education Foundation.

Kimmel, M. (1994). "Masculinity as Homophobia," in *Theorizing Masculinities* (eds H. Brod and M. Kaufman), Thousand Oaks, CA: Sage, pp. 119–41.

Kivel, P. (1992) *Men's Work*, New York: Ballantine Books.

Messner, M.A. (1997) *Politics of Masculinities: Men in Movements*, Thousand Oaks, CA: Sage.

Nylund, D. and Corsiglia, V. (1993) "Internalized Other Questioning with Men Who are Violent," *Dulwich Centre Publications* 2, 29–34.

Paschal, A.M. (2004) "I'm Doing What I Have to Do: African American Teens and their Experiences of Fatherhood," *Dissertation Abstracts International, A: The Humanities and Social Sciences* 64, 2663-A.

Rhein, L.M., Ginsburg, K.R., Schwarz, D.F., Pinto-Martin, J.A., Zhao, H., Morgan, A.P., and Slap, G.B. (1997) "Teen Father Participation in Child Rearing: Family Perspectives," *Journal of Adolescent Health* 21, 244–52.

Smith, P.B., Buzi, R.S., and Weinman, M.L. (2002) "Programs for Young Fathers: Essential Components and Evaluations Issues," *North American Journal of Psychology* 4(1), 81–92.

White, M. and Epston, D. (1990) *Narrative Means to Therapeutic Ends*, New York: W.W. Norton.

Chapter 11

Teen pregnancy and girl students with emotional and behavioral difficulties

Chrystal C. Ramirez Barranti

Girls with emotional or behavioral problems face additional challenges when they become adolescents or young adults. This chapter discusses these challenges and the implications for human service providers.

> Rea is waiting at the bus stop. It's morning – too early as far as she is concerned. Who wants to go to school anyway? Big waste of time, especially since she could be hanging around and hook up with Chuck. Sweet! He's got to be the hottest boy around the neighbourhood. Yep, and she's going to be his girl. Especially now that he wants to have sex with her. She never thought anyone would want to have sex with her – After all, she's one of those kids in Mr Wilkes' classes for special ed. But, wow, Chuck does! Chuck doesn't say anything about her being called SED and sometimes LD or even that other name, EBD. It's all bogus, that's for sure. Who cares what the teachers say anyway. The school bus door slams shut behind her. Well, looks like Chuck didn't come to school today. Hey, but maybe she'll see him later, after school. Yeah, that will be sweet, real hecka-sweet.

Rea (a fictional composite case) is one of many adolescent girls who has been identified as having severe emotional disturbance (SED). Her poor academic progress, coupled with her emotional and behavioral problems, has resulted in her being placed in the special education program at her school, the school system's attempt to provide intervention services. The provision of special education for students with severe emotional and behavioral disturbances has been mandated under the federal program, the Individuals with Disabilities Act (IDEA), which was first implemented in 1975 (Kavale *et al.* 2005).

Although IDEA was designed to assure that all children, regardless of emotional and/or behavioral difficulties, have access to education, the related problems and issues faced by children and youth identified as having SED, and by their families, almost always reach well beyond the confines of the school. For instance, poverty, minority status, child abuse, and domestic violence are just some of the related factors associated with students who are classified as having SED (Coutinho *et al.* 2002). Children and youth who struggle with SED often have social skill deficits that have ramifications in all of their social environments, such as school, friendship networks, community relationships, and the family. In Rea's case, multidimensional risk factors within her social environment, which includes individual, familial, school, neighborhood, and socio-political systems, may be dynamically transacting to bring her to the brink of becoming sexually active at 13 years of age. In fact, having SED, Rea may indeed be at greater risk than the average female adolescent for becoming a pregnant teenager (Yampolskaya *et al.* 2002).

Are girls with SED susceptible to additional or different risk factors for teenage pregnancy compared with the general female adolescent population? If so, can these particular risk factors help identify effective teen pregnancy prevention strategies for such girls? These questions are the focus of this chapter. The ecological perspective (Germain and Gitterman 1987) is used to provide multilevel lenses through which research findings can be organized and explored. First, a discussion concerning the definition and meaning of SED will be developed as it is important to understand what multidimensional factors define this population.

Following on from this understanding, an exploration of risk factors for teen pregnancy and identification of possible additional risk factors that may be associated with girls who are identified as having SED will be discussed. By identifying such risk factors for girls among the SED population, social workers and other human service workers may be able to determine specifically targeted interventions for pregnancy prevention. Likewise, the identification of protective factors assists in developing effective prevention strategies for this population of teenage girls. Reviewing the best practices and approaches of current adolescent pregnancy prevention programs can also provide direction for development of teen pregnancy prevention strategies that address the unique needs of female teenagers with SED.

Using an ecological perspective for exploring teen pregnancy and girls with severe emotional disturbances

The multidimensional nature of the combination of risk factors that place a child or youth at risk of developing SED and/or problematic and possibly antisocial behavioral patterns is a challenge for any human service provider and any scholar. Utilizing a theoretical model such as the ecological perspective (Germain and Gitterman 1987; Zastrow and Kirst-Ashman 2001) is helpful in considering risk factors as well as protective factors within the social environmental context of an individual with SED. The ecological perspective (Germain and Gitterman 1987; Zastrow and Kirst-Ashman 2001) is especially helpful in organizing, assessing, and making meaning out of the complex and multiple dimensions that interact to effect serious emotional and behavioral disturbances (Corcoran 2000). Placing the discussion of risk factors within the context of the ecological perspective not only provides a model to identify risk factors and protective factors, but facilitates effective interventions that address the inherent multidimensional complexity of SED and disruptive and/or antisocial behavioral patterns.

The ecological model enacts three levels of systems that continuously and dynamically interact with one another. As they interact, continuous reciprocal effects, which include change, take place. These multilevel systems are in continual, dynamic, and reciprocal transaction with one another. Three levels of systems are conceptualized: the individual level (micro level); the family, school, and community level (meso level); and the greater societal level (macro level). Any particular individual can be thought of as being nested within increasingly larger and more complex systems, all of which exist at three levels within their social environmental context. These transactional exchanges simultaneously impact on all of the systems involved in a particular social environment. Likewise, reciprocal transactions effect change that is always more than simply additive; the resulting effect is always more than the sum of the transactions themselves (Kauffman 2000). Figure 11.1 provides a pictorial representation of the social environmental context of a youth who is at risk for developing SED.

Emotional and behavioral disturbances

The transactional nature of a school's ecological milieu lends the school to easily reflect the behavioral and emotional health of its neighborhoods, community, and society at large. That is, our schools are truly microcosms of the communities they serve and of the greater society that supports them. It is no surprise then that, with our society growing ever more steeped in a culture of violence and disruptive behavior, our school communities should find themselves challenged with increasingly aggressive behavior and disturbed emotional responses from their students (Young *et al.* 2004). In fact, the number of children and youth who have been identified as developing SED and/or seriously disruptive behaviors has increased over the past two decades despite focused prevention and intervention efforts of school systems across the nation (Young *et al.* 2004). For example, some studies have estimated the prevalence of SED students to range from 4 to 10 percent of school-aged youth nationwide (Wood *et al.* 2005). Although prevalence statistics can be helpful in estimating how pervasive SED is among the national population of children and youth, the actual percentage of students who are identified as having SED and who receive special education services has a glaringly smaller value of 0.9 per cent (Kauffman 2000; Yeh *et al.* 2005).

Why is there such a difference between the estimated prevalence of SED and the proportion of students identified as having SED and receiving special education? The discrepancy between prevalence estimates and actual SED students identified and served has been partly attributed to the lack of clarity in the federal definition of SED provided in Public Law 94-142, or the IDEA (US House of

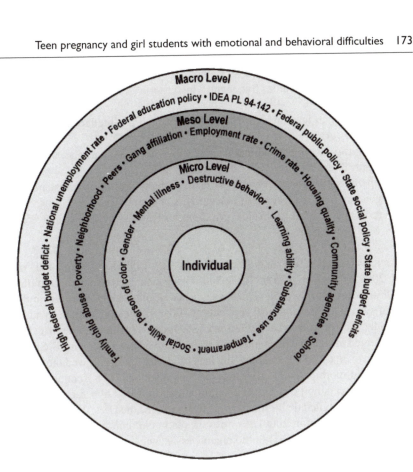

Figure 11.1 The ecosystem of a youth who is at risk for developing serious emotional disturbance.

Representatives 1997; Mason *et al.* 1999; Young *et al.* 2004). This lack of clarity found in IDEA is reflective of the lack of clear definitions and of the varying definitions of SED used by researchers, school professionals, school systems, and state agencies (Kauffman 2000; Kavale *et al.* 2005). The lack of a common definition of SED has serious consequences for children and youth who have severe behavior and emotional difficulties: many children and young people may remain unidentified, and as a result will not receive much needed services.

Kavale *et al.* (2005: 39) identified three primary features that must be covered in any definition of SED: severity, frequency, and chronicity. They noted that these three features provide the context for the definition of SED found in the federal IDEA. First enacted in 1975, Public Law 94-142, or the IDEA, was implemented to assure educational resources for children and youth who struggled with SED and other social, emotional, behavioral, and/or cognitive disturbances (Mason *et al.* 1999). Within IDEA a child or youth suffering with SED is defined as a student "exhibiting behavior disorders over a long period of time which adversely affect educational performance" (cited in Young *et al.* 2004). The federal definition of SED found in IDEA includes five identifying criteria (Kavale *et al.* 2005: 39):

1   an inability to learn which cannot be explained by intellectual, sensory, or health factors;
2   an inability to build or maintain satisfactory interpersonal relationships with peers and teachers;
3   inappropriate types of behavior or feelings under normal circumstances;
4   a general, pervasive mood of unhappiness or depression;
5   a tendency to develop physical symptoms or fears associated with personal or school problems.

As Kavale *et al.* (2005) and others (Mason *et al.* 1999; Kauffman 2000; Young *et al.* 2004; Clough *et al.* 2005; Cole 2005) have discussed, the definition of SED in IDEA is not entirely clear. The consequence of this lack of clarity is a glaring lack of systematic and uniform application of the SED classification. In addition, the inadequacy of the current definition of SED results in many children and youth being denied the special education and related resources that they need. Similarly, as Kavale *et al.* (2005) have noted, the lack of clarity has disallowed the inclusion of related co-morbid disorders such as learning disorders (LDs), conduct disorder (CD), attention deficit disorder (ADD), or attention deficit hyperactivity disorder (ADHD) (for detailed definition of these disorders see the DSM-IV-TR; American Psychiatric Association 2000). As a result, many children with such psychiatric disorders in addition to SED fail to receive assistance through appropriate special education services.

Now that the formal definition of SED has been presented, the reader may wonder just what risk factors are operating for children and youth who develop SED. Are these risk factors related to those factors that place girls at risk for teen pregnancy? The following section will attempt to address SED risk factors and explore the potential increase in the risk of teen pregnancy.

Factors that place children and youth at risk for SED

Young *et al.* (2004: 179) define risk factors as "conditions or influences that in-crease the likelihood that a child's behavior will deviate from the norm or that a problem condition will persevere into the child's teen and adult years." In other words, the presence of particular risk factors affects the probability that a child or youth will develop SED. Likewise, the presence of several risk factors most often exponentially increases the possibility that a child or youth will develop inappro-priate emotional and behavioral patterns. So, then, what are these risk factors that may place a child or youth at risk for SED?

When considering risk factors, it is helpful to place the discussion within the context of the ecological perspective. The ecological perspective posits that all systems are in continual, dynamic, and reciprocal transaction with one another. Systems can be conceptualized at the individual level (micro level), family, school, and community level (meso level), and at the greater societal level (macro level). These transactional exchanges impact all of the systems involved in a particular ecosystem simultaneously. Likewise, reciprocal transactions effect change that is more than simply additive; the resulting effect is always more than the sum of the transactions themselves (Kauffman 2000).

In considering a girl who is exposed to risk factors in her ecosystem that create a vulnerability to developing SED, four systems have been identified for consideration: individual characteristics, family characteristics, school characteristics, and cultural and larger societal characteristics (Young *et al.* 2004: 181–2). That is, risk factors can be found within the individual girl student, within the family, associated with peers, related to her school, and/or located within the community and larger society. Figure 11.2 helps to depict the levels of consideration within an ecological framework that utilizes the multiple systems levels of micro (individual), meso (family, peer group, school), and macro (community, socio-political).

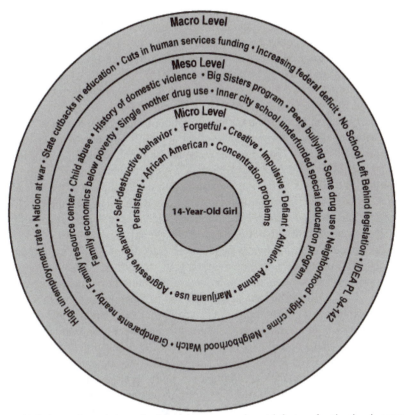

Figure 11.2 An ecological view of a girl student exposed to risk factors for the development of SED.

It is helpful to note that the more risk factors in one's ecological context, the greater the vulnerability for developing SED (Kauffman 2000; Young *et al.* 2004). In fact, when there is more than one risk factor, the increase in vulnerability to SED is more than the sum of these risk factors. Remember that the risk factors can exist within the individual (impulsivity), within the family system (child abuse), among peers (gang affiliation), in the neighborhood (high crime rate), in the school (lack of resources for academic support), and in the larger society (for example high unemployment transacting with the community and family to result in unemployed parent(s)). In fact, Kauffman (2000: 226) describes the effect of more than one risk factor as "multiplicative"' in nature.

Gender and race/ethnicity

Coutinho *et al.* (2002) have taken a closer look at the population of students who have been classified as having SED. Reviewing 1998 data from the US Department of Education's Office of Civil Rights' *Elementary and Secondary School Compliance Report*, they found the variables of gender and ethnicity to be influential in gaining increased understanding of the very real girls and boys who make up the prevalence and classification percentages of SED students. Caucasian males were found to be 3.8 times as likely as Caucasian females to be classified as having SED. Furthermore, African American girls were 1.4 times more likely than Caucasian girls to be classified as having SED. Likewise, African American boys were found to be 5.5 times more likely than Caucasian girls to be identified as having SED (Coutinho *et al.* 2002; Young *et al.* 2004).

These results point to important trends that implicate gender and race/ethnicity as contributing factors that impact classification of SED and consequent participation in related services. From a closer examination of the results identified above, it is apparent that girls are less likely than boys to be classified as having SED (Coutinho *et al.* 2002). Further investigation reveals that there is a dynamic transactional relationship of gender and race/ethnicity: Caucasian girls are less likely than girls and boys who are African American and boys who are Caucasian to be classified as having SED (Coutinho *et al.* 2002; Young *et al.* 2004).

While gender is an influential factor when considering representation among the total SED population, race/ethnicity is also a significant contributing factor. African American children and youth have been found to be overrepresented in the population of SED children, accounting for 24.5 percent of the total US SED student population (US Department of Education for Civil Rights 1994; Yeh *et al.* 2005). In stark contrast, however, Asian/Pacific Islander students are underrepresented as they make up only 3.7 percent of the SED population (US Department of Education for Civil Rights 1994). Likewise, Latino students are underrepresented in the SED population, although not to the same extent as Asian/Pacific Islander students. Latino students constitute 7.8 percent of the total SED population (US Department of Education for Civil Rights 1994). Caucasian students are the only ethnic group to be represented in the SED population at the expected rate

(McCabe *et al.* 2005), accounting for 65.5 percent of the total SED population (US Department of Education for Civil Rights 1994).

How should the reader interpret the meaning of the effect of race/ethnicity on classification of SED? The immediate conclusion would point to race/ethnicity and related discrimination and racism as an underlying factor. While this conclusion should not be discounted, McCabe *et al.* (2005) report findings from the *National Longitudinal Transition Study* which suggest an additional factor that may be responsible for the overrepresentation of African Americans among SED students. Data from this study reveal that race/ethnicity is indeed a contributing factor, but not the primary factor influencing the overrepresentation of African American children as SED (McCabe *et al.* 2005). A larger societal (macro-level) factor, poverty, has been found to be a primary contributor to the overrepresentation of African American students and other students of marginalized populations among the SED population (Wagner 1995; Yeh *et al.* 2005). Frankly stated, there is an overrepresentation of children and youth living in poverty among the SED population (Yeh *et al.* 2005). These findings reflect decades of research that has consistently found that persons of color are disproportionately represented among poor schoolchildren and youth (Kozol 1995; Polakow 2000).

Multilevel risk factors

From an extensive review of the literature several authors have identified particular risk factors that increase vulnerability for development of SED (Javitz and Wagner 1993; Bolger *et al.* 1995; Wagner 1995; Farmer *et al.* 1999; Mason *et al.* 1999; Hallahan and Kaufman 2000; Kauffman 2000; Coutinho *et al.* 2002; Yampolskaya *et al.* 2002; Young *et al.* 2004; Yeh *et al.* 2005). These are summarized in Table 11.1.

The multiplicative effect of risk factors has been associated with the concept of a "trajectory" of behavioral and emotional patterns (Smith 2005). In fact, Walker and Sprague (1999) and others (Young *et al.* 2004; Smith 2005) identified a risk factor trajectory that can move a SED-vulnerable child or youth from problem behaviors to more serious and possibly destructive emotional and/or behavioral patterns that may have long-term negative consequences. Such long-term outcomes can include school failure and dropout, criminal behavior and arrests, incarceration, drug and/or alcohol addiction, and/or gang affiliation (Mason *et al.* 1999; Kaufmann 2000; Young *et al.* 2004; Smith 2005). It is easy to conclude that such long-term outcomes can lead to major disadvantages in adulthood and serious costs to families, communities, and society at large. Needless to say, the risk factor trajectory emphasizes the critical need for early intervention for children and youth vulnerable to SED, or already suffering with SED, and for the families and communities in which they live.

In reviewing the literature on the potential risk factor trajectory and related outcomes, it is interesting to note that teenage pregnancy was rarely identified as a negative outcome. Is it reasonable, then, to deduce that the multiplicative risk

Table 11.1 Multilevel risk factors that increase vulnerability to SED

Micro level: individual	Meso level: family, school, peers, neighborhood	Macro level: larger systems such as culture, societal factors, policies (e.g., IDEA)
Temperament	*Family*	Socio-economic status
Gender	Poverty	High unemployment rate
Ethnicity/race	Unemployment	Increase in jobs that pay minimum hourly rate
Non-compliance with adults and authority figures	People of color	Continued ramification of racism and oppression of ethnic minority populations
Disruptive behavior	Substance abuse	Decrease in funding for social services
High level of anxiety	Child abuse and/or neglect	IDEA
Impulsiveness	Emotional abuse	Ineffective definition of SED
Easily distractible	Sexual abuse	Exclusion of psychiatric disorders for special education services
Easily upset under pressure	Spousal abuse	Acceptance of violence in media and recreation
Difficulty concentrating	Legal issues	
Low academic ability	Imprisonment	
Achievement	Parental psychiatric illness	
Truancy	No high school diploma (especially mother)	
Social skill deficits	Teen mother	
Difficulty with friendships	Hostile emotional environment	
Verbal aggression	Coercive parenting	
Physical aggression	Poor problem-solving	
Bullying of others	Single-parent household	
Difficulty with change	Lack of family rules	
Legal issues	Unhealthy family system boundaries	

Co-morbid psychiatric disorders
Conduct disorder
Oppositional defiant disorder
Attention deficit disorder
Attention deficit hyperactivity disorder
Depressive disorder
Anxiety disorders
Learning disorders
Substance abuse disorders

School
Lack of clear expectations for achievement
Teacher rejection
Lack of clarity for acceptable behavior
Low expectation for low-performing students
Improper placement of students
Poor adult models for behavior

Peers
Unsupportive peer group
Conduct deviant actions
Violence by peer group
Negative peer pressure
Bullying by peers
Gang affiliated
Peer rejection
Few or no peer friendships

Neighborhood
High crime rate
Drugs
High violence rate
Gang identified

Sources: summarized from Javitz and Wagner (1993), Bolger et al. (1995), Wagner (1995), Farmer et al. (1999), Mason et al. (1999), Hallahan and Kaufman (2000), Kauffman (2000), Coutinho et al. (2002), Yampolskaya et al. (2002), Young et al. (2004), and Yeh et al. (2005).

factors and the transactions among them do not place a girl student with SED at greater risk for teen pregnancy than those girls without SED? The next section examines this very question.

Examining risk factors for teen pregnancy: do girls with SED have a greater vulnerability for teen pregnancy?

Within the last decade there has been a downward trend in teenage pregnancy rates in the USA. In fact, the Guttmacher Institute's (2004) on-going research of teen pregnancy has found that the nationwide rate of adolescent pregnancy has dropped by 28 percent since 1990. Despite this welcome decline in adolescent pregnancy rates, the USA continues to have the highest teen pregnancy rate among all of the developed nations, with 84 out of every 1,000 American adolescent girls (15–19 years of age) becoming pregnant each year (Guttmacher Institute 2002, 2004). Despite the good news of a decline in teen pregnancy rates, there remains the bad news that many adolescent girls continue to become pregnant at great human as well as societal costs.

While recent studies indicate an annual pregnancy rate of 84 per 1,000 in the 15–19 years age group, these particular census studies do not tell us much about who these 84 girls are. That is, what are the possible multilevel risk factors that may have interfaced to lead these particular 84 teenagers in a population of 1,000 to become pregnant?

A strong body of literature has identified a number of risk factors related to adolescent pregnancy (Caldas 1994; Wagner 1995; Garrett and Tidwell 1999; Berry *et al.* 2000; Yampolskaya *et al.* 2002; Corcoran and Franklin 2004). These include such factors as low socio-economic status, poor family and peer relationships, living in single-parent households, a history of child abuse (physical, emotional, and/or sexual), a history of domestic violence, a high level of sexual knowledge, use of drugs and alcohol, poor school performance and/or failure, peer group behaviors, neighborhood composition, and level of access to sex education, family planning, and abortion. Table 11.2 provides a summary of these risk factors from the ecological perspective (the micro (individual), meso (family, peers, neighborhood), and macro (societal factors such as public policies, program funding, and access to services)) levels.

SED girls and additional risk factors for teen pregnancy

Given the multitude of multilevel risk factors for teen pregnancy for the general population of adolescent girls, the reader may be left wondering if there can be any further factors that could place a teenage girl of any population at any further risk. Are there risk factors for female teenagers with SED that are different from those found in the general population of adolescent girls? Adolescent girls with SED have a multitude of multilevel risk factors that have been identified earlier in this chapter. Do any of these risk factors overlap with those that may place an adolescent girl in the non-SED population at risk for early pregnancy? Are there risk factors unique to girls with SED and the experience of living with the symptoms of SED and destructive behavioral patterns that alone may place them at risk for adolescent pregnancy?

Despite the personal and societal reality that adolescent pregnancy continues to be a serious concern, it remains a mystery that there has been so little research concerning the SED population and teen pregnancy (Wagner 1995; Mason *et al.* 1999; Yampolskaya *et al.* 2002). The research that has been done has focused on identifying long-term outcomes associated with SED itself. For example, young people with SED are more likely to drop out of high school, to lack post-high school education, to be unemployed, and to be arrested; in addition, prevalence rates of sexual intercourse are higher than in the general population (Wagner 1995; Coutinho and Denny 1996; Doren *et al.* 1996; Valois *et al.* 1997; Mason *et al.* 1999). Mason *et al.* (1999) and Wagner (1995) have found that female teenagers with SED are significantly more likely than adolescent girls without SED to be teenage mothers.

Yampolskaya *et al.* (2002) conducted one of the few studies to explore risk factors and outcomes of teen pregnancy among adolescent girls with SED. Utilizing a sequential cohort design of age cohorts, longitudinal data were collected over 7 years as the researchers followed 190 girls with SED from the time they were 9 years of age until 18 years of age. Risk factors representing the micro, meso, and macro systems included psychopathology, self-esteem, race/ethnicity, dropout status, age of mother at time of birth of participant, marital status of parents, family income, family cohesiveness, housing arrangements, and poverty status. Of the 190 girls, 39 percent became pregnant by the age of 18.

What risk factors were found to be significant predictors of teen pregnancy among the sample? Race/ethnicity, family income, school dropout, diagnosis of conduct disorder, and diagnosis of substance abuse were found to be significantly associated with adolescent pregnancy among the sample of girls with SED (ibid.). The authors note:

> Specifically, girls of colour were almost twice as likely to get pregnant by age 18 as were European American girls. Girls from lower income families were more likely to get pregnant than were girls from higher income families, with the risk of becoming pregnant increasing 13 per cent per $5,000 reduction in family income. After dropping out of school, girls were over 3½ times more likely to get pregnant than were girls who did not . . . Girls with either conduct disorder or a substance use disorder were almost twice as likely to get pregnant early (i.e., by age 18) as were those without such disorders . . .
>
> Early pregnancy was marginally associated with the participants' mothers having been teenagers themselves when they gave birth. Neither self-esteem nor family cohesion was significantly associated with early pregnancy.
>
> (ibid.: 4)

Table 11.2 Multilevel risk factors for adolescent pregnancy

Micro level (individual)	Meso level (family, peers, school, neighborhood)	Macro level (larger societal factors)
Low self-esteem	Family	Socio-economic status
Poor school performance and/or failure	Poverty – low socio-economic status	High unemployment rate
Drops out of school	People of color (African American, Hispanic, etc.)	Increase in jobs that pay minimum hourly rate
Use of drugs and/or alcohol	Disrupted family structure	Continued ramification of racism and oppression of ethnic minority populations
Strained parental relationships	Single-parent household	Decrease in funding for social services
Experience of maternal rejection, deprivation, inconsistency	Loss of father or lack of father figure in early life	Public policy concerning sex education content (abstinence only)
Poor interpersonal communication skills	"Latchkey" child at early age	Pregnancy prevention programs (abstinence only)
Romanticism of dating relationships	Strained relationships between teenager and parent(s)	Lack of access for teens to family planning and abortion
Strong egocentrism – belief in invulnerability to pregnancy	Lack of family rules	Societal acceptance of sexualized environment in media and advertising
Low motivation to use contraceptives	Poor family cohesion	Culture norms regarding gender roles and sexuality
Feelings of discomfort regarding sexuality and sex	Lack of parental supervision	
Mental health problems	Lack of family closeness	
Depressive disorders	Inconsistent messages given regarding sexual behavior and pregnancy	
Lack of participation in religious community	Physical, emotional, and/or sexual abuse	
Lack of social support	Parental substance abuse	
	Domestic violence	
	Child protective services involvement – child in foster care	
	Lack of participation in religious community	

School

Lack of support programs for academic problems

Failure to identify school achievement problems

Sex education program content (abstinence only)

Peers

Drug and alcohol use

Peer pressure to become sexually active

Low academic achievement

Not active in school activities

Neighborhood

Urban

High concentration of single-headed households

High number of teenage pregnancies

Sources: summarized from Caldas (1994), Garrett and Tidwell (1999), Berry *et al.* (2000), Field *et al.* (2000), Lanctot and Smith (2001), Miller *et al.* (2001), Yampolskaya *et al.* (2002), and Corcoran and Franklin (2004).

Yampolskaya *et al.* (2002) utilized multivariate analysis to determine the effects the multiple risk factors had on early pregnancy among their sample of female teenagers with SED. The results of the analyses indicated that, of the risk factors identified in the study, only dropping out of school was significant in predicting early adolescent pregnancy. In fact, 58 percent of the participants who became pregnant had become pregnant after dropping out of school. In contrast, previous research exploring risk factors for and outcomes of teen pregnancy among the general population of adolescent girls showed that school dropout was more often an outcome of having become pregnant, rather than a precursor of teen pregnancy (Corcoran 1998; Stevenson *et al.* 1998; Corcoran and Franklin 2004).

Having identified risk factors that may predispose a teenage girl with SED to becoming pregnant, there might remain the question of whether or not the existence of SED places a girl at greater risk for early pregnancy. Using data from the National Adolescent and Child Treatment Study (NACTS), Yampolskaya *et al.* (2002) found that the pregnancy rates among the study sample of teenage girls with SED were significantly higher than those for adolescent girls in the general population. Yampolskaya's study provides pioneering research data for a population that has been almost forgotten in the adolescent teen literature. The study results provide initial findings that inspire and support the case for further, much needed, research in this area.

Strategies for adolescent pregnancy prevention among girls with SED

It is interesting to note that a number of studies found teenage girls with SED to be significantly more likely to be teen mothers than adolescent girls in the general population (Elster *et al.* 1990; Horwitz *et al.* 1991; Wagner, 1995; Mason *et al.* 1999). Similarly, Yampolskaya *et al.* (2002) found a much higher pregnancy rate among their sample of teenage girls with SED when compared with pregnancy rates among adolescent girls in the general population. The findings of these studies provide support for the importance of identifying teen pregnancy prevention strategies designed more specifically for adolescent girls with SED. Are there best practices and approaches that can be identified from teen pregnancy prevention programs that may be helpful for developing prevention strategies tailored for teenage girls with SED?

Best practices and effective components of adolescent pregnancy prevention programs

Several significant studies have rigorously examined adolescent pregnancy prevention programs (Kirby *et al.* 1994; Franklin *et al.* 1997; Corcoran and Franklin 2000; Kirby 2002). The results of these reviews have clearly indicated that programs that provide contraceptive information and incorporate contraceptive distribution have proven to be the most effective in reducing teenage pregnancy rates. More specifically, Corcoran and Franklin's (2000) analysis of teen pregnancy prevention program outcome studies has identified best practices for effective adolescent pregnancy prevention programs (pp. 48–9).

- Community clinic programs are more effective than school-based programs.
- The provision of information on contraceptives and contraceptive distribution is essential.
- Comprehensive sex education and skills training are critical components.
- Teenage pregnancy prevention programs are not a "one size fits all" curriculum. The age of and developmental issues among the target population must be taken into consideration for planning content and teaching–learning strategies.
- Abstinence and delay approaches are not effective with youth who are already sexually active.
- Social learning theory and skills training provide the most effective basis for curriculum development.

Kirby's (2002) rigorous review of 73 evaluation studies of programs aimed at reducing teen pregnancy, unprotected sex, and teen childbirth identified 10 characteristics of effective programs. These defining characteristics of effective prevention programs have been found to be built on curricula that:

a   focus on reducing behavior(s) that can lead to pregnancy;
b   are based on theoretical approaches found to be successful in reducing other health-related risk-taking behavior;
c   include the critical components of contraceptive knowledge and continually reinforce the connection between sexual activity and contraceptive use;
d   give basic and clear information about the risks of sexual activity and methods of avoiding sexual intercourse;
e   address social and peer pressures that can influence sexual activity;
f   use modeling and role playing to foster communication, refusal, and negotiation skills;
g   use engaging teaching methods that involve participants and increase personalization of the material;
h   design materials, present information, and develop behavioral goals appropriate to the age, developmental stage, culture, sexual orientation, and sexual experience of participants;
i   allow enough time to be thorough and complete; and
j   recruit and train motivated instructors and peers who have confidence in the program they would teach (ibid.: 4–5).

In addition to educational prevention programs, Kirby's (2002) review found that service learning programs have been effective in reducing teenage pregnancy rates. In fact, the results indicate that service learning programs have been found to be the most effective type of prevention programs in reducing adolescent sexual activity and teen pregnancy (Kirby 2002: 8–9). Kirby (2002) notes that the opportunity to develop positive relationships with caring adults, experiencing a sense of competence in relationships with others, and actually making a difference in the lives of others may be the protective factors that young people gain from participation in service learning programs.

Similar to the findings for the service learning programs described above, Kirby's (2002) analysis identified an intensive program that recruited students between the ages of 13 and 15 for participation throughout their high-school years. The Children's Aid Society-Carrera (CAS-Carrera) programs provide educational programs and activities 5 days a week during the school year. Paid employment and evening programs are encouraged during summer months:

> The CAS-Carrera programs used a holistic approach, providing multiple services: (a) family life and sex education; (b) an education component that included individual academic assessment, tutoring, help with homework, preparation for standardized exams, and assistance with college entrance; (c) a work-related intervention that included a job club, stipends, individual bank accounts, employment, and career awareness; (d) self-expression through the arts; and (e) individual sports.
>
> (ibid.: 9)

Three years after completing the program, the findings among girls who participated indicated exceptional results. For example, girls had typically delayed the beginning of sexual intercourse and were more likely to use condoms as a supplement to already highly effective contraceptive methods. Perhaps most encouraging was the finding of reduced pregnancy rates and teen birth rates.

Protective factors

While identifying risk factors for girls with SED is an important component in understanding the various multilevel forces that impact a teenager's ecological context, it is crucial to identify protective factors that may help mitigate their effect. In fact, when considering strategies to prevent pregnancy among adolescent girls with SED, it is paramount to consider protective factors in addition to the risk factors. Considering protective factors in conjunction with what is known about best practices and approaches for teen pregnancy in general may help guide the development of effective strategies for prevention among girls with SED.

Protective factors, like risk factors, can be found at all levels of a youth's ecological context. Such factors are conditions, characteristics, and/or events that can occur within an individual as well as throughout the multiple levels (micro, meso, and macro) of the individual's ecological context. Factors that help to mitigate negative influences and experiences, that provide a more nutritive ecological context, and which help to support resiliency are considered to be protective factors

(Young *et al.* 2004). For example, protective factors at the micro or individual level can include the ability to develop positive relationships, perhaps excel in extracurricular activities, or refrain from impulsive actions. At the meso or family, peer group, and school levels, protective factors may include a supportive family, participation in the church youth group, or a school that employs an early skills deficit identification strategy. Finally, at the macro level or policy levels, protective factors can be found in such areas as a strong economy, sufficient funding for supportive human services programs, or funding that supports strong special education programming.

Implications for adolescent pregnancy prevention strategies for teen girls with SED

Teenage girls with SED painfully struggle with the experience of difficult emotional responses and the consequences of seriously disruptive behaviors. Serious emotional and behavioral disturbance incurs many negative and discouraging consequences in all spheres of life, with perhaps the most visible being poor school achievement and overwhelming difficulties in learning. Such girls are often seriously at risk for dropping out of school, substance use and/or dependence, and becoming involved with the justice system (Wagner 1995; Coutinho and Denny 1996; Doren *et al.* 1996; Valois *et al.* 1997; Mason *et al.* 1999). In addition, recent studies have found that adolescent girls with SED are much more likely to become pregnant than are teenage girls in the general population (Wagner 1995; Valois *et al.* 1997; Mason *et al.* 1999; Yampolskaya *et al.* 2002). Perhaps the most startling difference between girls with SED and girls in the general population who become pregnant is in school dropout rates: teenage girls with SED are much more likely than teenage girls among the general population to have dropped out of school before becoming pregnant (Yampolskaya *et al.* 2002). This small, but hopefully growing, body of literature points to the critical need to develop effective strategies specifically tailored for teen girls with SED.

Risk factors for teen pregnancy are similar in girls with SED and in adolescent girls in the general population, i.e., being a person of color (specifically African American), being poor (low family income), and using substances (Caldas 1994; Wagner 1995; Coutinho and Denny 1996; Valois *et al.* 1997; Garrett and Tidwell 1999; Berry *et al.* 2000; Yampolskaya *et al.* 2002; Corcoran and Franklin 2004). Such similarities in risk factors may help identify the effective elements of best practices and approaches that have been discussed in the adolescent pregnancy prevention literature and which can be incorporated in specialized prevention strategies for teen girls with SED.

Implications for pregnancy prevention strategies

First and foremost, the research points to the critical importance of staying in school. Yampolskaya *et al.* (2002) recommend that pregnancy prevention programs for girls with SED include a strong component that reinforces the importance of remaining in school, doing what it takes to succeed academically, and emphasizes that completing school is a personal investment in one's self and one's future. This strategy is intimately woven throughout the multiple levels of micro, meso, and macro systems and indicates the significance of building and enhancing protective factors throughout the ecological context of each teenage girl with SED.

A comprehensive and successful pregnancy prevention program is one that is focused on reducing behavior(s) that can lead to pregnancy (Kirby 2002). Successful programs are based on theoretical approaches that have been found to be successful in reducing other health-related risk-taking behavior (Kirby 2002). In particular, such programs have been found to be more effective when they are informed by social learning theory that supports effective skill building (Corcoran and Franklin 2000). The inclusion of a strong skills training component is central especially when teens with SED are the target audience (Corcoran and Franklin 2000; Kirby 2002).

Effective teen pregnancy prevention programs are certainly not "one size fits all." Age, developmental issues, learning challenges, sexual experiences, sexual orientation, culture, and emotional and behavioral disturbance patterns must be taken into consideration when planning content and developing materials as well as teaching–learning strategies (Kirby 2002). This strategy mirrors an important characteristic of effective SED prevention programs (Young *et al.* 2004): the importance of placing a key emphasis on building new behaviors and developing effective social skills.

The focus on addressing the influence of social and peer pressures on sexual activity is especially important for female teenagers with SED given the potential risk factor that peers can constitute in their ecological context (Kirby 2002; Young *et al.* 2004). The building of new behaviors and social skills should include communication skills, negotiation skills, refusal skills, and conflict resolution skills (Corcoran and Franklin 2000; Kirby 2002). It is important to use highly engaging teaching methods that have proven effective in skills training such as modeling and role playing (Kirby 2002).

Rigorous reviews of pregnancy prevention evaluation studies have shown the importance of including information on contraceptives and the continual reinforcement of the connection between sexual activity and contraceptive use, and, critically, the value of making contraceptives available to youth (Corcoran and Franklin 2000; Kirby 2002). Abstinence only and delay approaches have been found to be ineffective with youth who are already sexually active (Kirby 2002). This is an important finding, considering that teenage girls with SED are more likely than adolescent girls in the general population to be sexually active (Mason *et al.* 1999; Yampolskaya *et al.* 2002). Therefore, the prevention strategy of building knowledge about contraceptives, reinforcing the importance of contraceptive use in sexual activity, and making contraceptives available to teenage girls with SED is fundamental to preventing early pregnancy among this population. This critical piece cannot be left out of any prevention program if it is to be successful with this population.

The need for a sense of belonging, to feel that one has something meaningful to contribute to others, that one matters, makes a difference, and the need to experience success and achievement are important to every person. These basic human needs, which are fundamentally interwoven with self-esteem and self-image, may not be easily met for an adolescent girl with SED. She may not feel success in school or other contexts, she may not feel welcome, and she may have poor social skills that keep her friendless. Kirby (2002) identified what may be considered an atypical pregnancy prevention program that may help to address such unmet needs while at the same time reducing the risk for early teen pregnancy: service learning programs.

Service learning programs are structured programs that bring students into the community to provide service to others. Such programs involve students in meaningful activities while providing an environment for preparation and reflection, and an opportunity to work with others. The service learning programs that were reviewed by Kirby (2002) documented a significant reduction in sexual activity and teen pregnancy. One program also found a reduction in school failure (Kirby 2002). The application of a service learning program as a strategy for pregnancy prevention among girls with SED may effectively address a multitude of targeted areas of concern: pregnancy prevention, interpersonal skill development, self-esteem building, experiences with success and efficacy. These protective factors can provide a mitigating force that can enhance resiliency while building a trajectory of experiences for success rather than failure.

Conclusion

Female teenagers who suffer from severe emotional disturbances and negative behavioral patterns experience extreme challenges in many, and sometimes all, of the social arenas in which they live. In fact, the many risk factors that have made them vulnerable to SED exist at the micro, meso, and macro levels of their ecological contexts. It is some of these same risk factors which may increase their vulnerability to early pregnancy (Wagner 1995; Mason et al. 1999; Kauffman 2000; Couhtinho et al. 2002; Young et al. 2004). Risk factors such as coming from a low-income or poor family, being a person of color (specifically African American), having a diagnosis of conduct disorder, and/or having a substance abuse disorder have been found to place adolescent girls with SED at greater risk for pregnancy.

However, probably the most important finding, given the primary context in which a girl's SED is first labeled and made visible, is the risk factor of dropping out of school. Female teenagers with SED who drop out of school are significantly more likely than adolescent girls in the general population to become pregnant (Yamploskaya et al. 2002). It is not surprising to note that all young people with SED are at high risk for dropping out of school as a consequence of their emotional difficulties, disruptive behaviors, and difficulties with learning (Clough *et al.* 2005). Special education programs that are successful in teaching young people with SED how to manage difficult emotions and behavior, and how to develop new behaviors and social skills, all while achieving academically would go a long way in providing protective factors that could help prevent early pregnancy. The development and implementation of pregnancy prevention programs for female teenagers with SED could supplement a successful school experience to provide additional protective factors.

References

American Psychiatric Association (2000) *The Diagnostic and Statistical Manual of Mental Disorders IV T-R*. Washington, DC: American Psychiatric Association.

Berry, H.E., Shillington, A.M., Peak, T., and Hohman, M.M. (2000) "Multi-ethnic Comparison of Risk and Protective Factors for Adolescent Pregnancy," *Child and Adolescent School Work Journal* 17, 79–96.

Bolger, K.E., Patterson, C.J., Thompson, W.W., and Kupersmidt, J.B. (1995) "Psychosocial Adjustment Among Children Experiencing Persistent and Intermittent Family Economic Hardship," *Child Development* 66, 1107–129.

Caldas, S.J. (1994) "Teen Pregnancy: Why it Remains a Serious Social, Economic, and Education Problem in the U.S.," *Phi Delta Kappa* 75, 402.

Clough, P., Garner, P., Pardeck, J.T., and Yuen, F. (2005) "Themes and Dimensions of EBD: A Conceptual Overview," in *Handbook of Emotional and Behavioural Disorders* (eds P. Clough, P. Garner, J.T., Pardeck, and F. Yuen), London: Sage, pp. 3–17.

Cole, T. (2005) "Emotional and Behavioural Difficulties: an Historical Perspective," in *Handbook of Emotional and Behavioural Disorders* (eds P. Clough, P. Garner, J.T., Pardeck, and F. Yuen), London: Sage, pp. 31–44.

Corcoran, J. (1998) "Consequences of Adolescent Pregnancy/Parenting: a Review of the Literature," *Social Work in Health Care* 27, 49–67.

Corcoran, J. (2000) "Ecological Factors Associated with Adolescent Sexual Activity," *Social Work in Health Care* 30, 547–88.

Corcoran, J. and Franklin, C. (2000) "Preventing Adolescent Pregnancy: a Review of Programs and Practices," *Social Work* 45(1), 40–53.

Corcoran, J. and Franklin, C. (2004) "Adolescent Pregnancy and Parenting: a Bio-psychosocial Framework," in *Intervention with Children and Adolescents: an Interdisciplinary Perspective* (eds P. Allen-Meares and M.W. Fraser), Boston: Pearson, pp. 398–416.

Coutinho, M.J. and Denny, K. (1996) "National Leadership for Children and Youth with Serious Emotional Disturbance: Progress and Prospects," *Journal of Child and Family Studies* 5, 207–27.

Coutinho, M.J., Oswald, D.P., and Forness, S.R. (2002) "Gender and Sociodemographic Factors and the Disproportionate Identification of Culturally and Linguistically Diverse Students with Emotional Disturbance," *Behavioural Disorders* 27(2), 109–25.

Doren, B., Bullis, M., and Benz, M. (1996) "Predicting the Arrest Status of Adolescents with Disabilities in Transition," *Journal of Special Education* 29, 363–80.

Elster, A.B., Ketterlinus, R., and Lamb, M.E. (1990) "Association Between Parenthood and Problem Behavior in a National Sample of Adolescents," *Pediatrics* 85, 1044–50.

Farmer, T.W., Farmer, E.M.Z., and Gut, D. (1999) "Implications of Social Development

Research for School Based Interventions for Aggressive Youth with Emotional and Behavioural Disorders," *Journal of Emotional and Behavioural Disorders* 7, 130–6.

Field, T., Pickens, J., Prodromidis, M., Malphurs, J., Fox, N., Bendell, D., Yando, R., Schanberg, S., and Kuhn, C. (2000) "Targeting Adolescent Mothers with Depression Symptoms for Early Intervention," *Adolescence* 35(138), 381.

Franklin, C., Grant, D., Corcoran, J., O'Dell, P., and Bultman, L. (1997) "Effectiveness of Prevention Programs for Adolescent Pregnancy: a Meta-analysis," *Journal of Marriage and the Family* 59, 551–67.

Garrett, S.C. and Tidwell, R. (1999) "Differences Between Adolescent Mothers and Non-mothers: an Interview Study," *Adolescence* 34(133), 91–105.

Germain, C.B. and Gitterman, A. (1987) "Ecological Perspective," in *Encyclopaedia of Social Work*, 18th edn (ed. A. Minahan), Silver Springs, MD: National Association of Social Workers, pp. 488–99.

Guttmacher Institute (2002) *Facts in Brief: Teenagers' Sexual and Reproductive Health*, New York: Guttmacher Institute.

Guttmacher Institute (2004) *U.S. Teenage Pregnancy Statistics: Overall Trends, Trends by Race and Ethnicity, and State-by-state Information*, New York: Guttmacher Institute.

Hallahan, D.P. and Kauffman, J.M. (2000) *Exceptional Learners: Introduction to Special Education: Theories and Recommendations*, Boston: Allyn and Bacon.

Horwitz, S.M., Klerman, L.V., Kio, H.S., and Jekel, J.F. (1991) "Intergenerational Transmission of School-age Parenthood," *Family Planning Perspectives* 23, 168–73.

Javitz, H. and Wagner M.M. (1993) *The National Longitudinal Study of Special Education Students: Sample Characteristics and Procedures, Wave 2 (1990)*, Menlo Park, CA: SRI International.

Kauffman, J.M. (2000) *Characteristics of Emotional and Behavioral Disorders of Children and Youth*, 7th edn, Upper Saddle River, NJ: Merrill.

Kavale, K.A., Forness, S.R., and Mostert, M.P. (2005) "Defining Emotional or Behavioural Disorders: the Quest for Affirmation," in *Handbook of Emotional and Behavioural Disorders* (eds P. Clough, P. Garner, J.T., Pardeck, and F. Yuen), London: Sage, pp. 45–58.

Kirby, D., Short, L., Collins, J., Rugg, D., Kolbe, L., Howard, M., Miller, B., Sonenstein, F., and Zabin, L. (1994) "School-based Programs to Reduce Sexual Risk Behaviour," *Family Planning Perspectives* 23, 6–16.

Kirby, D. (2002) "Effective Approaches to Reducing Adolescent Unprotected Sex, Pregnancy, and Childbearing," *Journal of Sex Research* 39(1), 51 (available from the Questia data base, www.questia.com; retrieved August 8, 2004).

Kozol, J. (1995) *Amazing Grace: The Lives of Children and the Conscience of a Nation*, New York: HarperCollins.

Lanctot, N. and Smith, C.A. (2001) "Sexual Activity, Pregnancy, and Deviance in a Representative Urban Sample of African American Girls," *Journal of Youth and Adolescence* 30, 349.

Mason, C.A., Chapman, D.A., and Scott, K.G. (1999) "The Identification of Early Risk Factors for Severe Emotional Disturbances and Emotional Handicaps: an Epidemiological Approach," *American Journal of Community Psychology* 27, 357–81.

Miller, B.C., Benson, B., and Galbraith, K.A. (2001) " Family Relationships and Adolescent Pregnancy Risk: a Research Synthesis," *Developmental Review* 21, 1–38.

Polakow, V. (ed.) (2000) *The Public Assault on America's Children: Poverty, Violence, and Juvenile Injustice*, New York: Teachers College Press.

Smith, C.R. (2005) "Advocacy for Students with Emotional and Behavioural Disorders," in *Handbook of Emotional and Behavioural Disorders* (eds P. Clough, P. Garner, J.T., Pardeck, and F. Yuen), London: Sage, pp. 285–98.

Stevenson, W., Maton, K.I., and Ted, D.M. (1998) "School Importance and Dropout Among Pregnant Adolescents," *Journal of Adolescent Health* 22, 376–82.

US Department of Education Office for Civil Rights (1994) *Elementary and Secondary School Compliance Report*, Washington, DC: US Department of Education Office for Civil Rights.

US House of Representatives (1997) *Report No. 105-95*, Washington, DC: US House of Representatives.

Valois, R.F., Bryant, E.S., Rivard, J.C., and Hinkle, K.T. (1997) "Sexual Risk Taking Behaviours Among Adolescents with Severe Emotional Disturbance," *Journal of Child and Family Studies* 6, 409–19.

Wagner, M.M. (1995) "Outcomes for Youths with Serious Emotional Disturbance in Secondary School and Early Adulthood," *The Future of Children* 5, 90–112.

Walker, H.M. and Sprague, J.R. (1999) "The Path to School failure, Delinquency and Violence: Causal Factors and Some Potential Solutions," *Intervention in School and Clinic* 35, 67–73.

Wood, P., Yeh, M., Pan, D., Lambros, K., McCabe, K., and Hough, R. (2005) "Exploring the Relationship Between Race/Ethnicity, Age of First School-based Services Utilization, and Age of First Specialty Mental Health Care for At-risk Youth," *Mental Health Services Research* 7, 185–96.

Yampolskaya, S., Brown, E.C., and Greenbaum, P.E. (2002) "Early Pregnancy Among Adolescent Females with Serious Emotional Disturbances: Risk Factors and Outcomes," *Journal of Emotional and Behavioural Disorders* 10(2), 108 (retrieved February 28, 2005, from EBSCO HOST Research Databases Academic Search Elite).

McCabe, K., Lambros, K., Hough, R., Landsverk, J. Hulburt, M., Culver, S., and Yeh, M. (2005) "Racial/ethnic representation across five public sectors of care for youth with EBD," in *Handbook of Emotional and Behavioural Disorders* (eds P. Clough, P. Garner, J.T. Pardeck, and F. Yuen), London: Sage, pp. 165–88.

Young, K.R., Marchant, M., and Wilder, L.K. (2004) "School-based Interventions for Students with Emotional and Behavioral Disorders," in *Intervention with Children and Adolescents: an Interdisciplinary Perspective* (eds P. Allen-Meares and M.W. Fraser), Boston: Pearson, pp. 175–204.

Zastrow, C. and Kirst-Ashman, K.K. (2001) *Understanding Human Behavior and the Social Environment*, 5th edn, Belmont, CA: Wadsworth/Thompson Learning.

Index

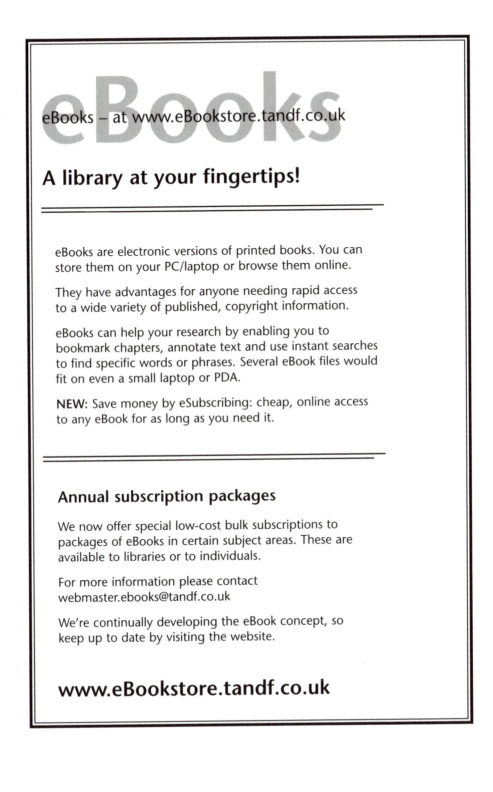